I0795649

IMAGES
of America

MAIN STREET NEW HAMPSHIRE

IMAGES
of America

MAIN STREET NEW HAMPSHIRE

Bruce D. Heald

ARCADIA
PUBLISHING

ISBN 978-0-7385-1342-33

Published by Arcadia Publishing
Charleston, South Carolina

Printed in the United States of America

Library of Congress Catalog Card Number: 2003110391

For all general information, contact Arcadia Publishing:
Telephone 843-853-2070
Fax 843-853-0044
E-mail sales@arcadiapublishing.com
For customer service and orders:
Toll-Free 1-888-313-2665

Visit us on the Internet at www.arcadiapublishing.com

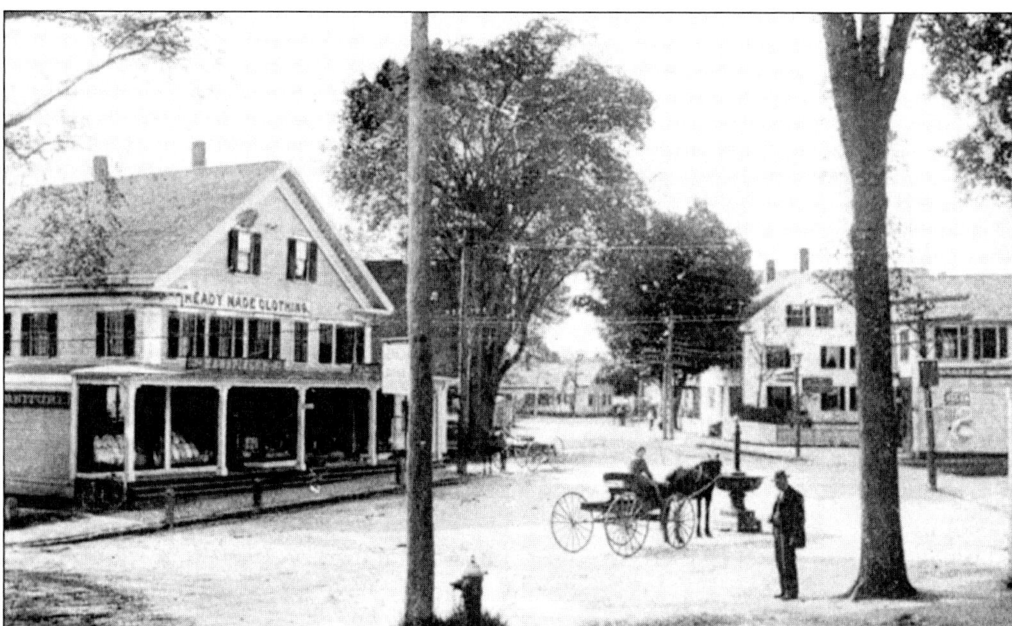

This view of Meredith's Post Office Square looks south and dates from 1910.

Contents

ACKNOWLEDGMENTS

I would like to give special thanks to the following people and organizations for their contributions: Robert and Barbara Bennett, the Ashland Historical Society, Peter Francesco, Stephen Holden, David Ruel, Matthew E. Thomas, and the Works Progress Administration for the state of New Hampshire.

INTRODUCTION

When you think of New Hampshire, you will likely picture a quaint village with a Main Street and a town common in the center. Ionic porticoes, elms, bandstands, honor rolls, white steeples, tavern signs, small-paned windows, and green turf may come to mind. For those of us who grew up in New Hampshire, Main Street was the center of our social, political, and economic life.

Driving through New Hampshire, one can see that Main Streets vary in size. Seen are Main Streets boasting town squares, lined with white, well-kept old homes, and guarded by the sleepless sentinel of tall, white Colonial church spires seen through the elms. The sense of earlier times comes to us. We remember the roll of the drums and the bustling babble of men in homespun guard carrying their firearms. We remember the times for relaxation and robust pleasures, for the free flow of rum, for wrestling and marching, and for boasting and fighting. Main Street was the place of meetings, speeches, cheers, the rumble of war, and the tramping of determined feet upon the sod. It was the place of band concerts and gala crowds beneath the lights of a starry sky. Main Street was the hub of activity. It was where we assembled at the country store, barber shop, soda shop, train station, town hall, and library.

Main Street, New Hampshire, brings to mind Memorial Day ceremonies, the planting of a symbolic tree, a volley of gunfire commanding our attention to battles past, a fading bugler's call, and the day of our independence. The village still lies beneath its arching elms, a changeless avenue in a time of change. Sunlight and shade shine upon the village green. Spring birds are in the trees, and young lovers stroll upon the quiet paths where their parents strolled before them. The church clock strikes, and the sound echoes, then dies among the hills. The church spire stands as before, touching the clouds in the sky.

The roots of so many Americans are found in these peaceful village Main Streets that bring to us not only a sense of dignity, serenity, and quiet beauty, but also of homecoming. Main Street, New Hampshire, is not a place but rather an experience, a feeling, an emotion. It was a central place to shop, gossip, and socialize. It was the soul of American life, a place where customs grew and took root.

To the casual observer, Main Street's role as the center of village activity has become obsolete. Some attribute this to the convenience of the automobile and the new development and popularity of the shopping malls. Whatever the reason, there is a revival in the making for Main Streets in many New Hampshire communities. From the 1980s to the present, a popular reincarnation and revitalization project has grown throughout New Hampshire.

The National Trust for Historic Preservation has developed a pilot Main Street program nationally, and for the past 15 years, the National Main Street Center has worked in more than 1,350 communities throughout the country. The New Hampshire Main Street community approach states: "This revitalization approach advocates a return to community self-reliance, empowerment, and the rebuilding of commercial districts based on its traditional assets: unique architecture, personal service, local ownership, and a sense of community. The Main Street approach to downtown revitalization requires the effort of the entire community. The merchants, property owners, local government officials, and civil leaders must agree to support common goals for revitalization and join together in a partnership. The promotion of the downtown as a single unified commercial area—in the same way that a major shopping mall is promoted—will help attract customers and strengthen Main Street's role as a visible business center."

From 1997 to the present, the New Hampshire Main Street program has made significant investments, and New Hampshire Main Street communities are making a strong comeback. As the New Hampshire Main Street program has stated, "Downtown revitalization efforts set the tone for new investment in downtown."

The purposes of this volume are to reflect upon the romance of our state's past and to relive the memories of our Main Streets. More than 200 images have been assembled in this book, including Main Streets of Concord, Keene, Nashua, Rochester, Laconia, and most of the smaller villages throughout the state. Main Street is a place where we feel the pulsing heart of something time cannot change.

— Bruce D. Heald, Ph.D.

One

Alexandria to Concord

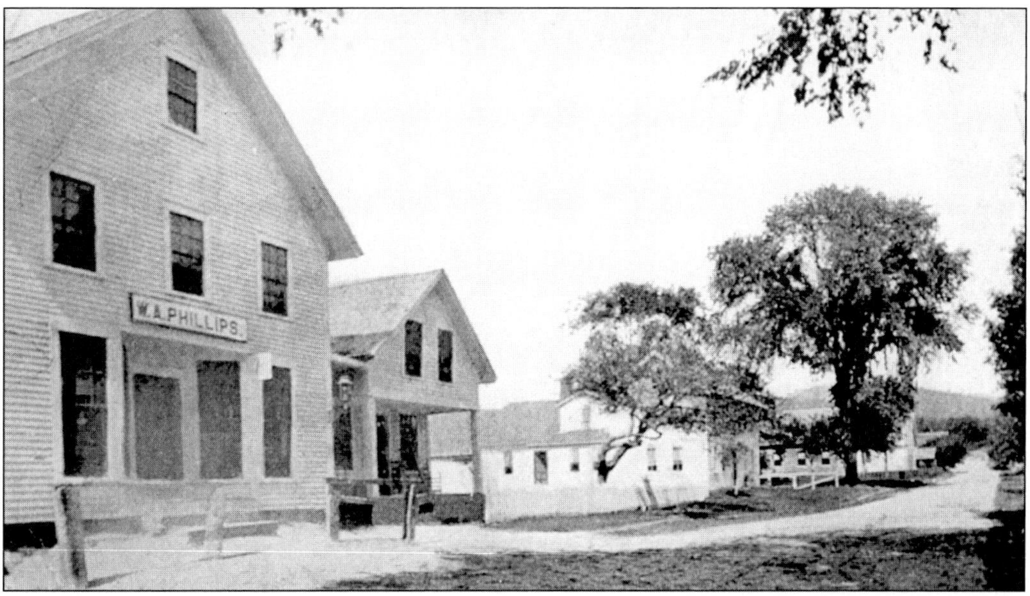

Seen here is Main Street in Alexandria in the late 1800s. The simplicity of the business district reflects the rural lifestyle of the mid-19th century. Like other towns in this section of the state, Alexandria was a part of the Masonian grant of New Chester. The acres of valuable land in the intervale of the Fowler River attracted settlers as early as 1769, although the town was not incorporated until 1782.

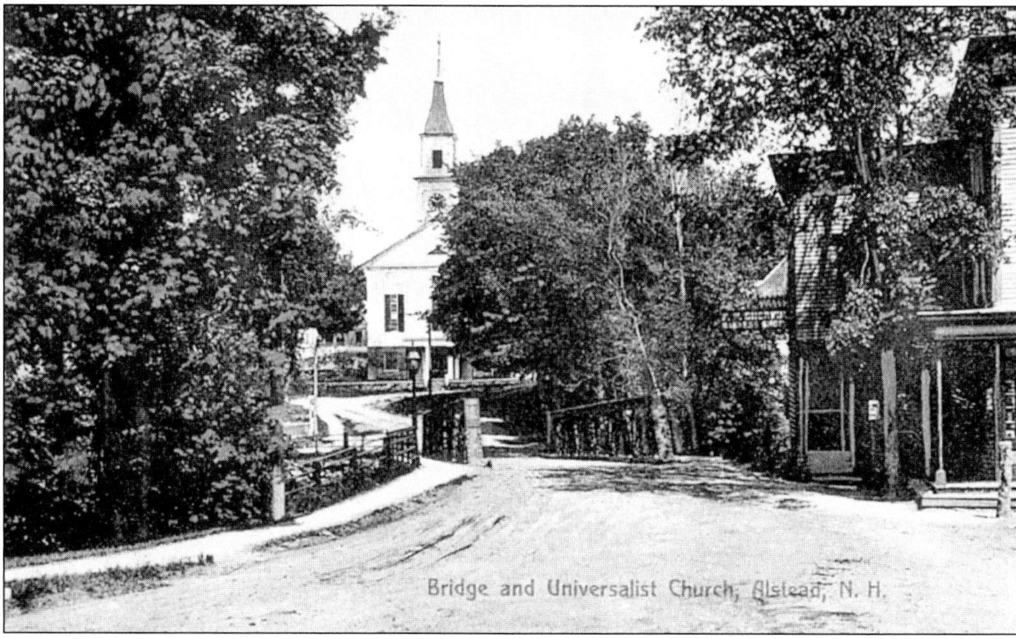

This 1910 view shows Main Street and the bridge in Alstead. Looking across the bridge to the Universalist church on the hill, we see the small village divided by Cold River. Alstead was granted a charter in 1772. Alstead is one of the towns that wavered its allegiance between New Hampshire and Vermont. In April 1781, the town began to transact business under the state of Vermont, but it returned to the authority of New Hampshire in January 1782.

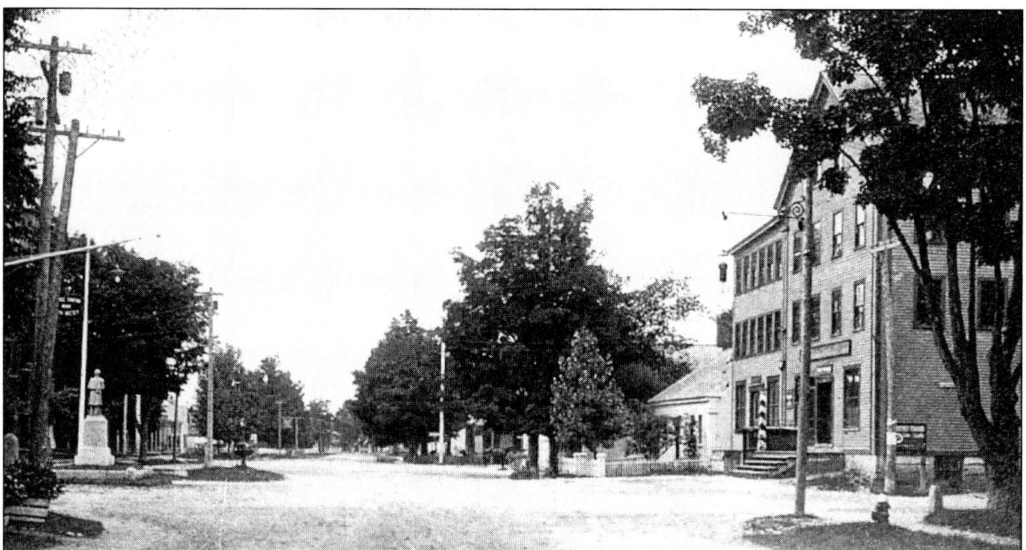

This view of Main Street in Alton, looking south, dates from the late 1800s. At this time, Main Street was a one-street settlement through which flowed the Merry-Meeting River, the chief inlet of Lake Winnipesaukee. Alton, once called New Durham Gore, was settled in 1770. When it was incorporated in 1796, the citizens requested that it be called Roxbury, but Governor Wentworth gave it the name of an English town. Today, Alton is largely a summer resort.

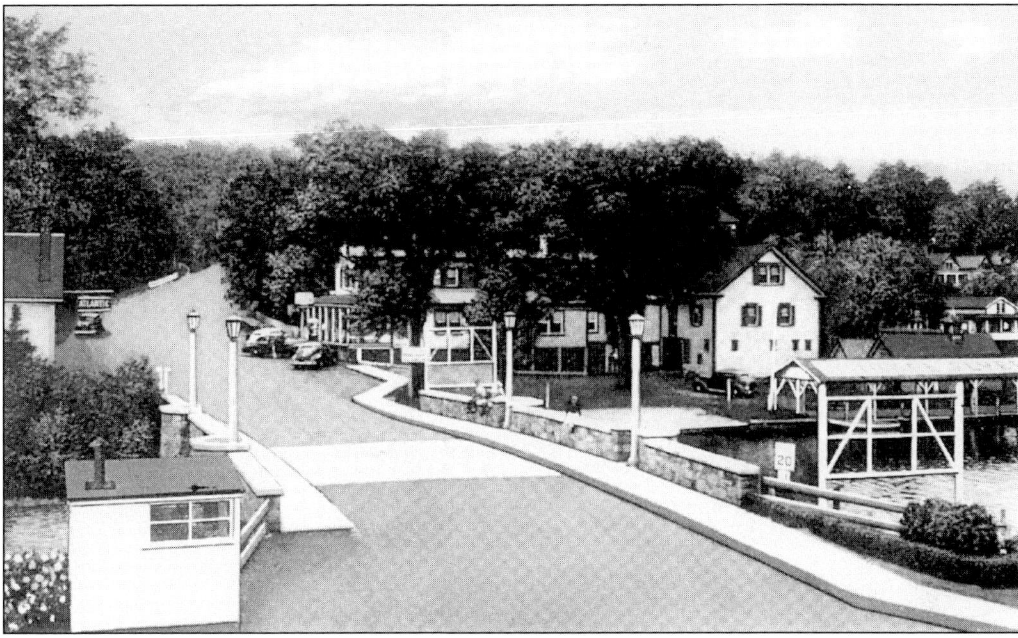

This is a *c.* 1940s view of Main Street in Alton Bay looking west. Alton Bay is largely a summer resort and a port for the *M/V Mount Washington*. This part of the lake was once known as Merry-Meeting Bay.

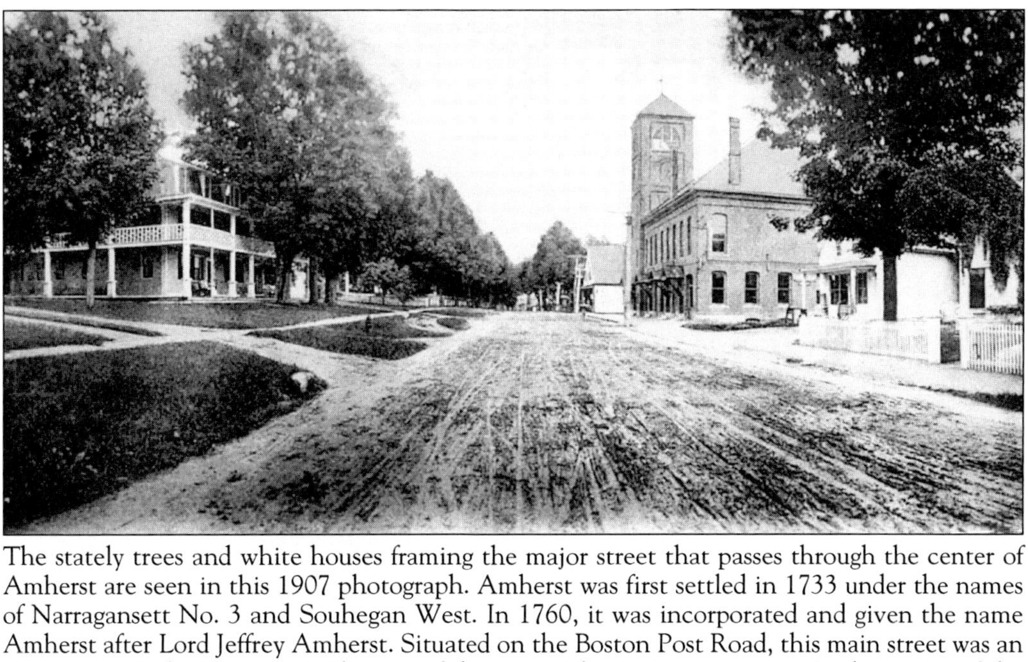

The stately trees and white houses framing the major street that passes through the center of Amherst are seen in this 1907 photograph. Amherst was first settled in 1733 under the names of Narragansett No. 3 and Souhegan West. In 1760, it was incorporated and given the name Amherst after Lord Jeffrey Amherst. Situated on the Boston Post Road, this main street was an important coaching center, and many of the present houses were taverns. In the center of the village stands a square brick building that housed the general store and post office.

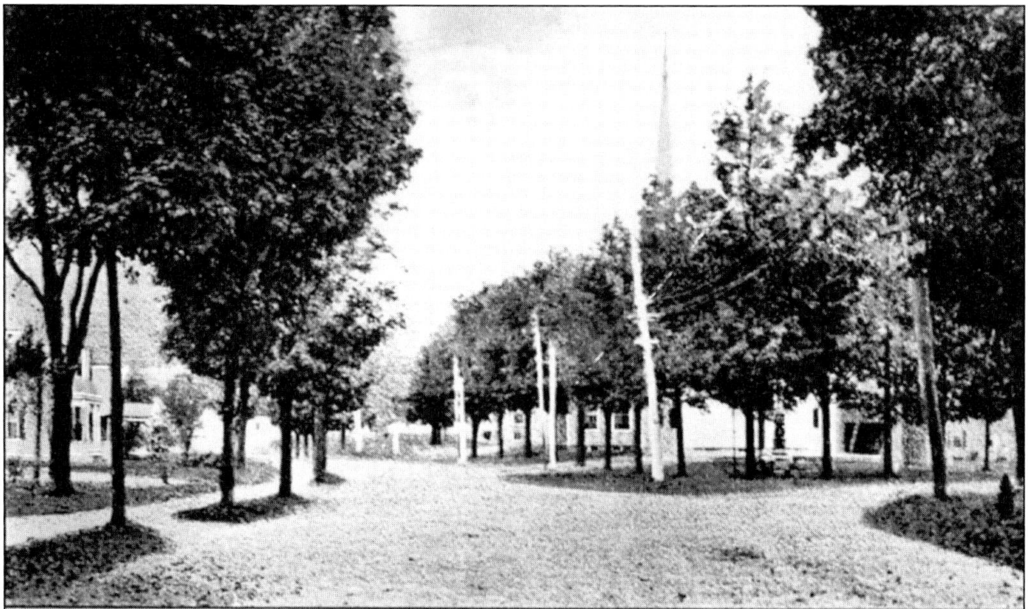

MAIN AND CONCORD STREETS, ANTRIM, N. H.

Seen here are the main street and business district in Antrim in 1905. Antrim lies on a hillside, sloping toward the Contoocook River. Sand was once taken from the river and brought to nearby Stoddard to be used in the making of the famous Stoddard glass. Although the name Antrim was taken from a town in the north of Ireland, the first settler was a Scotsman who came to the area in 1741. A few years later, other settlers arrived, bringing with them their stern Presbyterian faith. Antrim was incorporated in 1777.

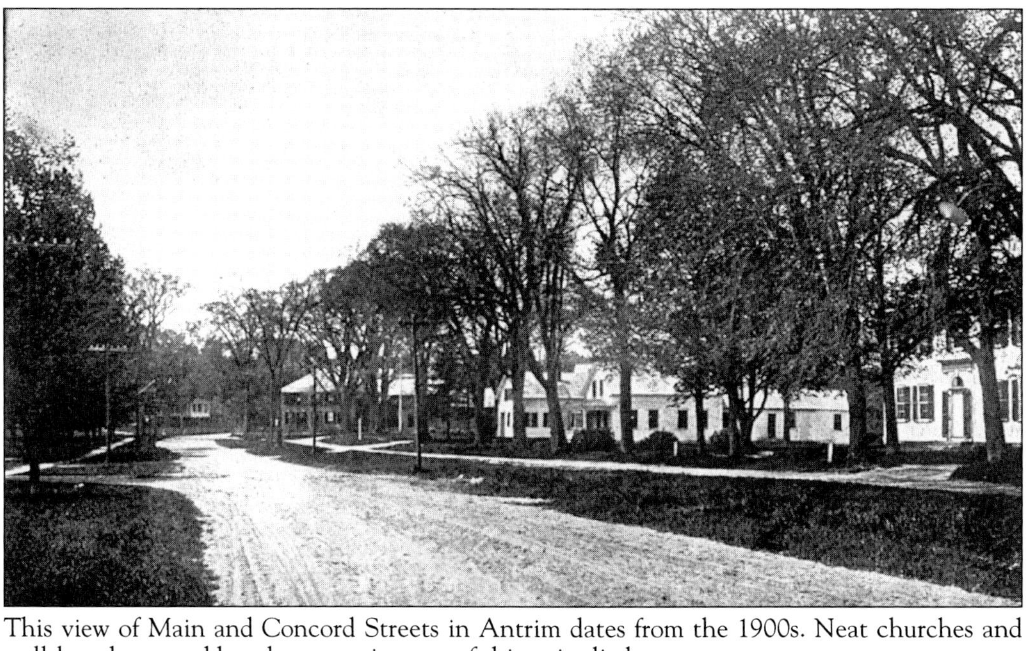

This view of Main and Concord Streets in Antrim dates from the 1900s. Neat churches and well-kept homes add to the attractiveness of this quiet little town.

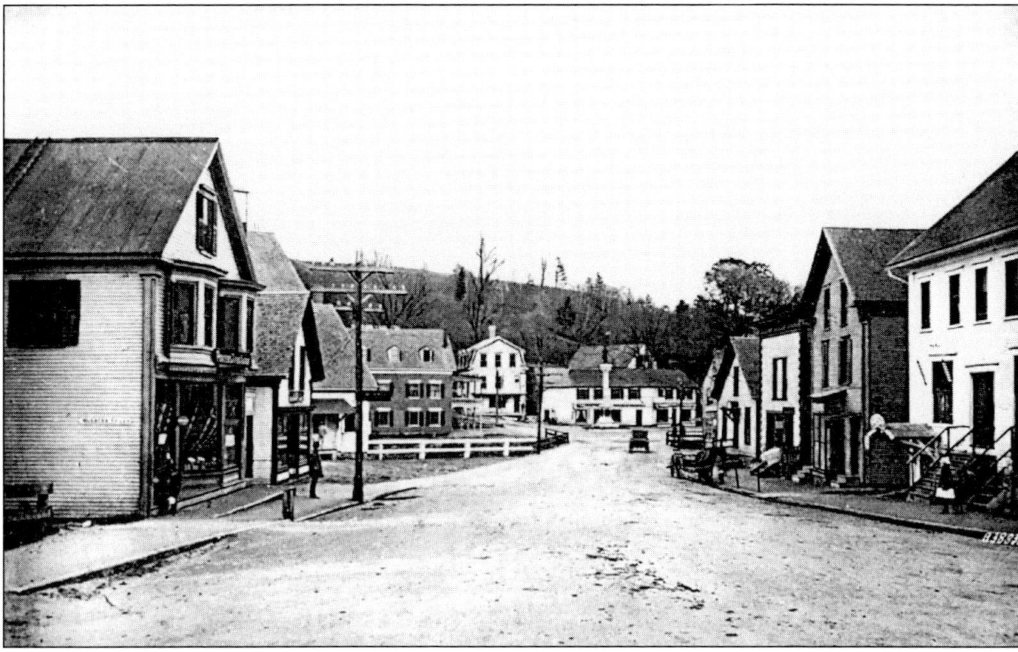

Ashland's South Main Street and Soldiers' Monument are seen in this 1900s view looking east. The business manufacturing interests of Ashland were mostly centered in this section. Ashland is a fine example of a thriving New England community.

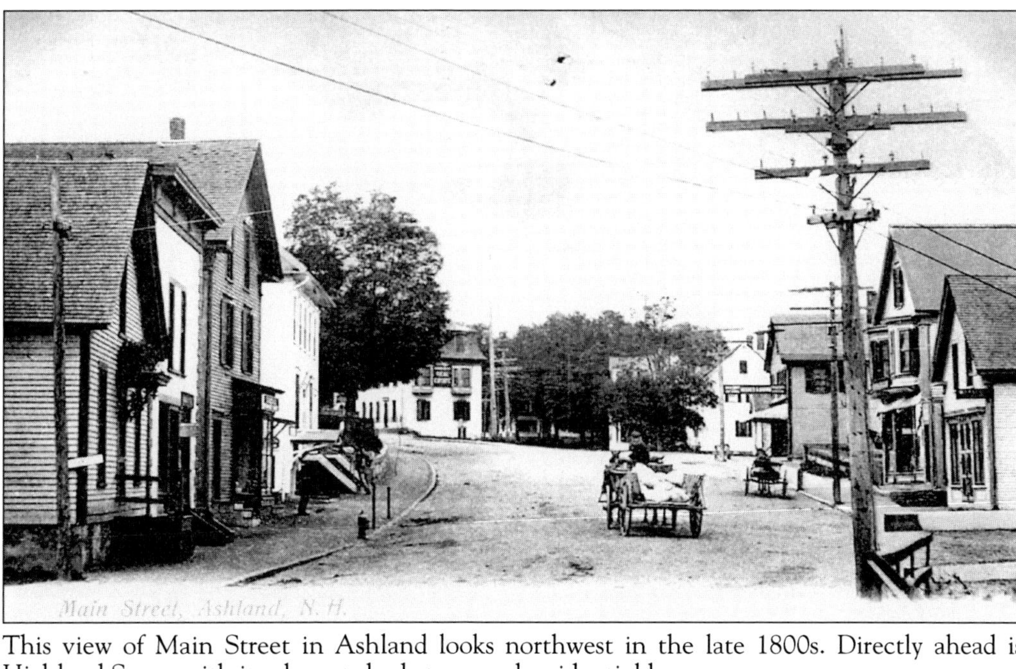

This view of Main Street in Ashland looks northwest in the late 1800s. Directly ahead is Highland Street with its elegant shade trees and residential homes.

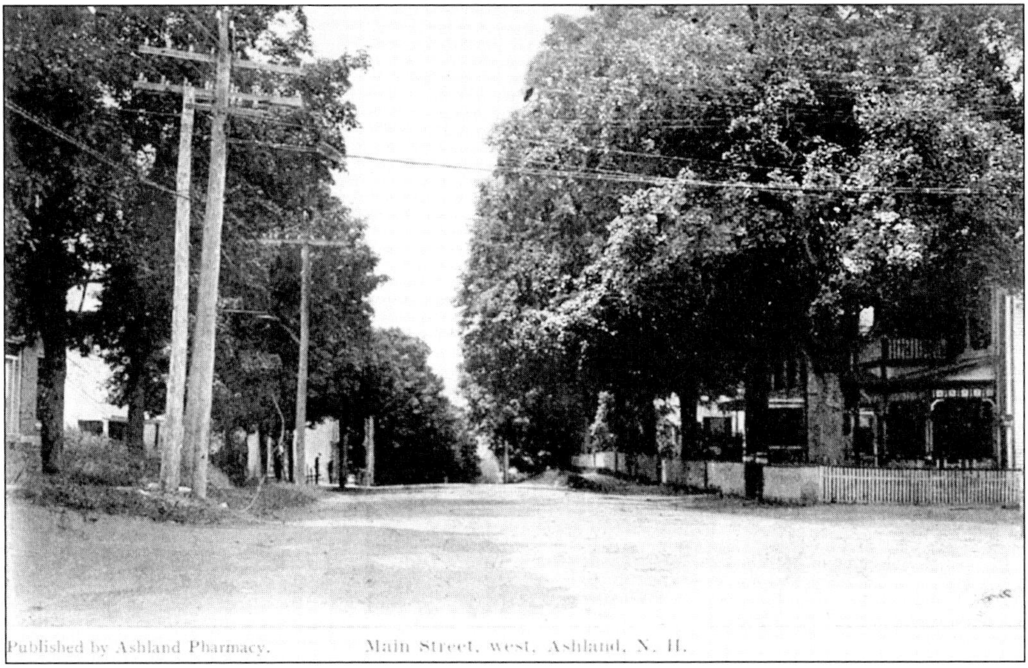

This early-1900s view of Main Street looks west toward the residential section of Ashland. Outside the business district, gracious shade trees frame the thoroughfare to the neighboring town of Plymouth.

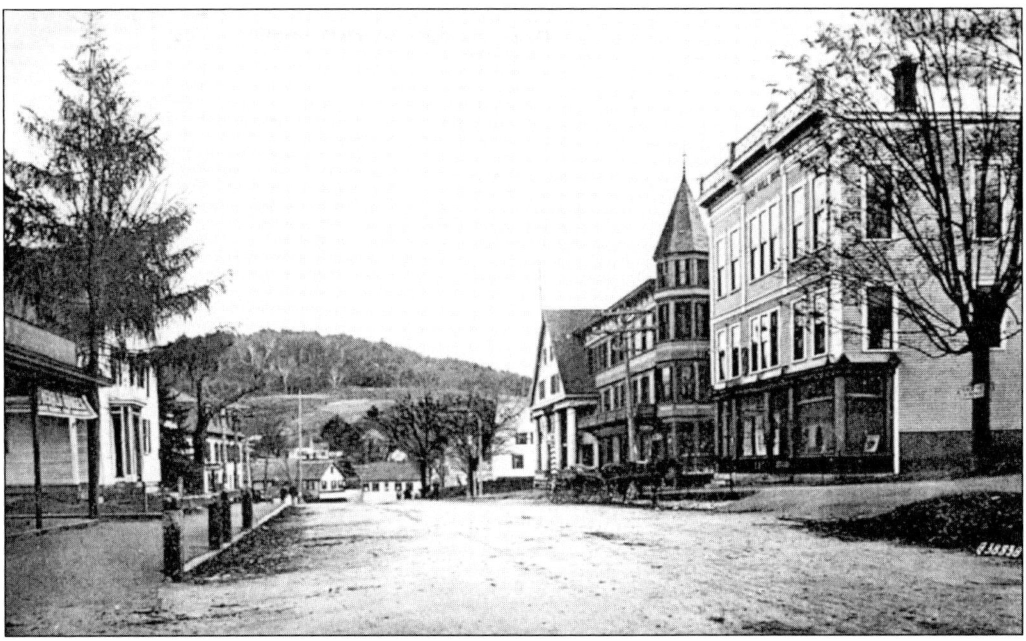

Seen is North Main Street in Ashland in this *c.* 1900 view looking southeast. Farm pastures on the hillside could be seen from the business district of Main Street. In the early days of settlement, Ashland was a part of Holderness; it was incorporated independently in 1868.

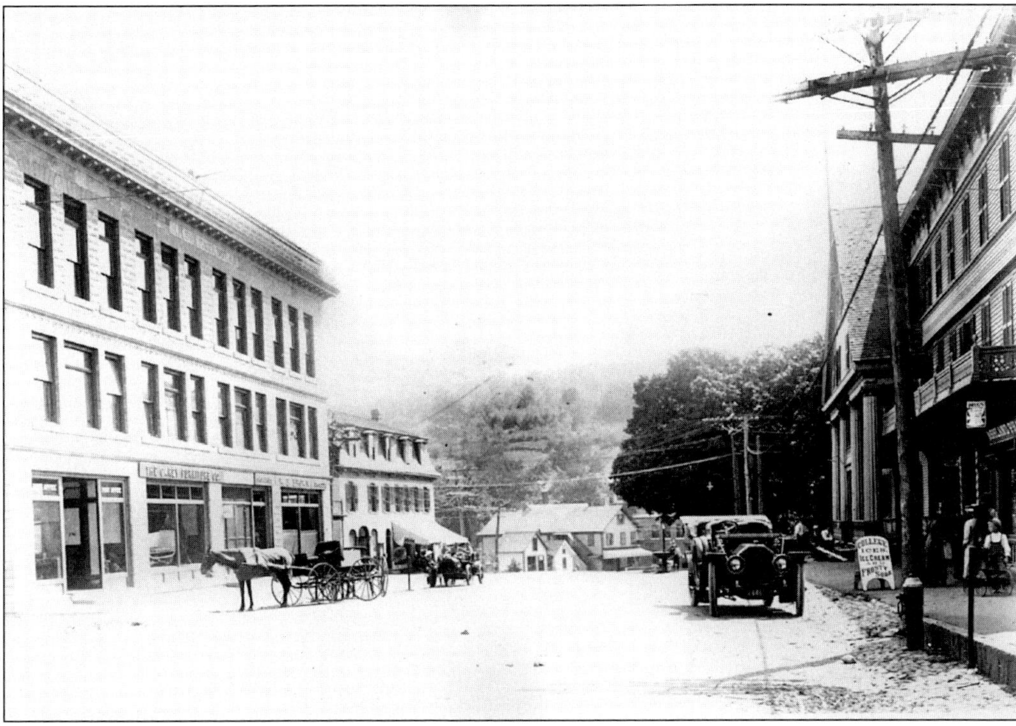

Ashland's Main Street is alive and well with the old and new modes of transportation. This view looks southeast to Monument Square *c.* 1900.

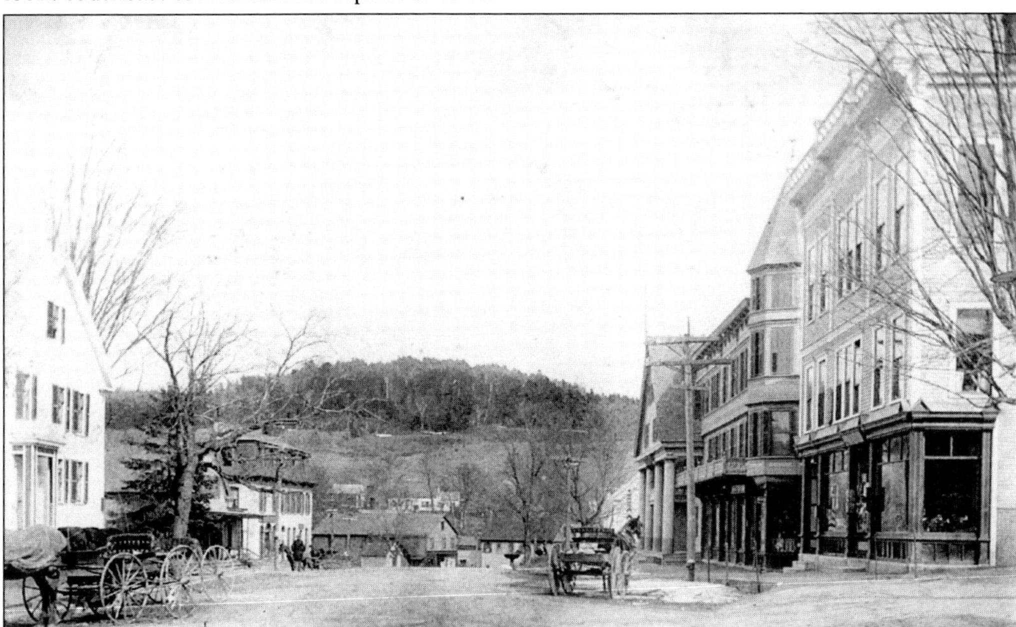

This *c.* 1900 view of North Main Street in Ashland looks southeast. During the last half of the 19th century, the village experienced a boom of activity. The creation of some of the finest boardinghouses, hotels, and inns, together with well-equipped livery stables for drives around the area, made Ashland a popular stop in the Lakes Region of the Squam Lakes.

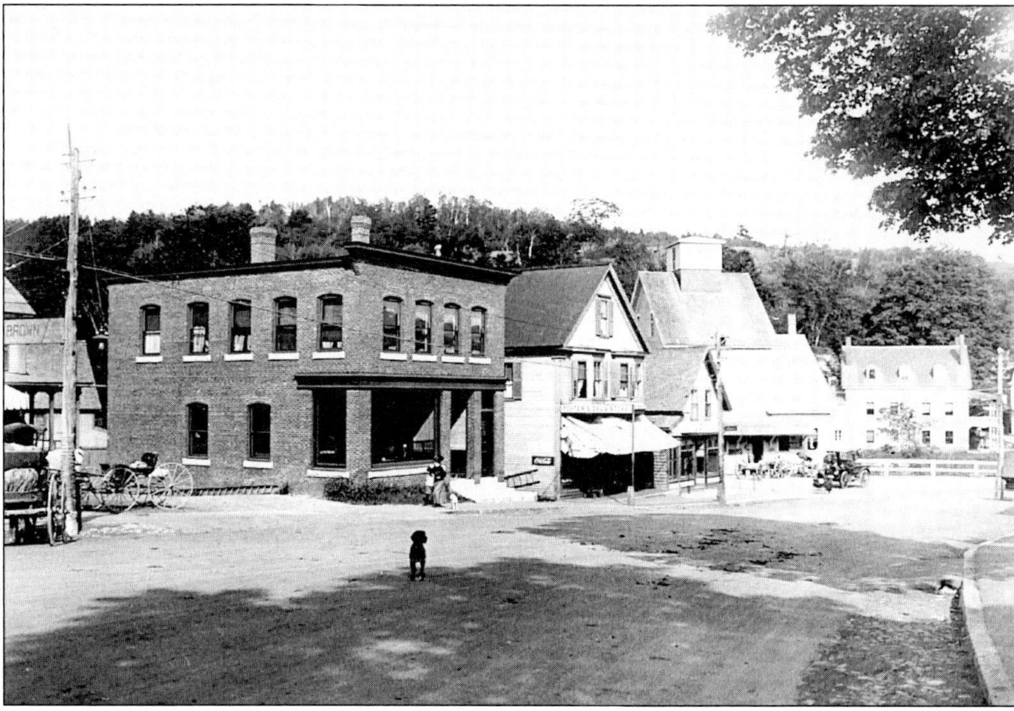

The town bank (left) is seen in this *c.* 1900 view of South Main Street in Ashland. As the town grew, the business district on Main Street expanded.

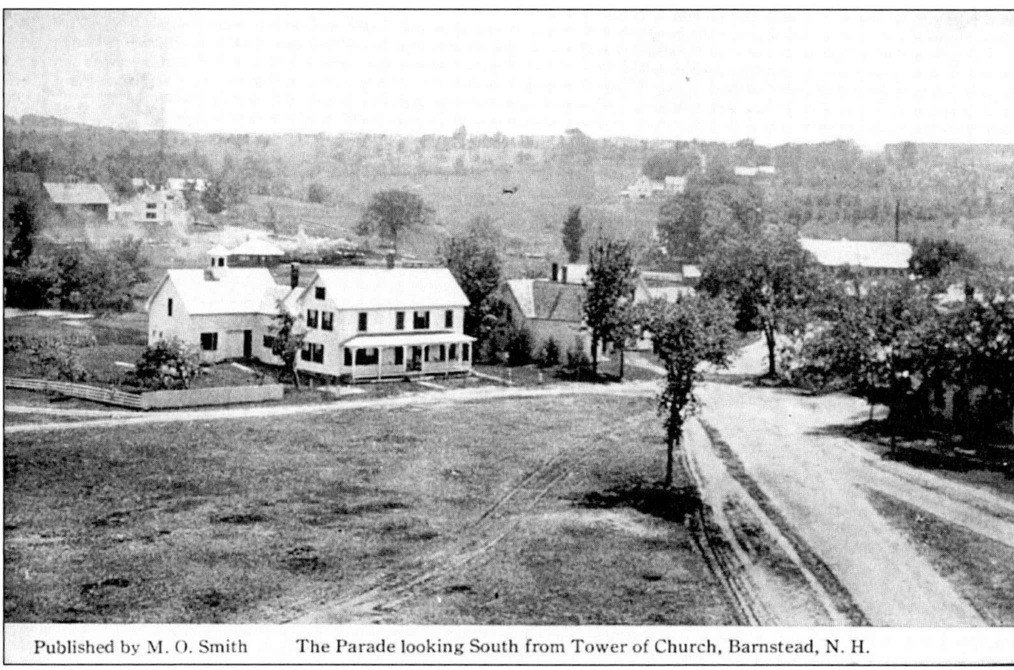

This photograph of a main road looks south from the church tower in Barnstead in 1921. This compact little town was granted to the Reverend Joseph Adams, uncle of Pres. John Adams, and other Newington residents in 1727; settlement began in 1768.

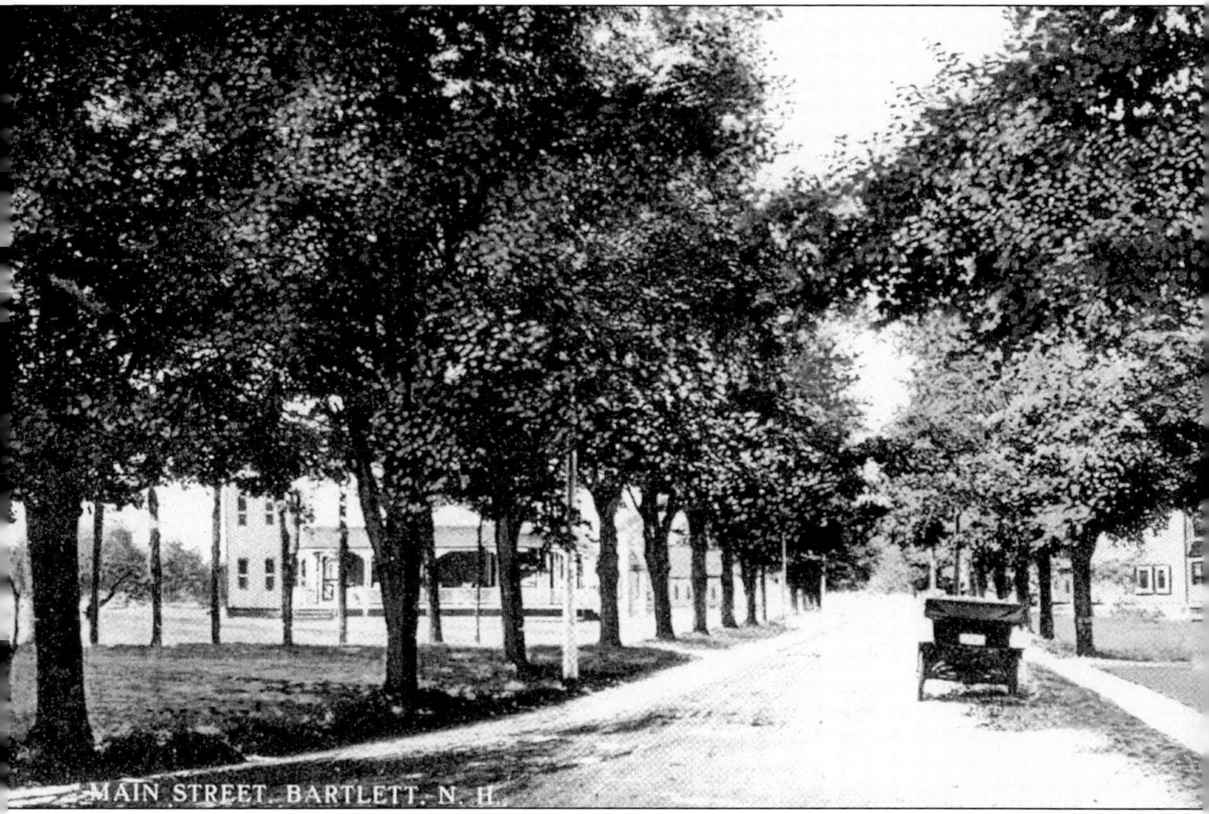

The restful appearance of the well-spaced elms and maples provides a tone of elegance to Bartlett, seen in this early-20th-century view. The town was probably settled from Conway. The land was originally granted as a reward for services during the French and Indian War to William Stark and others. At its incorporation in 1790, the town took the name of the last of the state's presidents, Josiah Bartlett. Although extensive deposits of iron ore are in the town, farming was the chief industry until later years, when Bartlett became a popular resort.

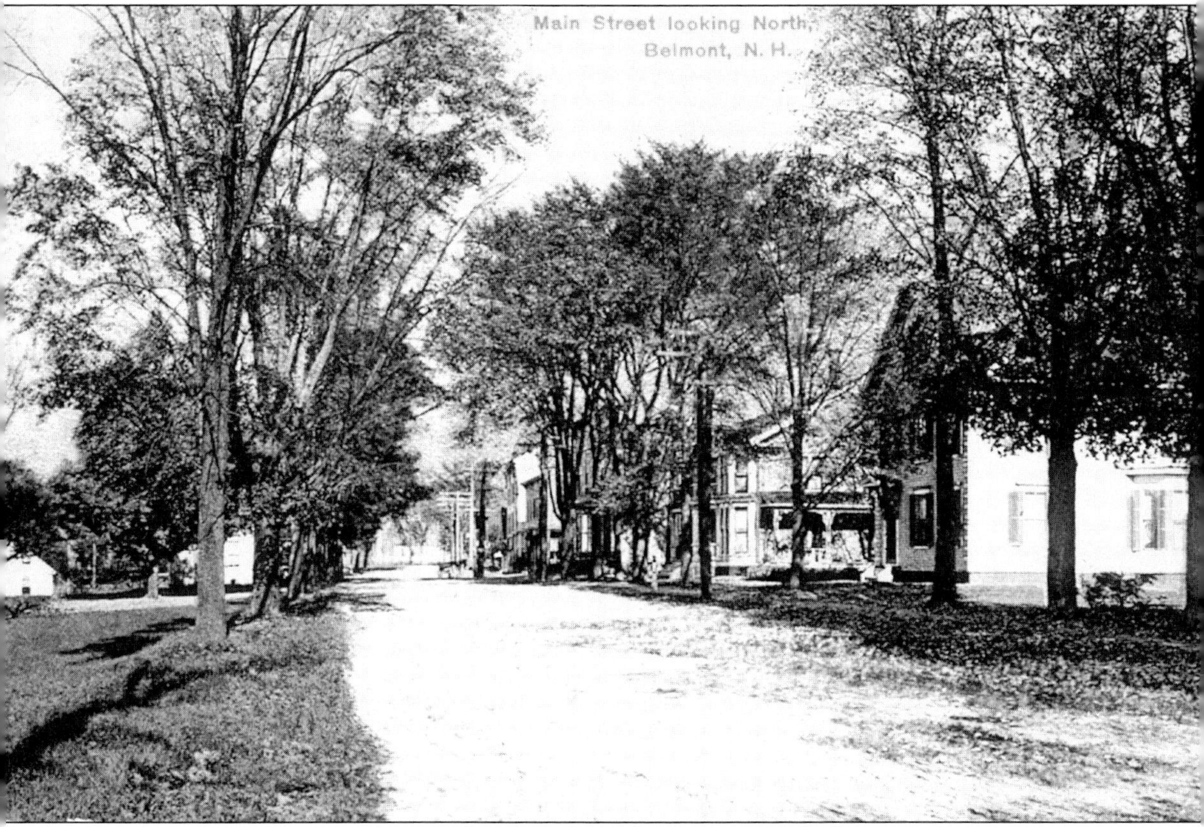

This *c*. 1900 view of Main Street in Belmont looks north. The shading trees, typical of many New Hampshire towns, greet visitors entering the business district. The town was originally a part of Gilmanton, which was first chartered in 1727 to a group of settlers from Exeter. Like most early towns, Gilmanton became separated into parishes, among them Upper and Lower Gilmanton, Gilford, Gunstock, and Gilmanton Iron Works. Belmont was known as Upper Gilmanton until it was incorporated in 1859.

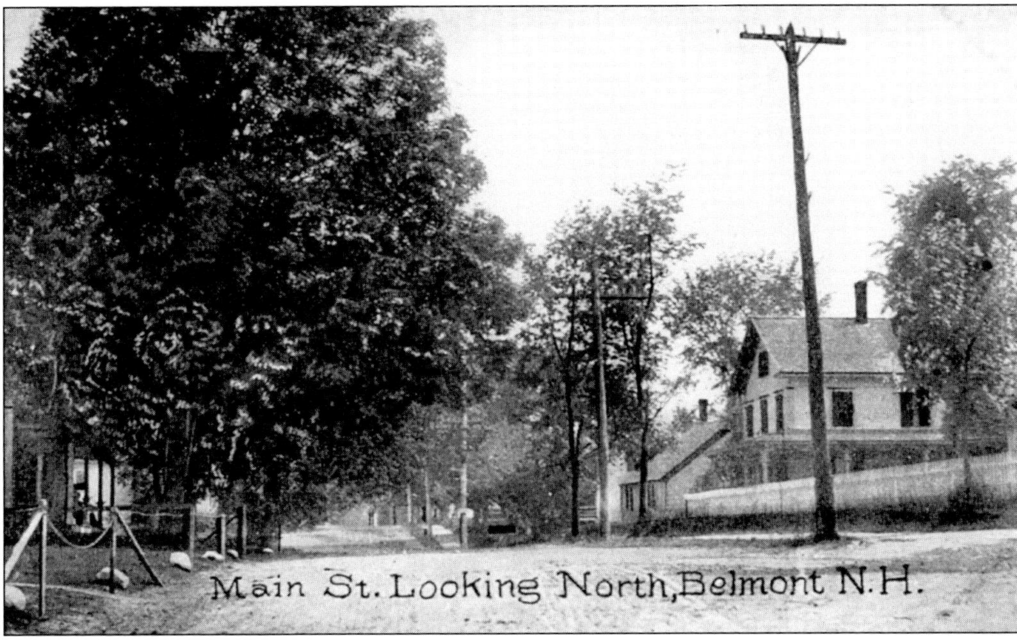

Beyond the center of town, Belmont's Main Street extends into the residential section, where fine, white Colonial homes frame the thoroughfare. Following the Civil War, the voters in what is now Belmont met and petitioned the legislature to rename their town. The name Belmont was taken from August Belmont, the well-known financier during the Civil War days; however, so far as is known, August Belmont was unaware of the petition. This view dates from *c.* 1900.

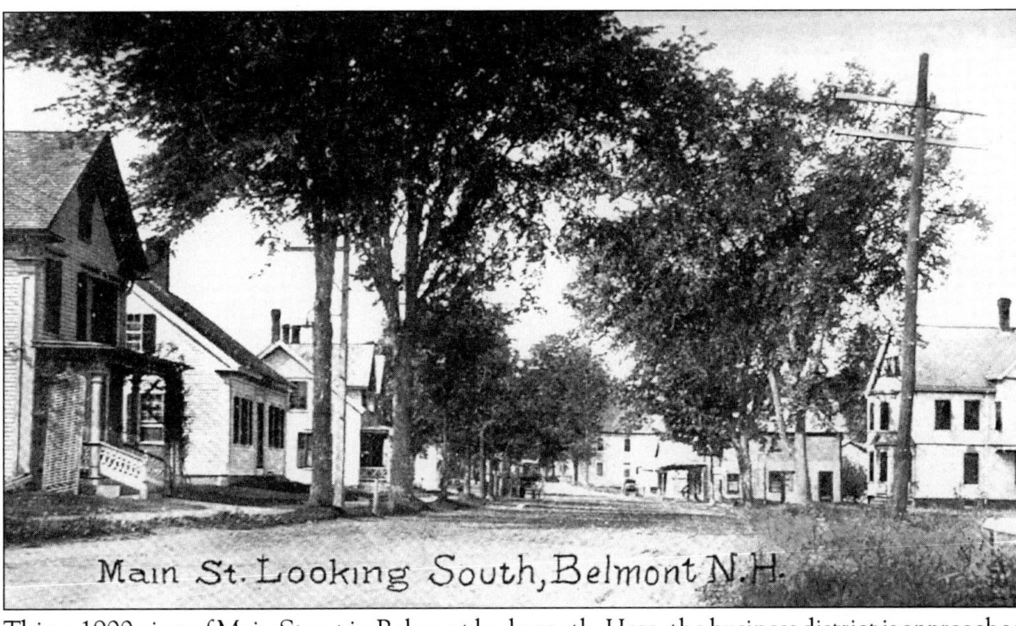

This *c.* 1900 view of Main Street in Belmont looks south. Here, the business district is approached from the north. Gilmanton was at one time New Hampshire's second most populous town, ranking after Portsmouth. It was nearly triple its present land area in the Colonial period, before Belmont and Gilford separated from it.

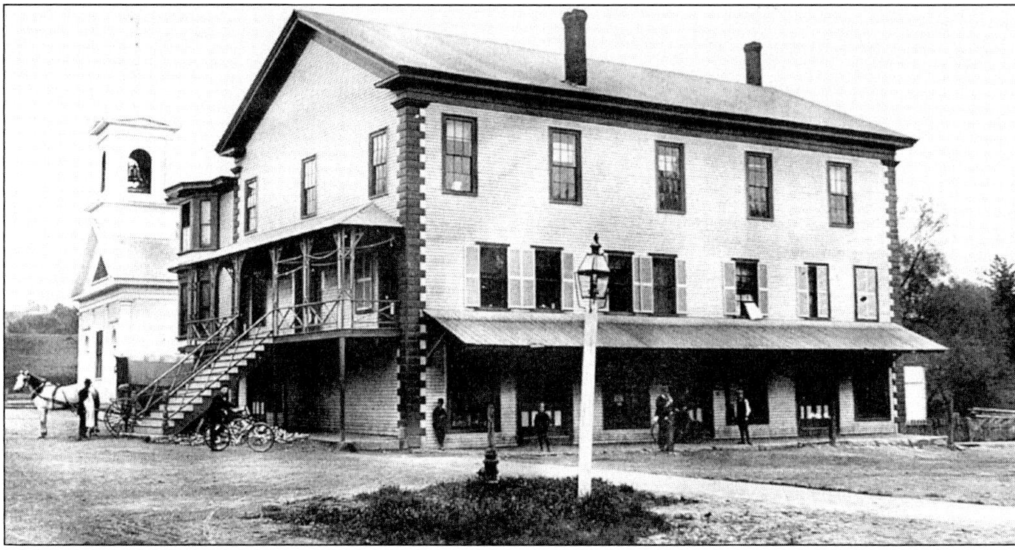

An old store and hall stood near the monument at the north end of Main Street in Belmont. The structure was built by George Riley in 1874 and was later owned by Haven Grant and Fred Hall. The building was torn down in 1927. The South Church can be seen at the rear, along with Alvin Bean's meat cart.

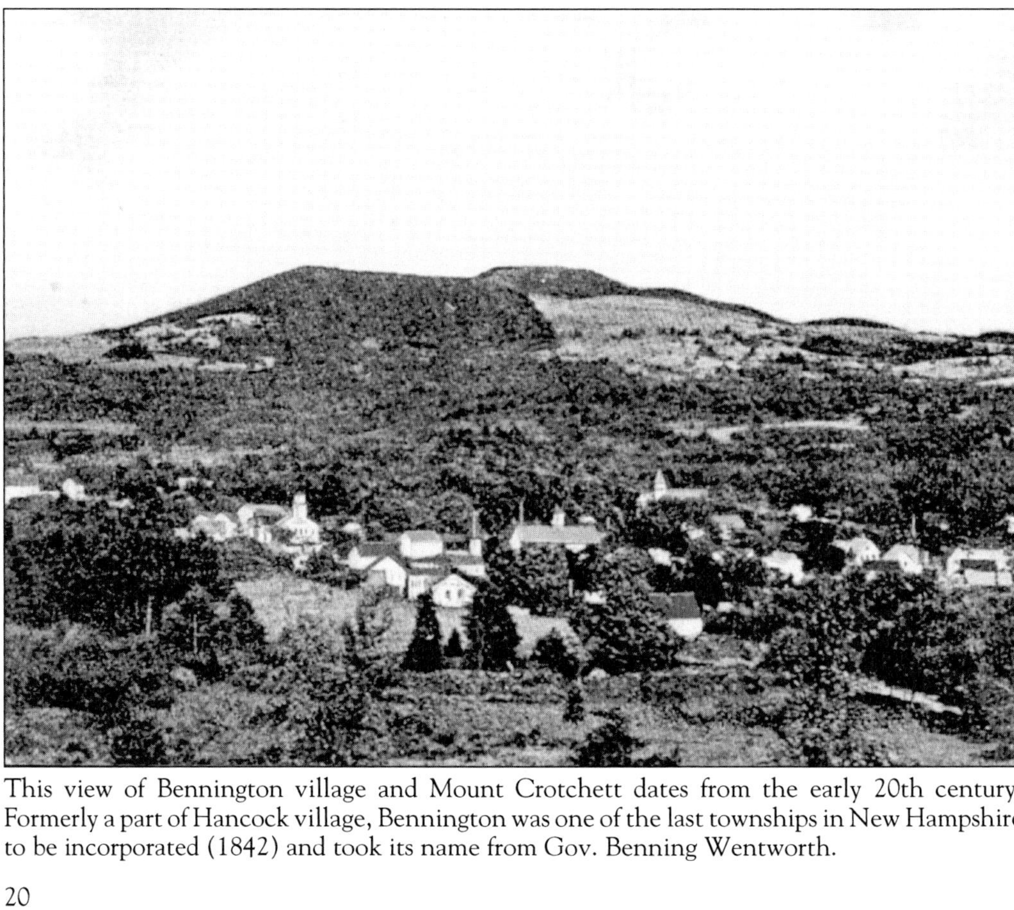

This view of Bennington village and Mount Crotchett dates from the early 20th century. Formerly a part of Hancock village, Bennington was one of the last townships in New Hampshire to be incorporated (1842) and took its name from Gov. Benning Wentworth.

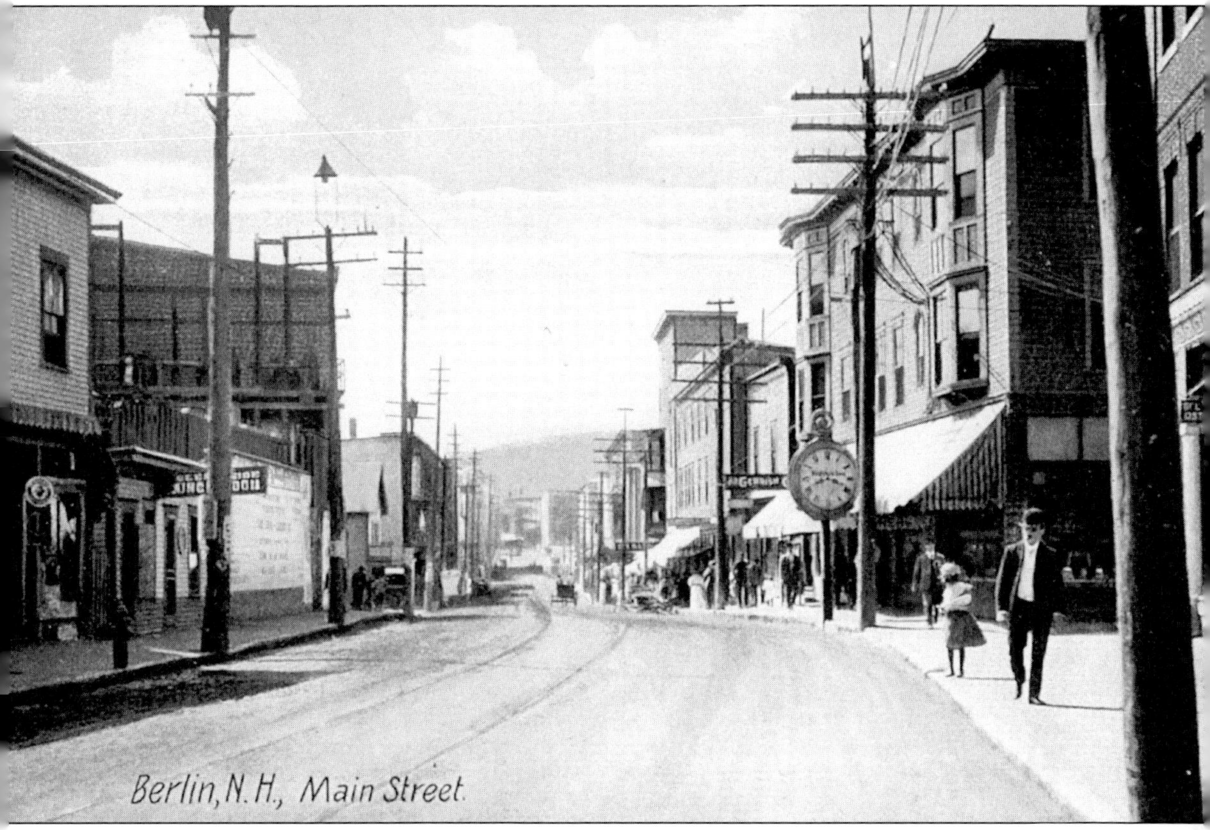

Berlin's bustling Main Street had a prosperous business district in the early 20th century. In the late 1760s, plantation lines were run in this vicinity, but it was not until the last day of 1771 that the New Hampshire Assembly granted a charter to Sir William Mayne and others under the name of Maynesborough. The first settlers were farmers, but tillable land proved extremely scarce, and the later prosperity of the city was due to the acres of encircling forest and the proximity of the Androscoggin River. Berlin is a member of the New Hampshire Main Street community, a program begun in 1997 to preserve the historic nature of the state's Main Streets.

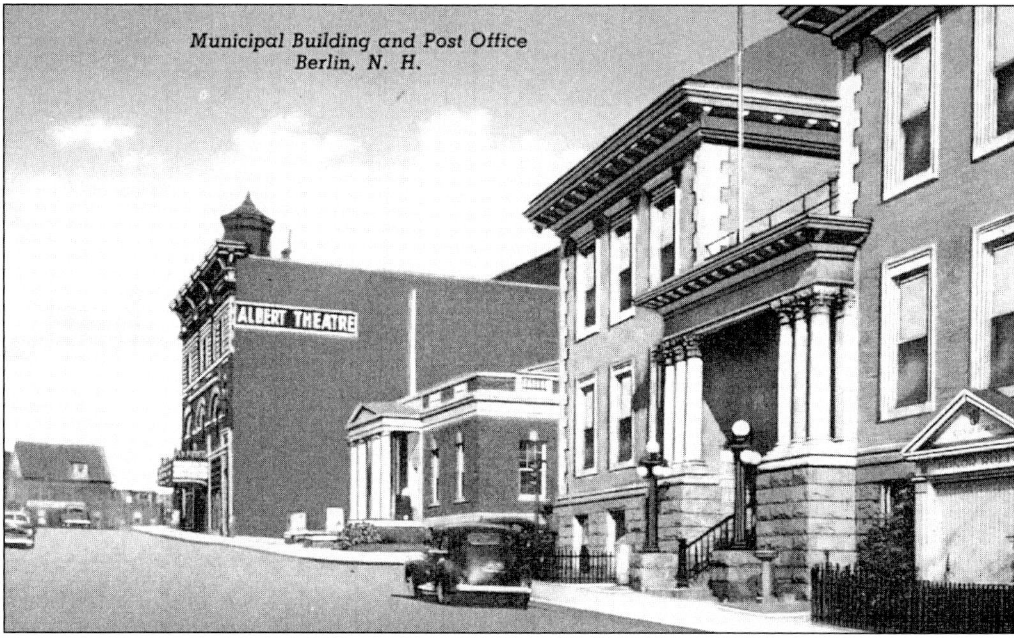

The municipal building and post office on Main Street in Berlin are seen here in the 1940s. The community and Main Street flourished through the main industry of logging. The first logging camp was erected *c.* 1825 by Thomas Lary and Thomas Green. Soon thereafter, Berlin began to prosper, and the Brown Lumber Company, the city's dominant enterprise, was born.

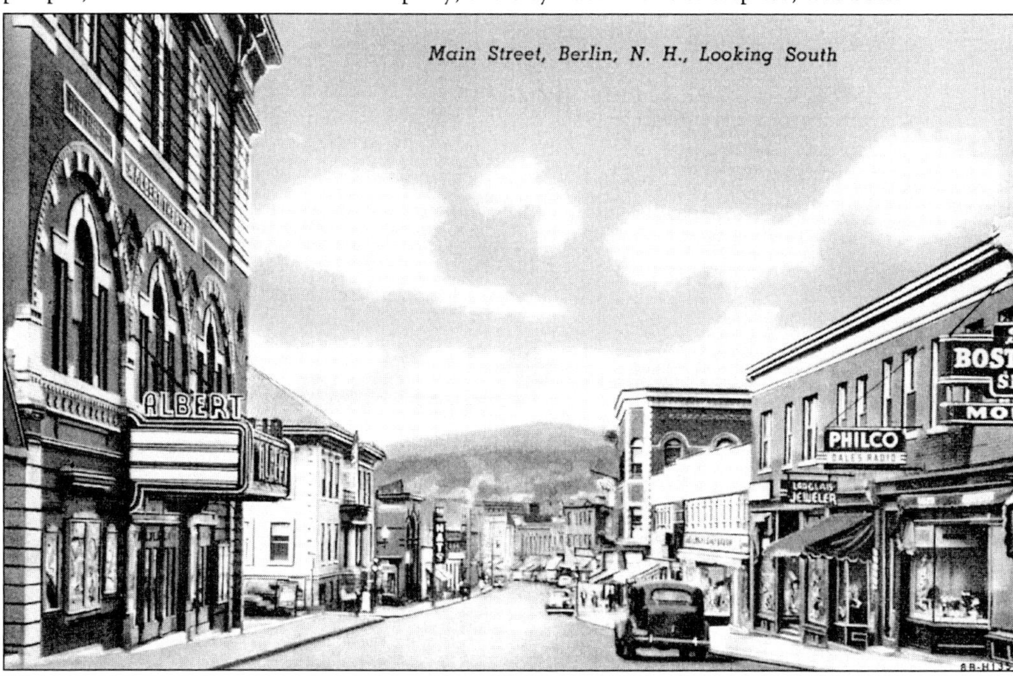

This 1940s view of Main Street in Berlin looks south. The rise of the mills greatly increased the population of Berlin, bringing in many French-Canadians and Norwegians. In 1897, Berlin had 8,000 people and was incorporated into a city. Within 30 years, the population doubled, reaching a population of more than 20,000 inhabitants.

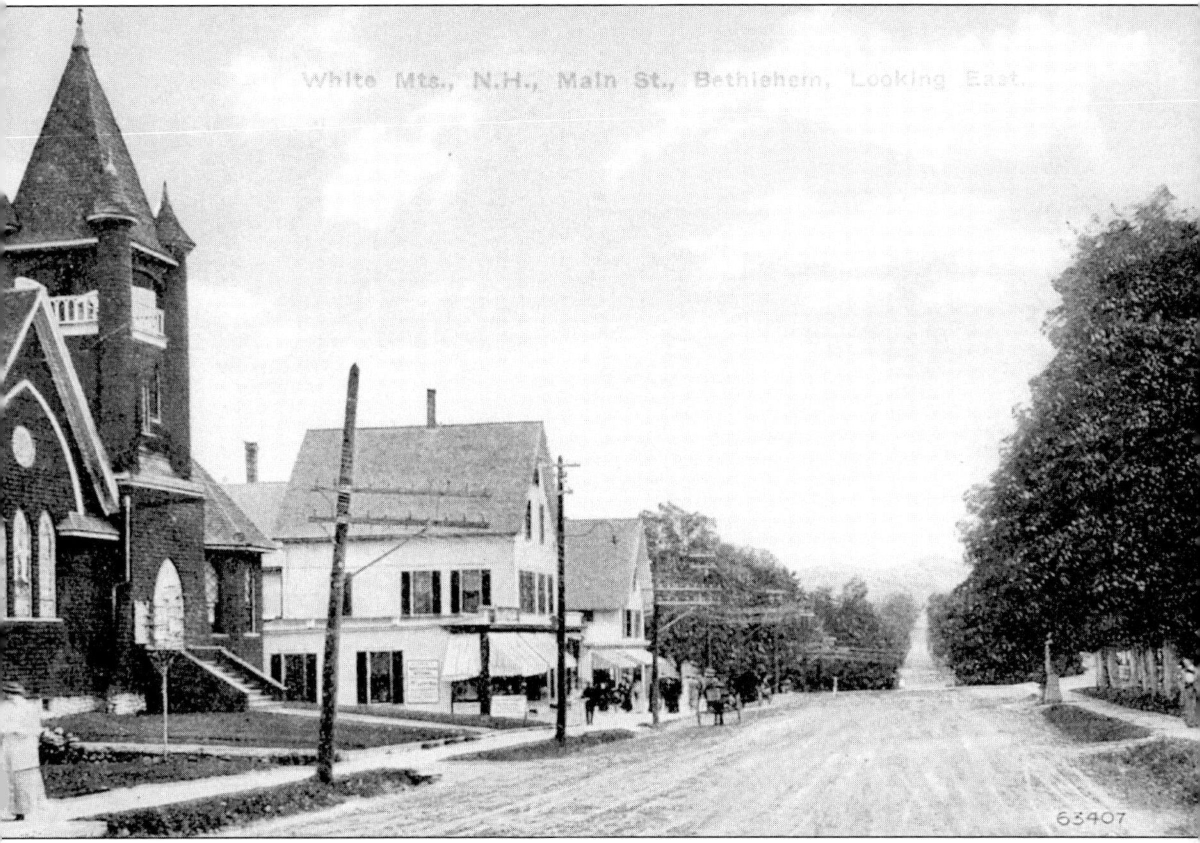

Bethlehem's Main Street stretches for two miles in an almost straight line from east to west along the northern slope of Mount Agassiz and slips down into the wide Ammonoosuc Valley. The charm of Bethlehem has drawn a large number of summer tourists to the White Mountains. This view looks east in the early 20th century.

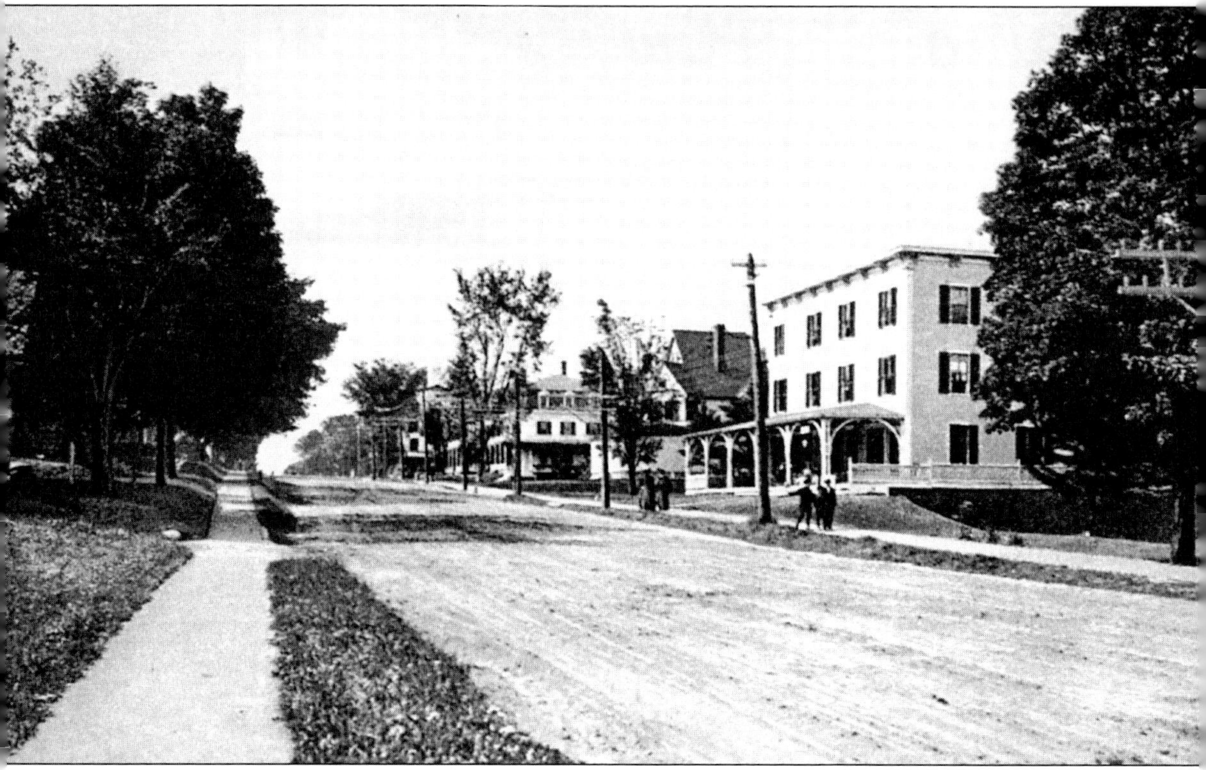

Bethlehem's Main Street is seen in this view, which looks west and dates from 1907. The original chartered town of Lloyd Hills (1774), named for Byfield Lloyd, a friend of Gov. Benning Wentworth, was never settled. A petition for incorporation was made in 1798, and when the incorporation was granted the following year, the name Bethlehem was chosen. This town reputedly owes its development as a summer resort to an accident. In 1863, Henry Howard of Rhode Island, later the state's governor, was on a journey in the White Mountains. As the coach was descending Mount Agassiz, it overturned with serious injuries to some of the occupants. The travelers remained some weeks in Bethlehem until the injured people had been restored to health. During this time, Howard became attracted to the beauty of the place. He made extensive purchases of land, formed a company to develop it, and provided money for establishing modest summer hotels. The fact that this region is most favorable for victims of hay fever was discovered later, and Bethlehem became the headquarters of the American Hay Fever Association.

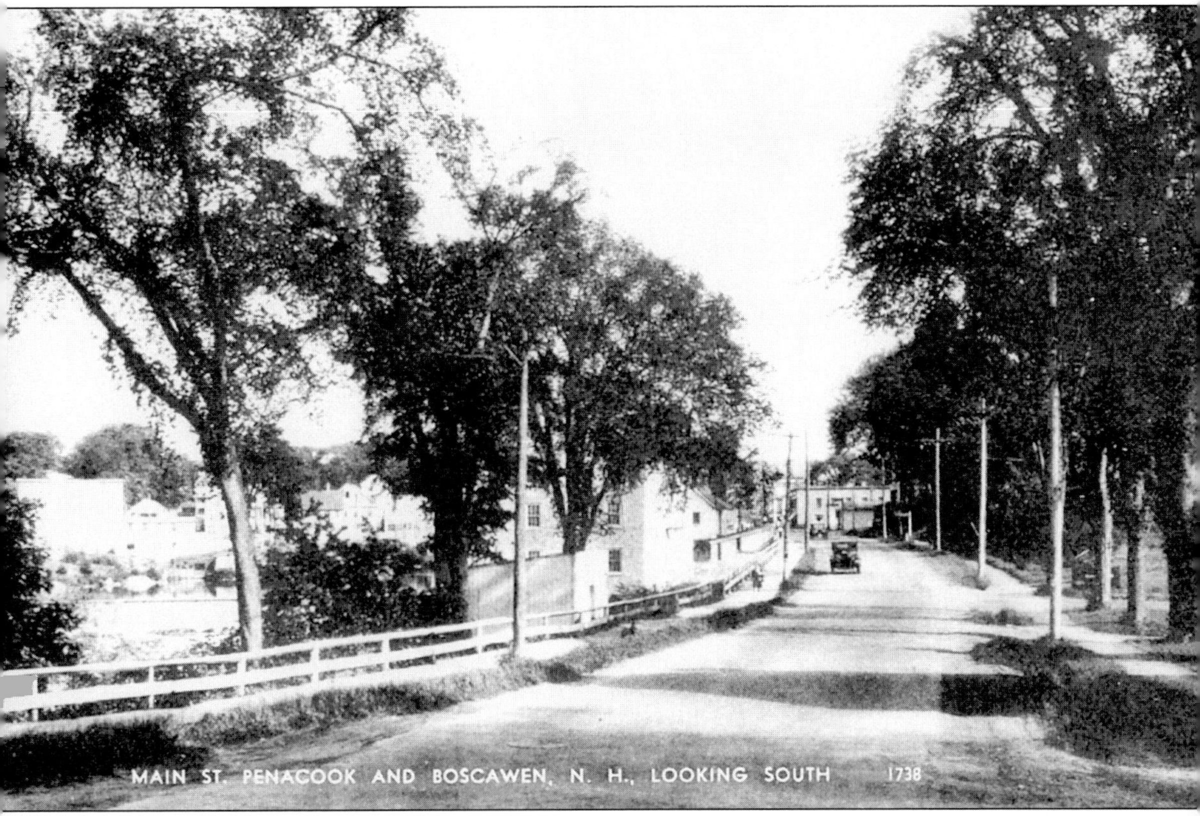

This is a view of Main Street looking south in Boscawen and Penacook in the 1930s. This Main Street, one of the most interesting two-mile stretches in New Hampshire, is lined with fine old elms that shade the old white houses. In 1733, the General Court of Massachusetts Bay granted a seven-square-mile tract of land on the west side of the Merrimack River to John Coffin and others and designated it as "the Plantation of Contoocook." The town was settled and grew rapidly. In 1760, the town was incorporated and named in honor of Admiral Boscawen, a British commander who assisted at the siege of Louisburg in 1758. A century later, the section of Boscawen west of the Blackwater River was set off and incorporated as the town of Webster.

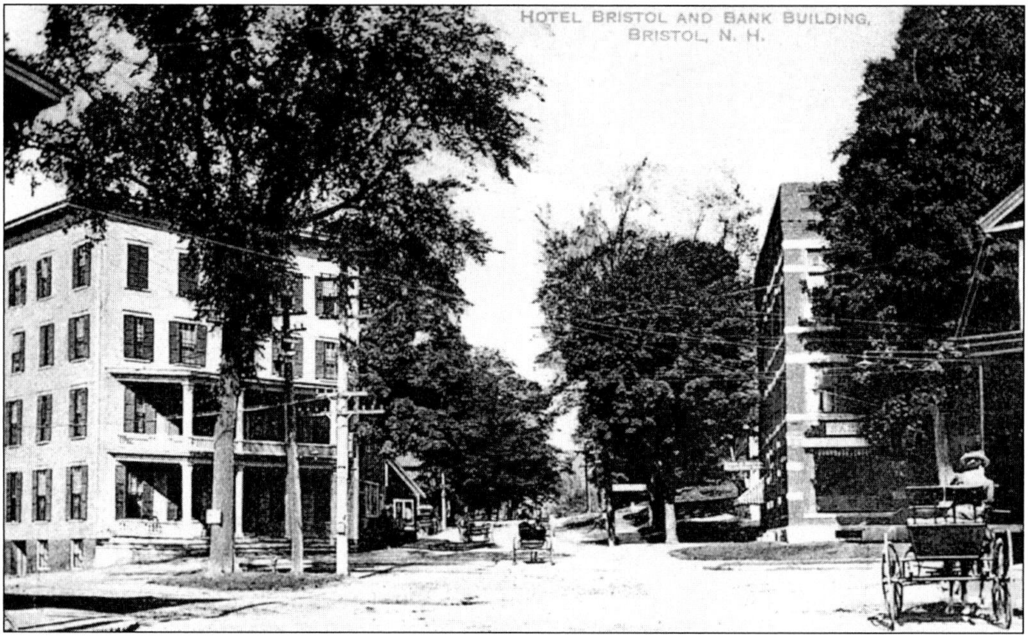

The Hotel Bristol and the bank are seen in this late-1800s view of Main Street in Bristol. At the center's intersection is an atmosphere of country restfulness. The town, granted in 1753, was set off and incorporated in 1819, taking the name of Bristol, England. At first a farming town, it was spurred to industrial activity by the opening of a railroad from Franklin in 1848. It has become a thriving resort community on the shore of Newfound Lake.

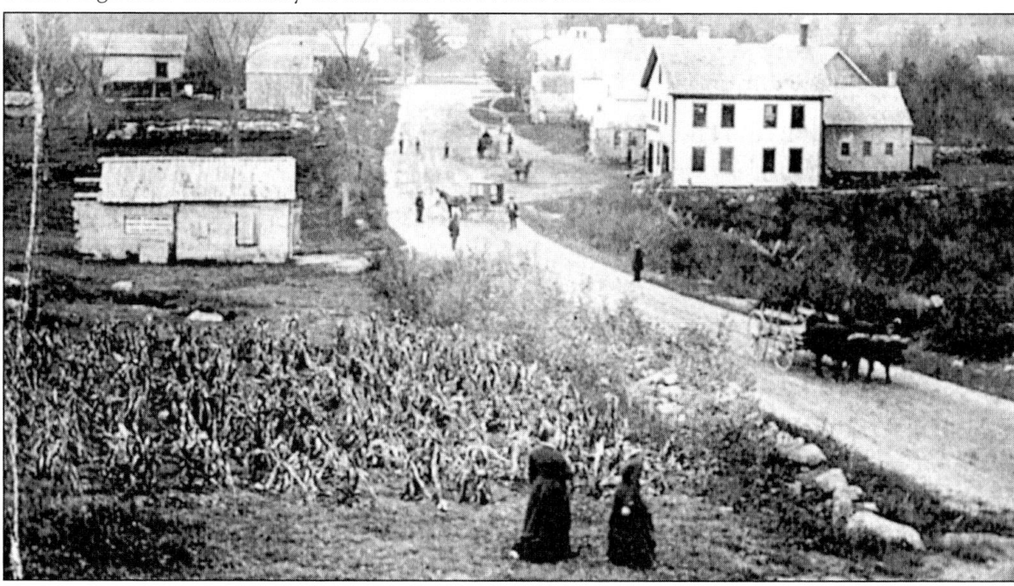

This October 1856 view of Candia Depot looks north. It is believed that this photograph was taken on the day a liberty pole was raised on High Street. Note the little cluster of houses about the general store and railroad station. David McCluer and other pioneers came from Chester Center and settled this little hilltop village, which acquired the name of Charmingfare, c. 1743. For the next 20 years, Charmingfare was a part of the town of Chester. In 1763, a charter for incorporation was granted under the name of Candia.

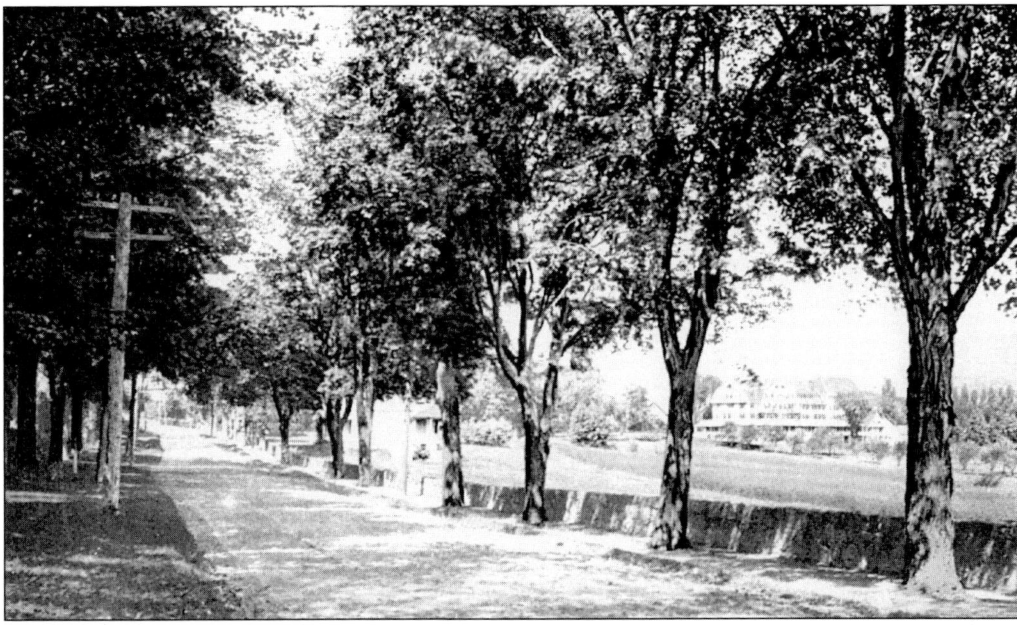

This is a 1906 view of Main Street (Meredith Road) in Center Harbor, with the Colonial Hotel in the distance. Note the bandstand in the center and the village at the end of the road. This settlement was originally named Moultonborough Addition and was later known as Senter Harbour. On the slope west of Lake Winnipesaukee were numerous summer hotels and private homes grouped around the village center. Center Harbor was incorporated in 1797.

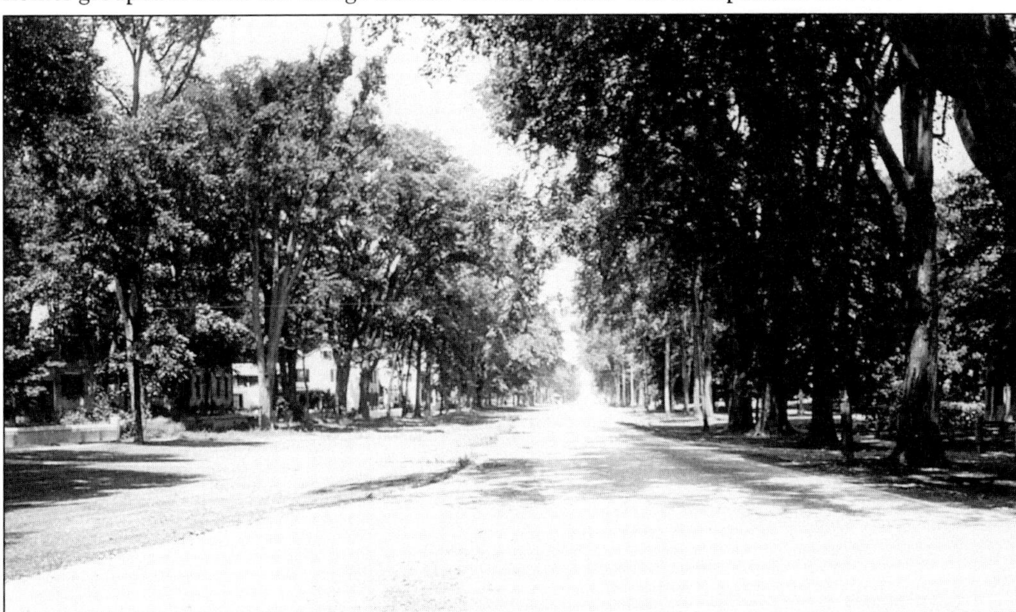

Lower Main Street in Charlestown, one of the most charming towns in New Hampshire, is seen in this 1943 view. Beautiful old elms, wide lawns, lovely gardens, and dignified Colonial homes line the wide Main Street, which was the training green for Revolutionary soldiers. Charlestown, originally granted by the Massachusetts Bay Colony as No. 4, was granted once again in 1753.

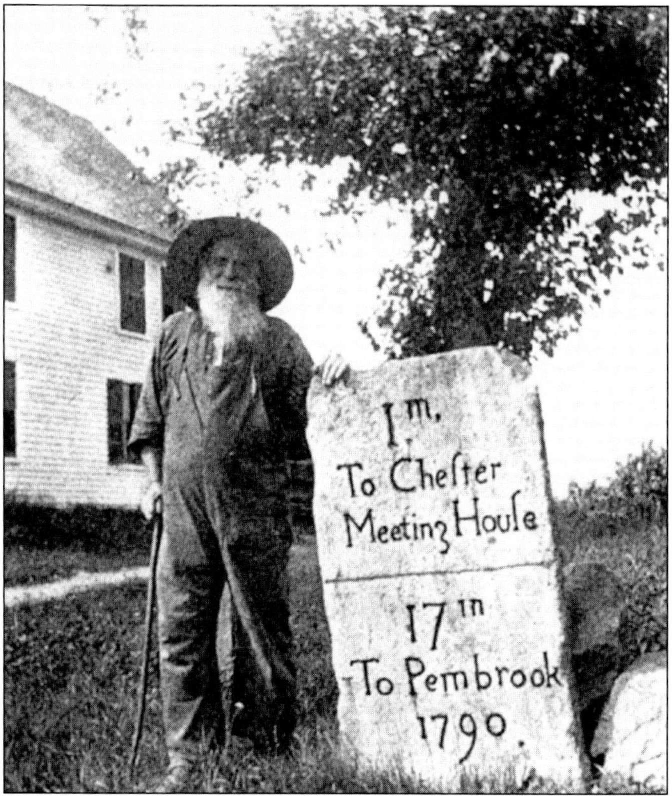

This milestone, one of many in Chester, was erected in 1790. The inscription reads, "1 m[ile] to Chester Meeting House—17 m[iles] to Pembrook." The photograph was taken in 1926.

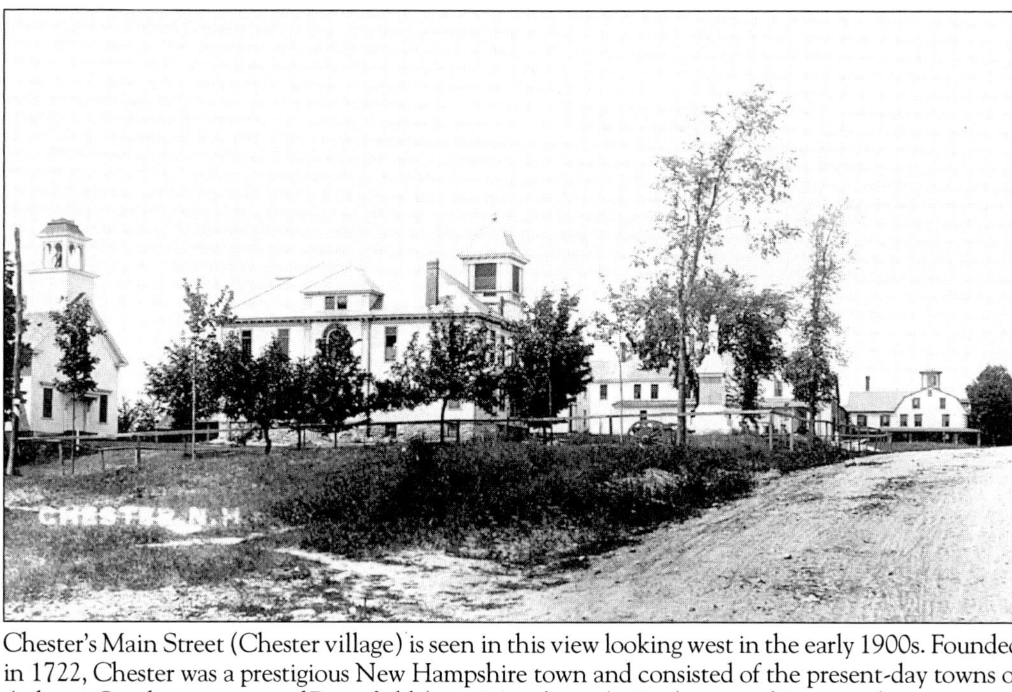

Chester's Main Street (Chester village) is seen in this view looking west in the early 1900s. Founded in 1722, Chester was a prestigious New Hampshire town and consisted of the present-day towns of Auburn, Candia, a portion of Derryfield (now Manchester), Hooksett, and Raymond.

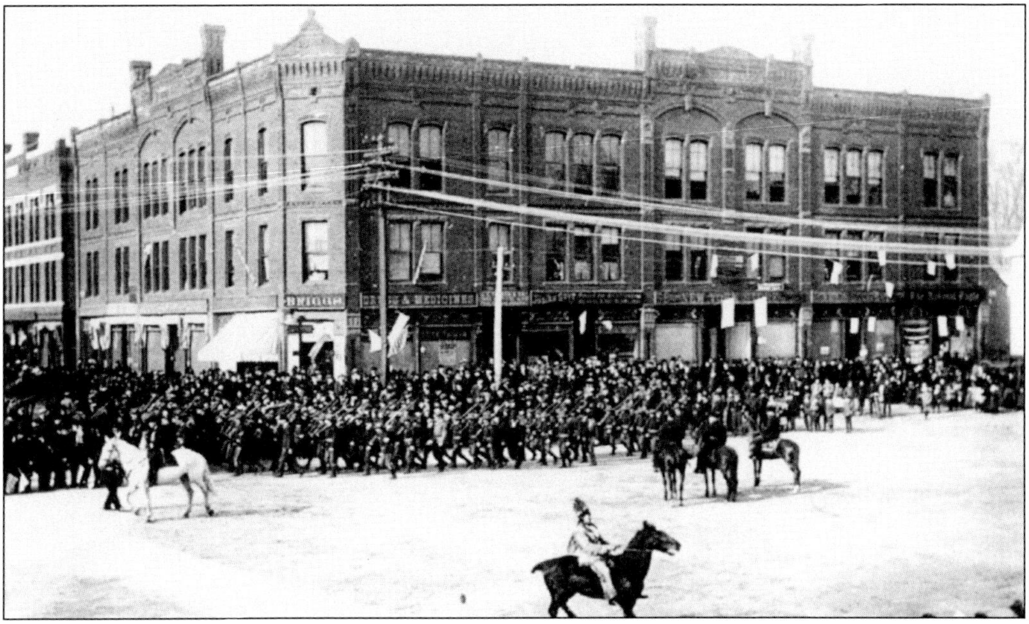

This is an 1891 view of the Union Block at Tremont Square in Claremont. A parade of marching men has brought the town out in full force for a special celebration. The town was granted in 1764, taking the name of Claremont in honor of Gov. Benning Wentworth's friend Lord Clive, whose English estate bore that name. Only three of the 69 grantees ever settled here, and they were preceded by two Connecticut men, Moses Spafford and David Lynde, in 1762.

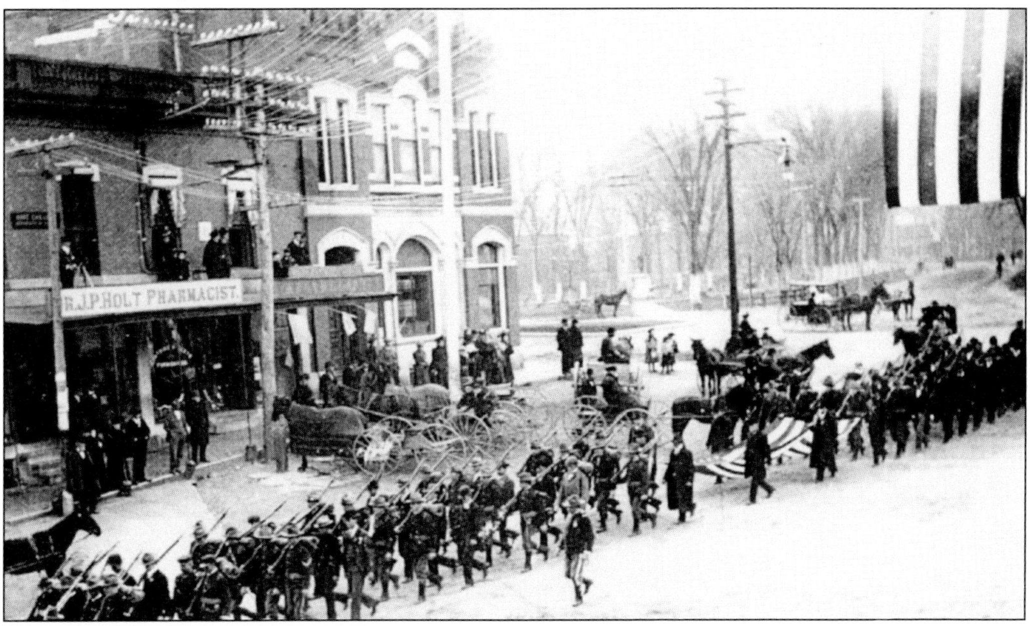

The Claremont National Bank is seen here in Tremont Square in 1891. The parade continues through the center of town on the wide Main Street. The settlement spread almost immediately to Town Hill, where many of the old houses, some of them former taverns and early farms, still remain. Claremont's growth has steadily increased through the years, and the town has become an industrial, cultural, and resort center in the Connecticut Valley.

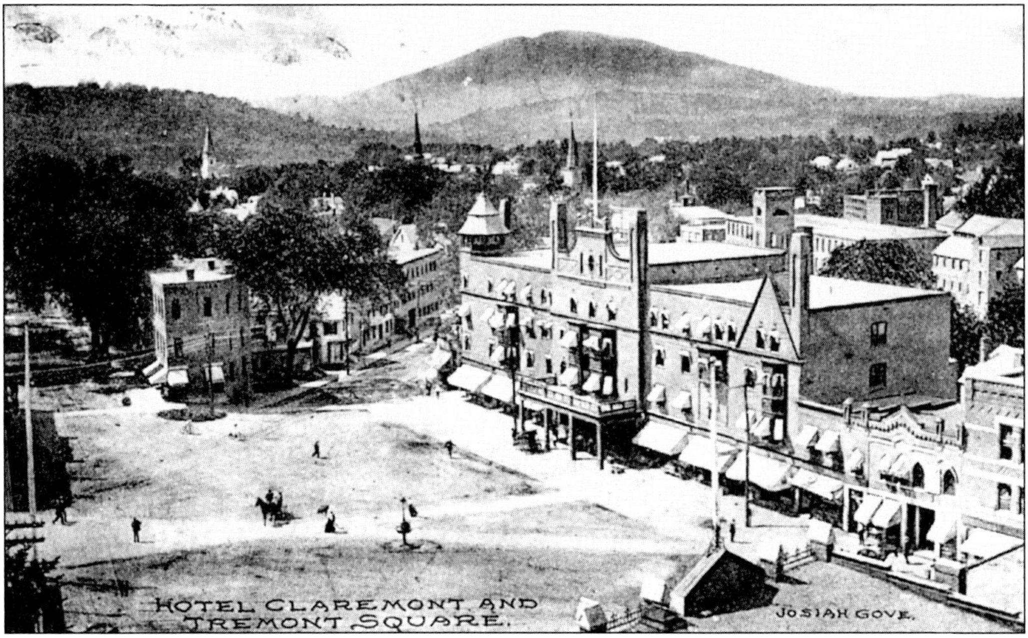

This 1905 view of Main Street at Tremont Square shows the Hotel Claremont on the right. The center of the town is Tremont Square, from which radiates the business section of two- and three-story brick buildings, nearly all of which have been remodeled. Since this is the business district not only for the people of Claremont but also for surrounding villages in both New Hampshire and Vermont, the square is a busy place. Claremont is a member of the New Hampshire Main Street community.

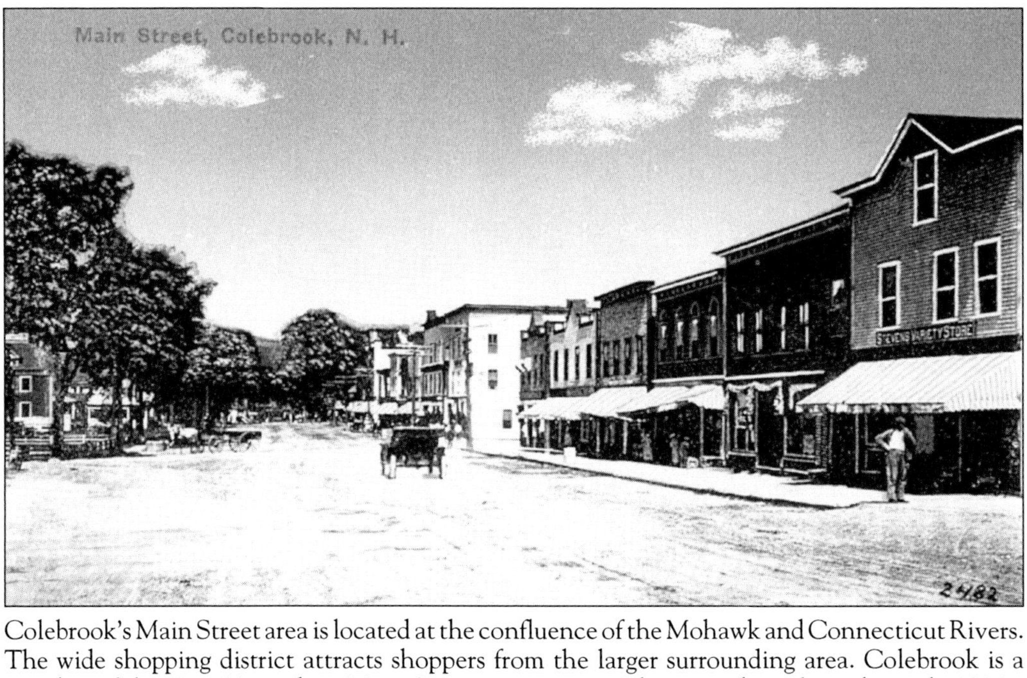

Colebrook's Main Street area is located at the confluence of the Mohawk and Connecticut Rivers. The wide shopping district attracts shoppers from the larger surrounding area. Colebrook is a member of the New Hampshire Main Street community. This view dates from the early 1900s.

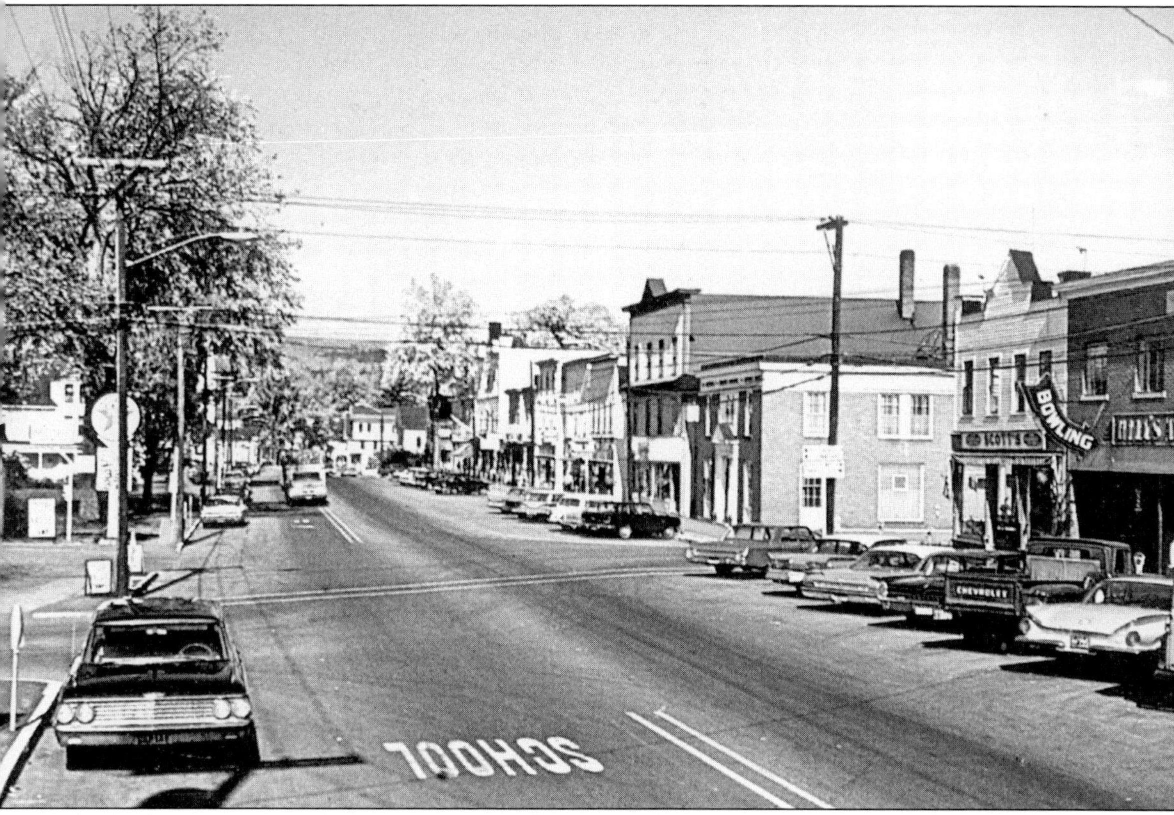

This early-1900s view of Main Street in Colebrook looks north. Over the past 50 years, Main Street has continued to expand and prosper in the North Country. The town was first granted with Stewartstown and Columbia in 1770 to Sir George Colebrook, Sir James Cockburn, John Stuart (Stewart) of London, and John Nelson from the island of Granada in the West Indies. It was given the name Colebrook when it was incorporated in 1796.

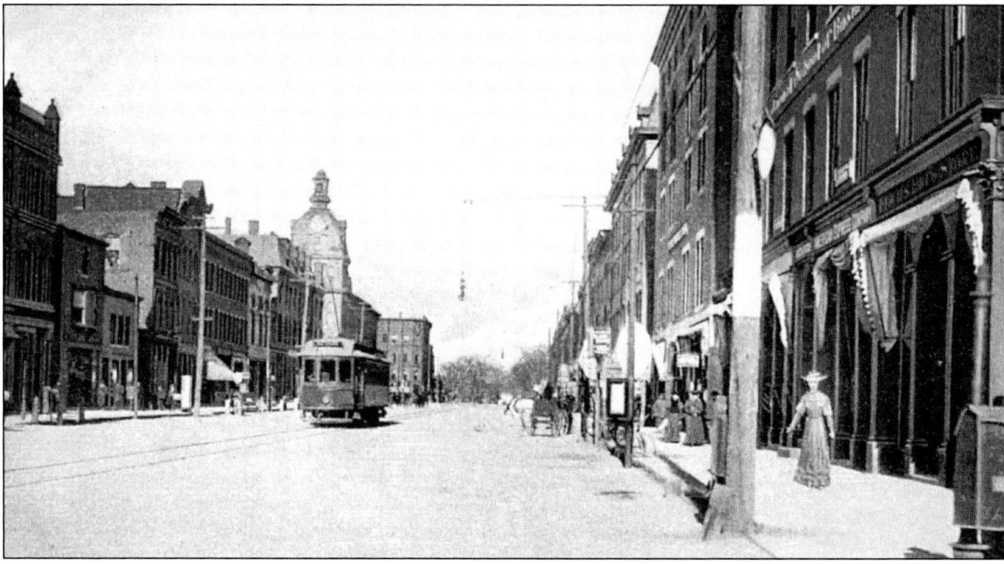

Concord's Main Street is seen in this 1909 view. The capital of New Hampshire, with its flourishing business district, has an air of importance. Concord is a member of the New Hampshire Main Street community.

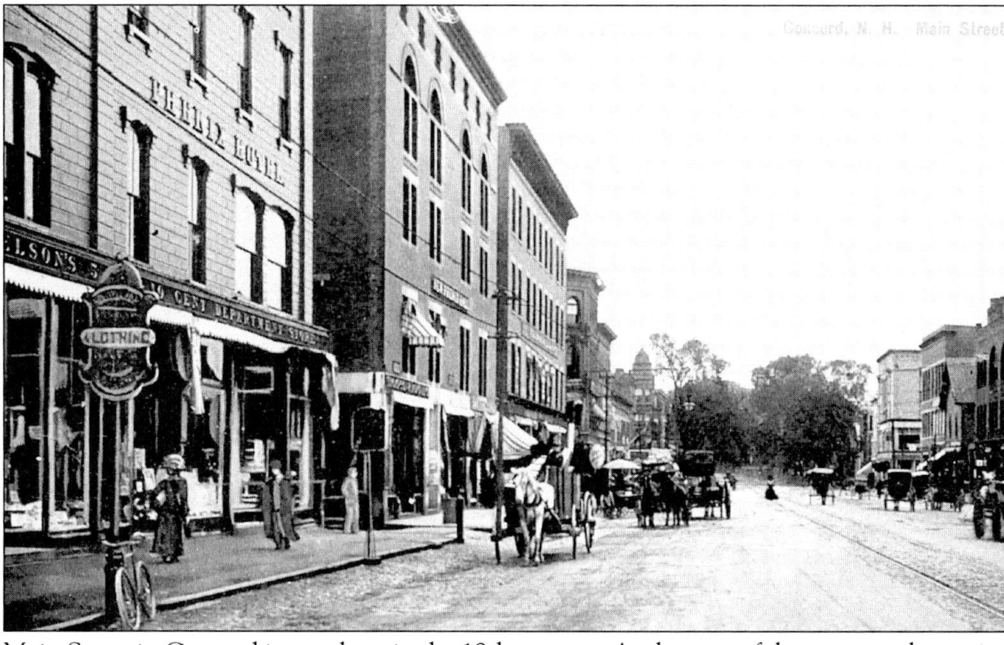

Main Street in Concord is seen here in the 19th century. At the turn of the century, the capital became the political, economic, and social center of activity for the state. Main Street has kept up with the growing needs of the city.

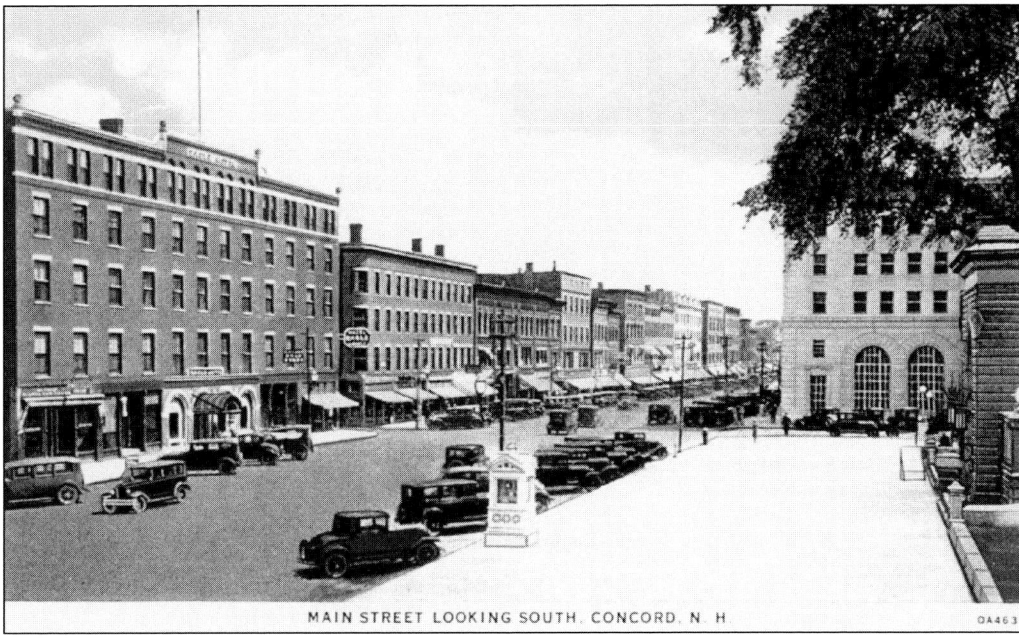

This view of Main Street in Concord looks south and dates from the 1930s. Situated on the west bank of the Merrimack River, the city has a compact business district. The seat of government is located on Main Street, in the center of the city, which has been the capital of New Hampshire since 1808. It was founded as the plantation of Penny Cook by a grant in 1659 from the Massachusetts Bay Colony to Richard Waldron and others. In 1725, it was regranted by Massachusetts to a group including Ebenezer Eastman, an early settler.

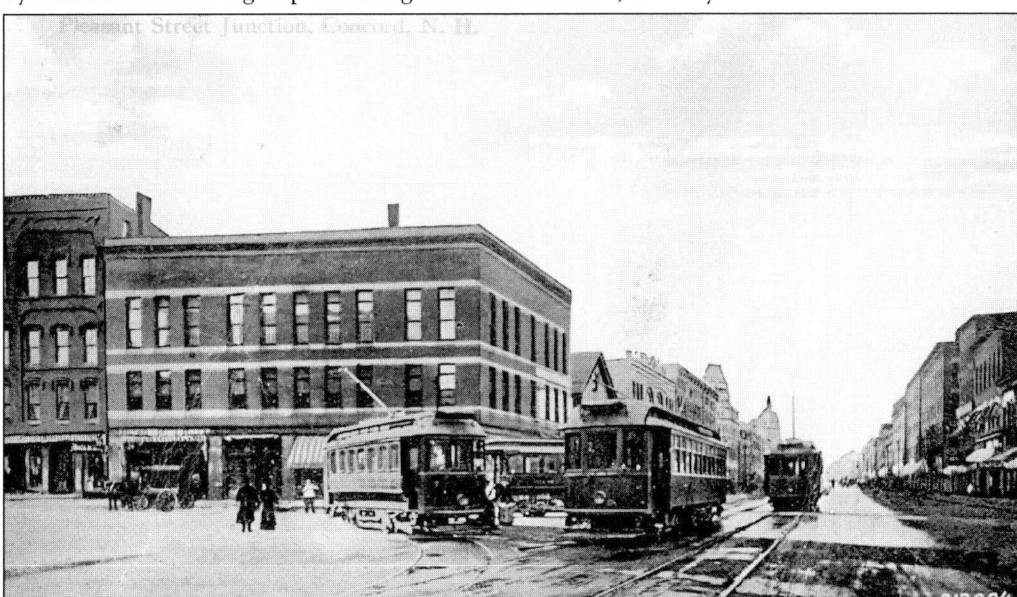

The Pleasant Street junction in Concord is seen in this early-1900s view. Concord was considered the key city in transportation, the crossroads of New Hampshire's railroads and highways. Note the number of streetcars. In 1733, the town was incorporated by Massachusetts as Rumford, and it was reincorporated by New Hampshire as Concord in 1765.

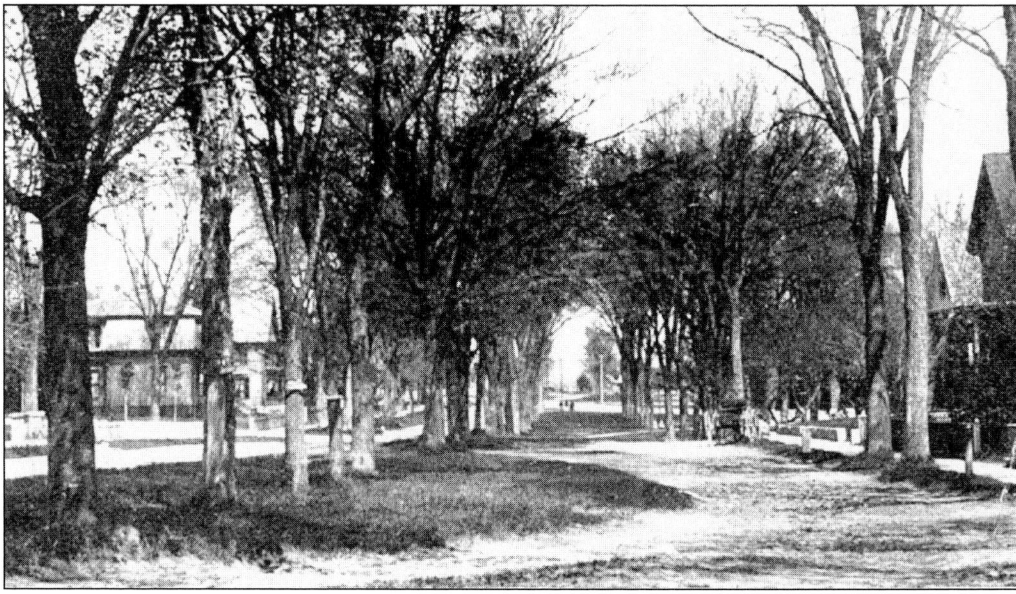

This is a *c.* 1900 view of North Main Street in Concord. The residential part of Concord, framed with beautiful shady trees, lies mainly to the west and north of the Merrimack River and includes the homes of many people of prominence in the state. This community is grouped within an area of seven blocks between Main Street and State Street.

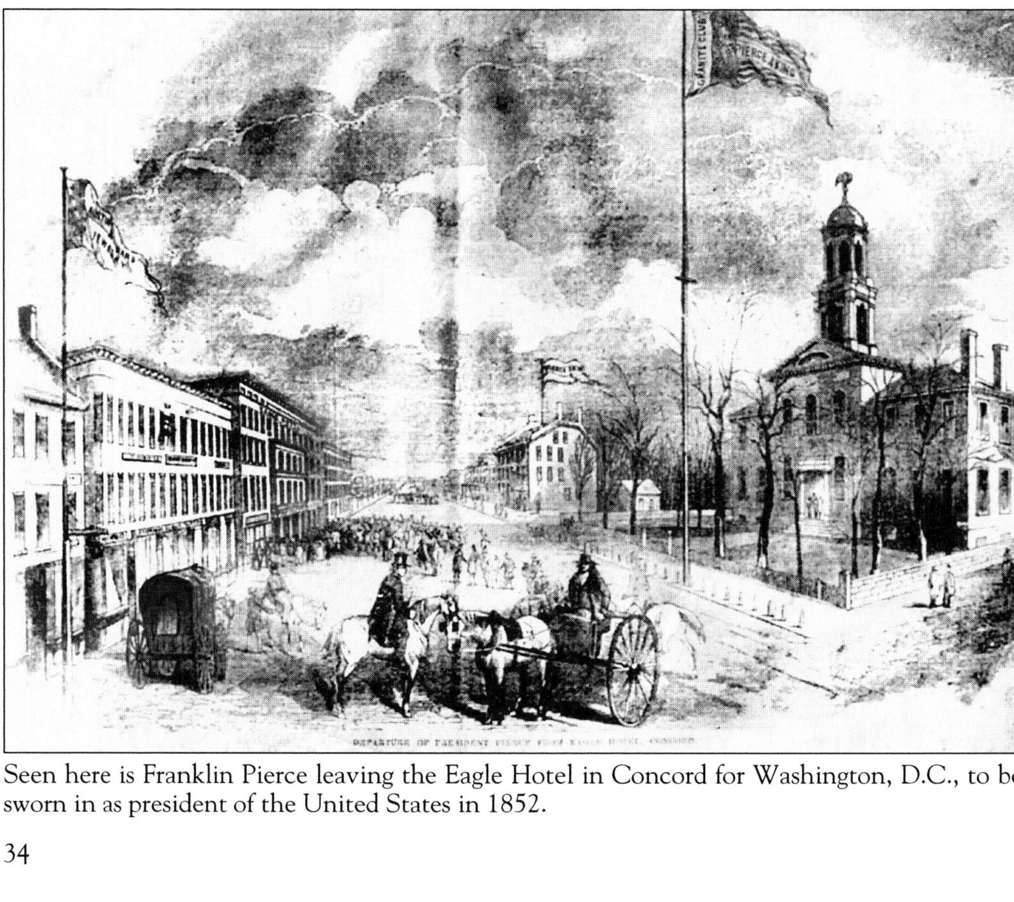

Seen here is Franklin Pierce leaving the Eagle Hotel in Concord for Washington, D.C., to be sworn in as president of the United States in 1852.

Two

DANBURY TO GILMANTON

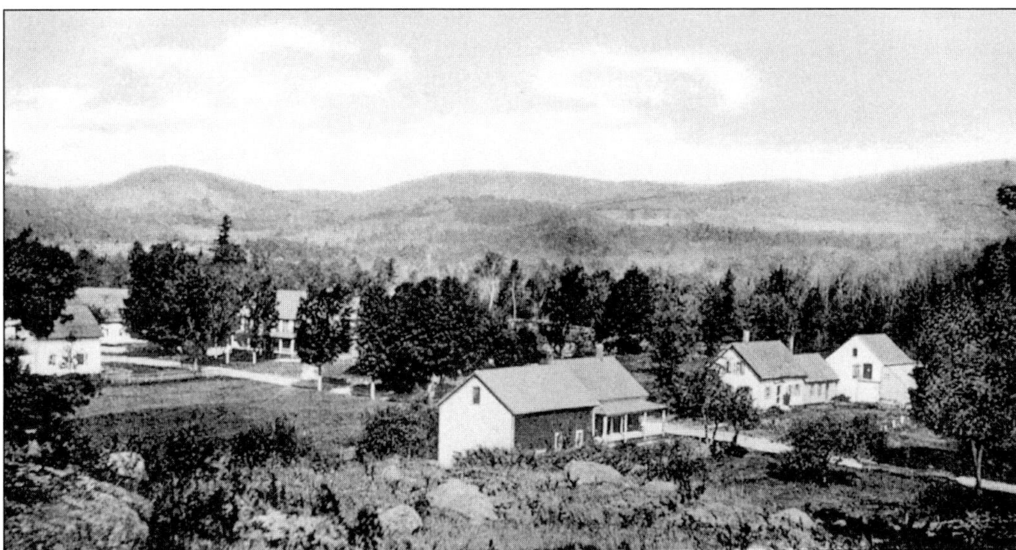

This bird's-eye view of Main Street in Danbury dates from 1937. This quiet town was originally in Alexandria Township. In 1771, the town's first settler, Anthony Tyler, came up the Smith River and made a home in the southeastern part of the present town. According to a petition to the General Assembly, the name of the town was Cockermouth until 1788, when its inhabitants asked that it be changed. Danbury was set off and incorporated in 1795.

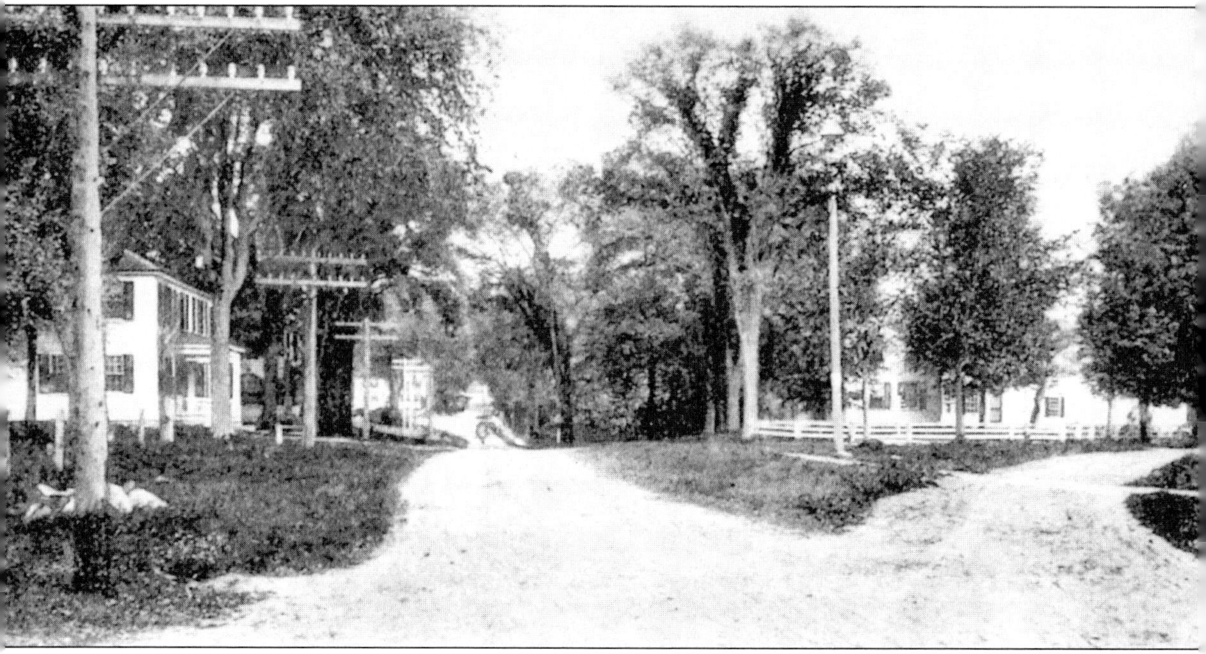

This is the Old Turnpike in Derry in 1907. Originally a part of Nutfield, and later Londonderry, Derry was settled by Scotch-Irish immigrants and remained a parish of that town until its incorporation in 1827. It eventually became a lively manufacturing village surrounded by hills, valleys, ponds, and meadows. East Derry, a small residential village, is where the earliest settlement of Derry Township took place. East Derry was the most important section of the town until 1804, when the Londonderry Turnpike made Derry village the business center. In 1849, the status of the village was changed when the Manchester and Lawrence Railroad was built, creating small factories along the right of way in the present village of Derry. Old white houses with spacious lawns, flower gardens, and plentiful trees make this a charming and restful village. Derry is a member of the New Hampshire Main Street community.

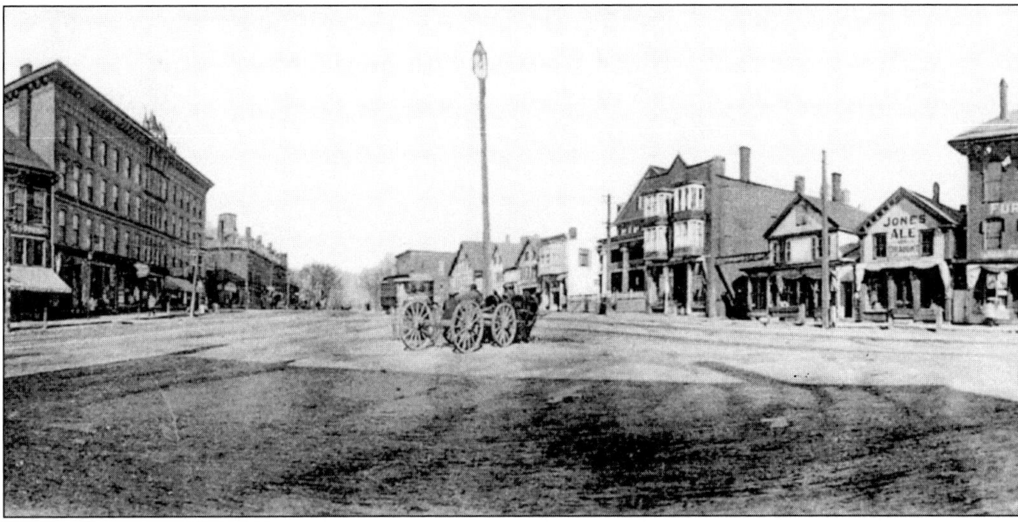

The important manufacturing city of Dover spreads over two hills at the fall line of the Cocheco River, with the Piscataqua and Bellamy Rivers flowing down on either side to meet in Great Bay. Dover is five miles northwest of the original settlement at Dover Point. At the time of this 1906 photograph of Franklin Square, the square was made up of shops, mills, and the simple houses of the mill workers. The square was a very busy place on Saturday evenings, when people came from the surrounding towns intent on an evening of entertainment.

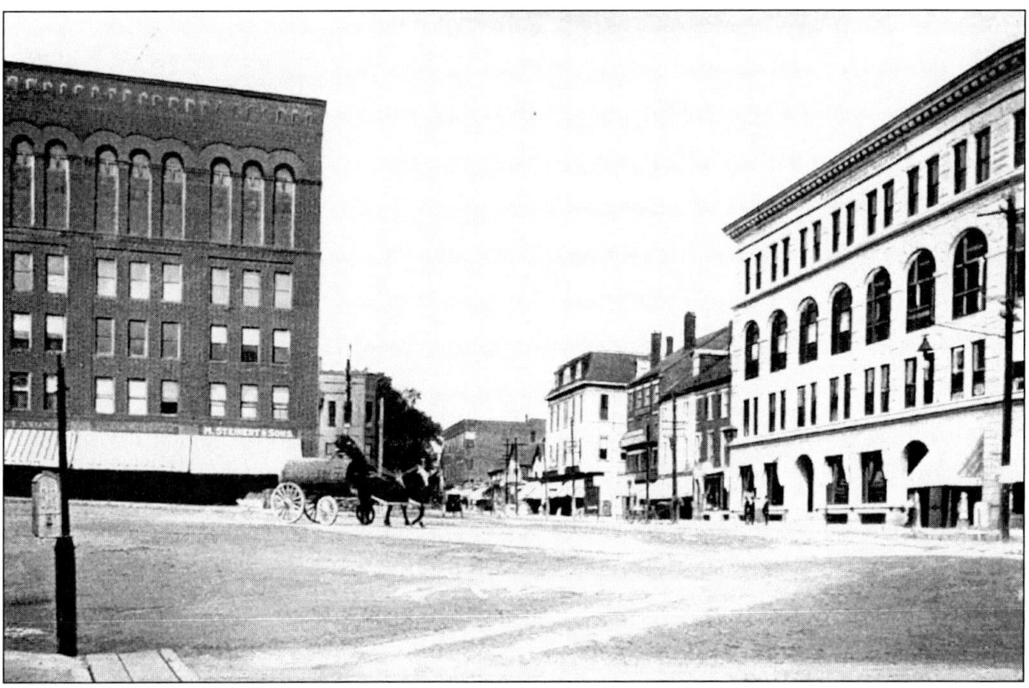

Dover's Central Square is seen here, in a view dating from 1906. Central Avenue, the main business street, crosses the Cocheco River and leads to the northern section of the city, which centers around Franklin Square. Dover is a member of the New Hampshire Main Street community.

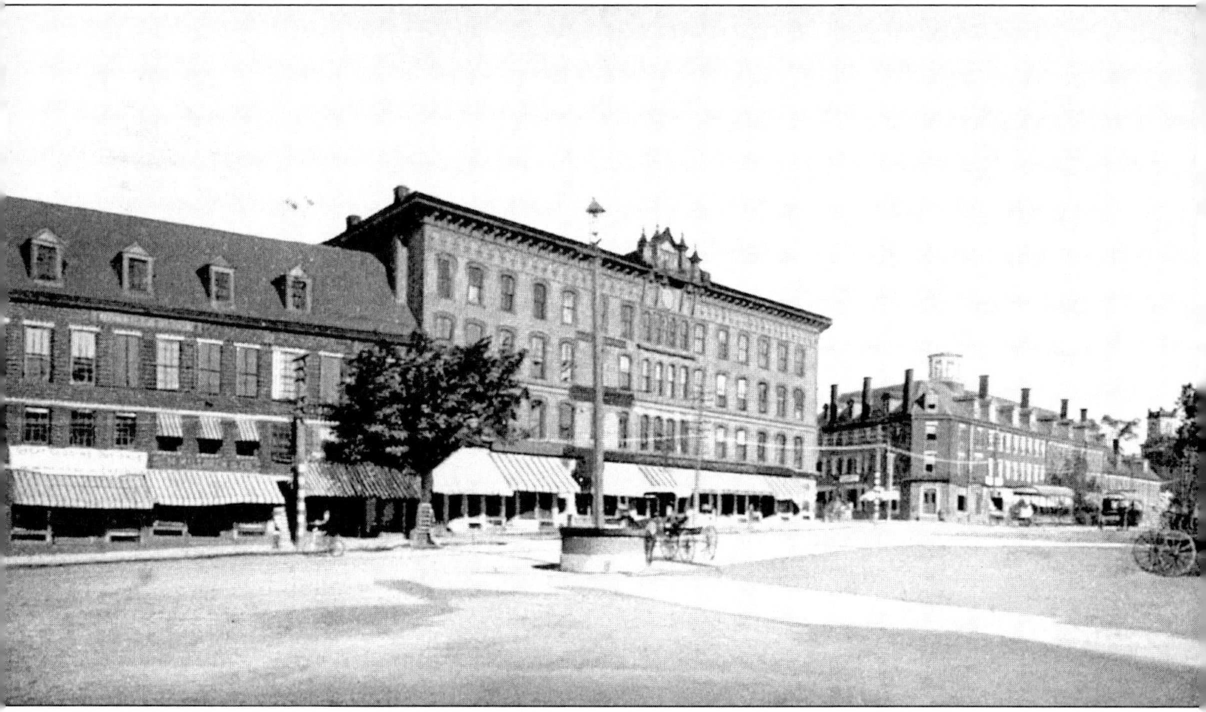

This is a view of the Upper Square in Dover in 1905. When farming and fishing gave way to the Industrial Revolution, the city was impacted dramatically. Due to the many changes, Dover has retained a strong appropriation of its history, evidenced in the collections of antiquities in the Woodman Institute. During the Revolutionary years, Dover's chief minister, the Reverend Jeremy Belknap, later author of the *History of New Hampshire,* stirred up much activity with his fiery sermons. Dover has had a number of names. For a time, it was known as Bristol, in connection with the first settlement. For about two years, to please a minister who came from Northam, England, the name Northam was used. The name Dover soon began to appear on the records and to supersede all others. Dover was incorporated as a city in 1855.

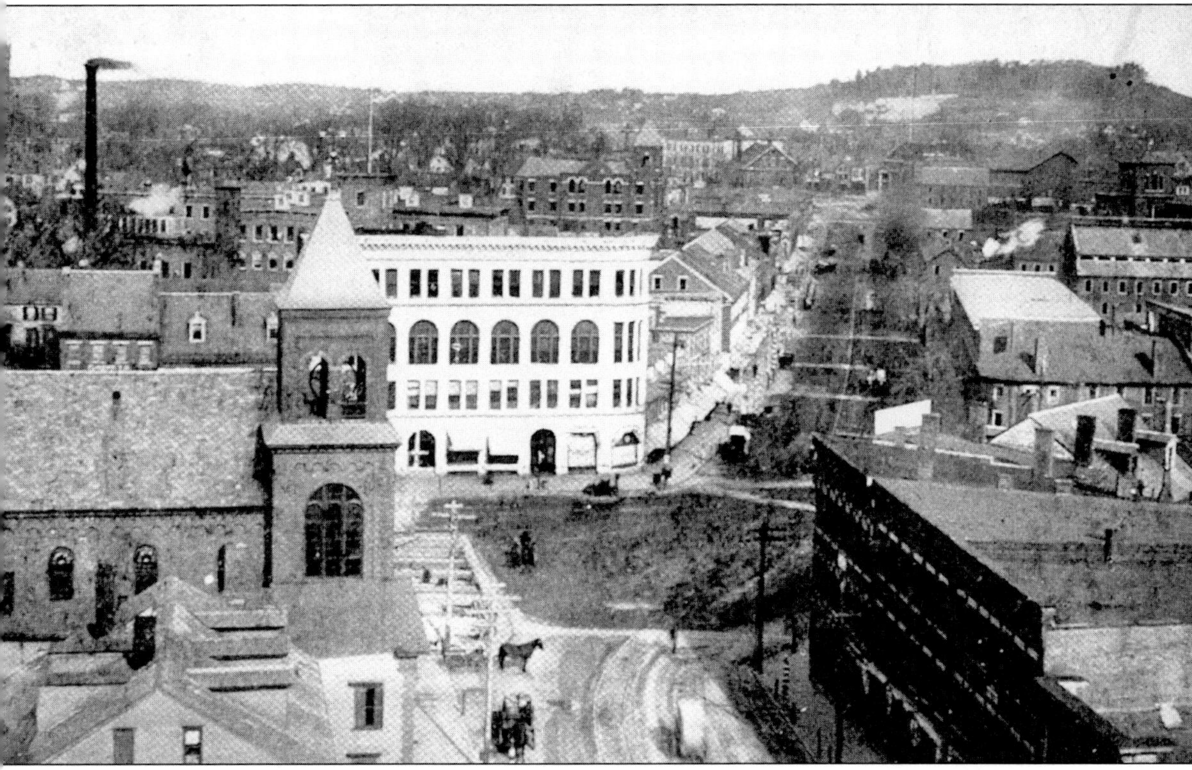

This bird's-eye view of Central Avenue and Garrison Hill was taken from the city hall tower in Dover in the early 1900s. Industrial Dover got its start with the use of waterpower from the falls of the Cocheco by Major Waldron, who established sawmills and gristmills there. In 1812, when the war and the embargo interfered with mercantile pursuits, cotton mills were erected. The success of this enterprise gave great impetus to the cotton industry in Dover. For nearly 100 years, the cotton industry was supreme in Dover. The changing tenor of the city was reflected in the successive wave of immigrants who tended the looms.

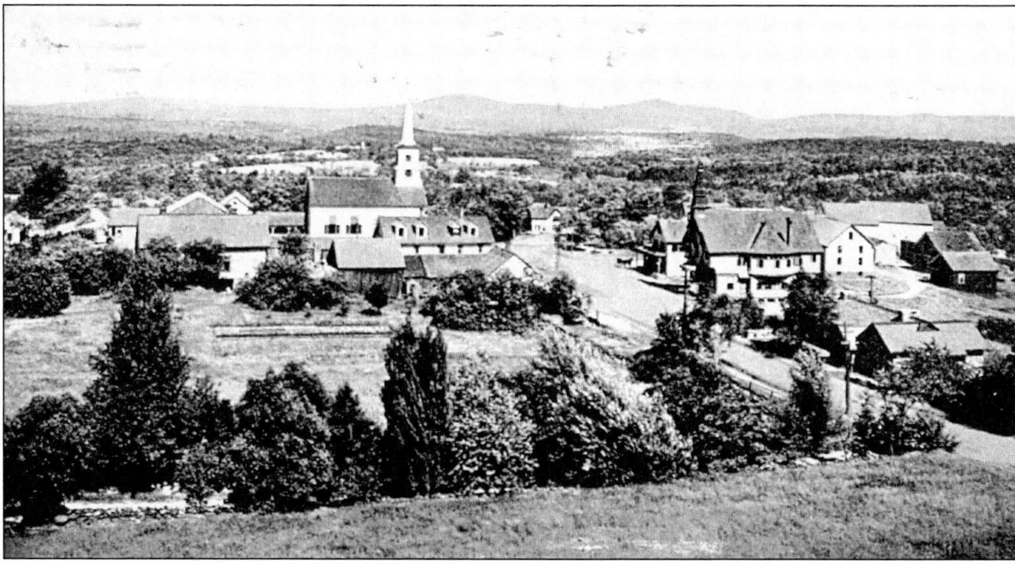

Dublin is one of the highest towns in New Hampshire, and its beautiful lake and mountain scenery, seen in this 1907 view of Main Street from the west, have made it an attractive summer resort. In 1749, the town was granted by the proprietors of the Masonian Grant to Matthew Thornton and others, but the first settlement was not made until William Thornton established himself in 1752. In 1763, a spurt of immigrants from Massachusetts and eastern New Hampshire increased the population, and the town of Dublin was incorporated in 1771.

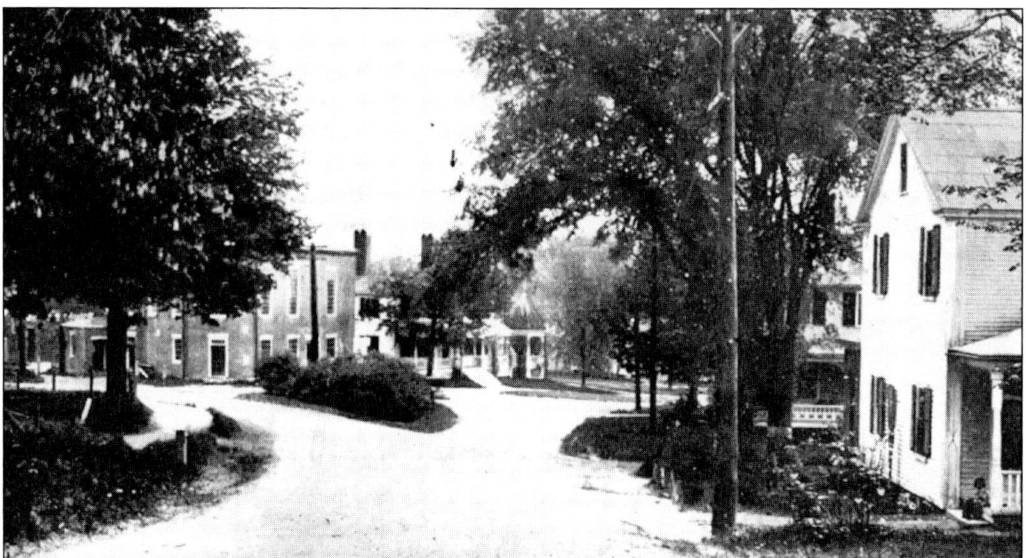

This is a view of Main Street in Durham *c.* 1927. This town of elm-shaded streets is the seat of the University of New Hampshire. The oldest section of Durham lies on the banks of Oyster River. As early as 1635, a group of settlers sailed up the Piscataqua River from Dover Point and settled at the mouth of Oyster River in what is now Durham. At its incorporation under the name of Durham, it included Lee (which separated in 1766), a part of Madbury (cut off in 1768), and a portion of Newmarket (which was turned over to that town in 1870). Durham is a member of the New Hampshire Main Street community.

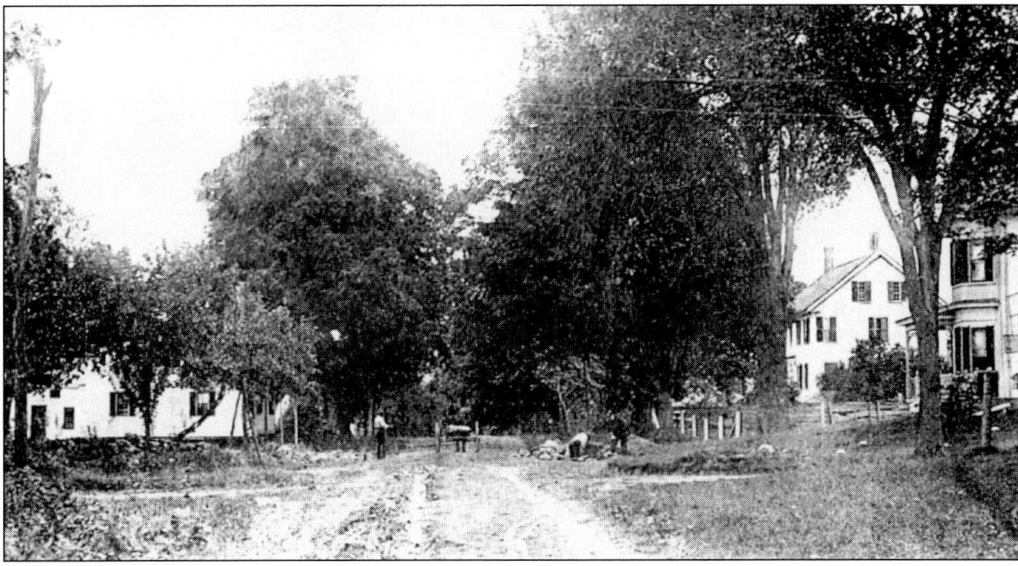

This view of Main Street at Four Corners in North Dunbarton dates from 1908. Dunbarton is a quiet little village stretching along the ridge of the highest hill for miles around. The town was granted in 1733 by the Massachusetts General Court and was then known as Narragansett No. 6. The exact date of its first settlement is unknown, but prior to 1746, James Rogers and Joseph Putney built a cabin here and named the settlement Montalona for their hometown in northern Ireland. In 1751, Archibald Stark and others purchased this tract of land from the heirs of the Mason claim and named it Starktown. In 1765, the town was incorporated as Dunbarton, for the town of Dunbarton, Scotland, from which the Starks emigrated in 1720.

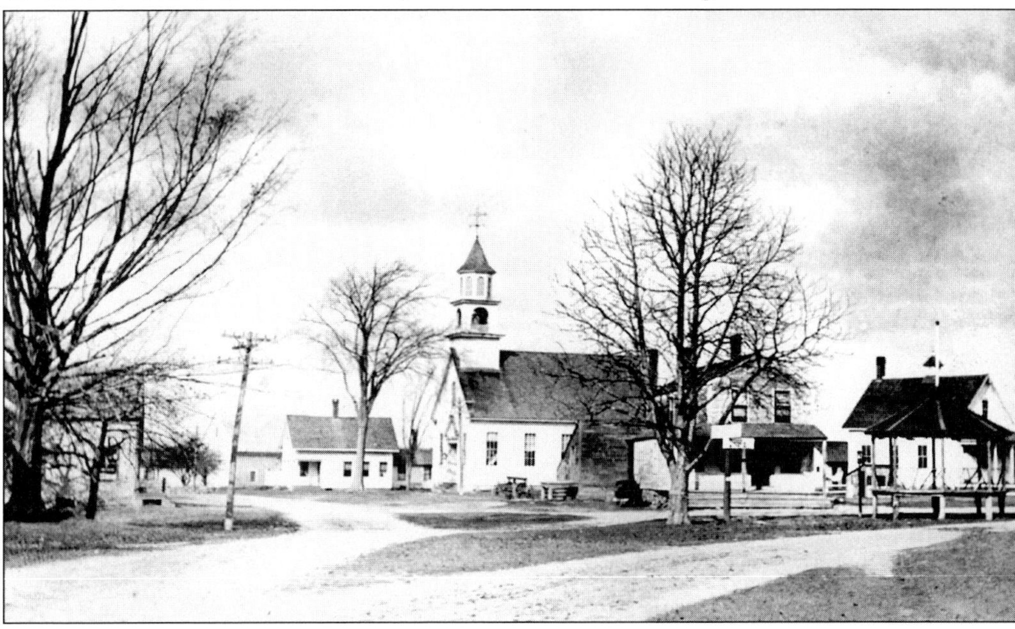

East Hampstead, seen here, is a part of Hampstead, which was incorporated in 1749. Typical of each settlement is the church, with its tall spire projecting above the rest of the building. Note the Union Church, wooden guidepost, bandstand, and one-room schoolhouse behind the bandstand. This *c.* 1910 view looks north.

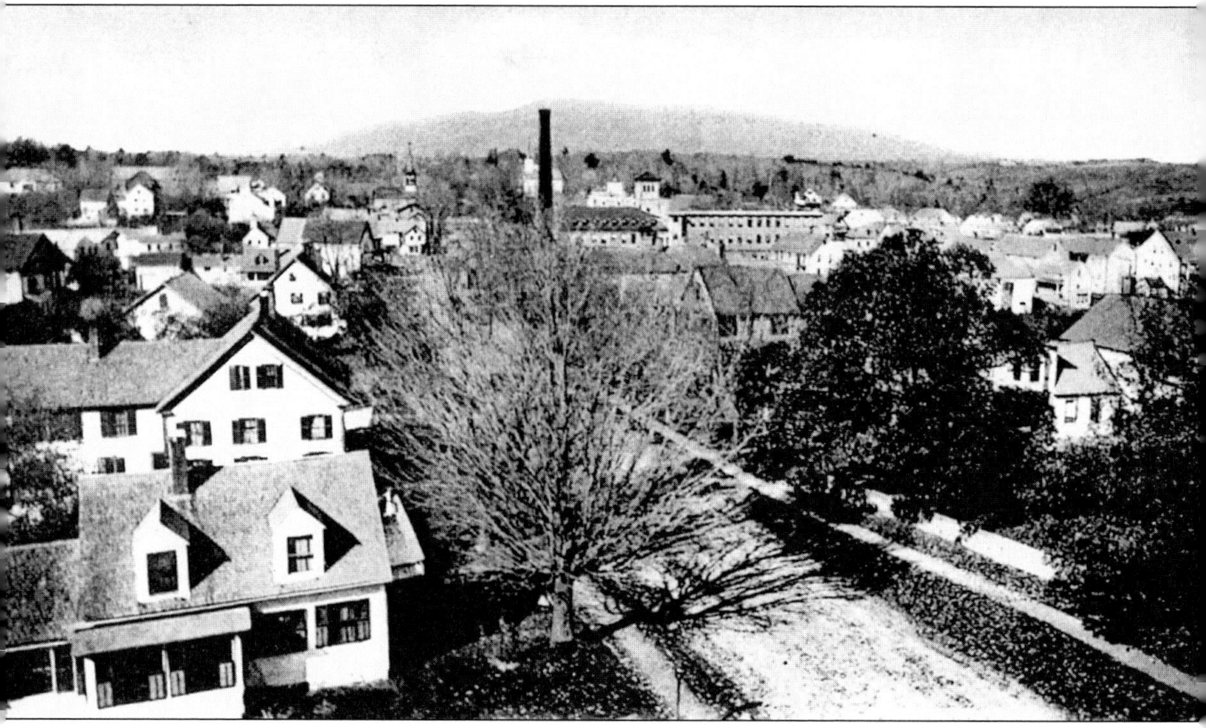

This bird's-eye view of East Jaffrey and Monadnock Mountain was taken in 1907. East Jaffrey, located on both banks of the Contoocock River, was once the industrial center of Jaffrey Township. Largely a product of the 19th century, it is a community of simple Victorian houses and some modern homes. The area was called Rowley Canada when it was originally granted in 1736. The town was rechartered as Monadnock No. 2 in 1749 and was sometimes known as Middle Monadnock or Middletown. A regrant was made in 1767 by John Wentworth, and six years later, it was incorporated as Jaffrey in honor of George Jaffrey, a member of one of the prominent families of Portsmouth. Jaffrey is a member of the New Hampshire Main Street community.

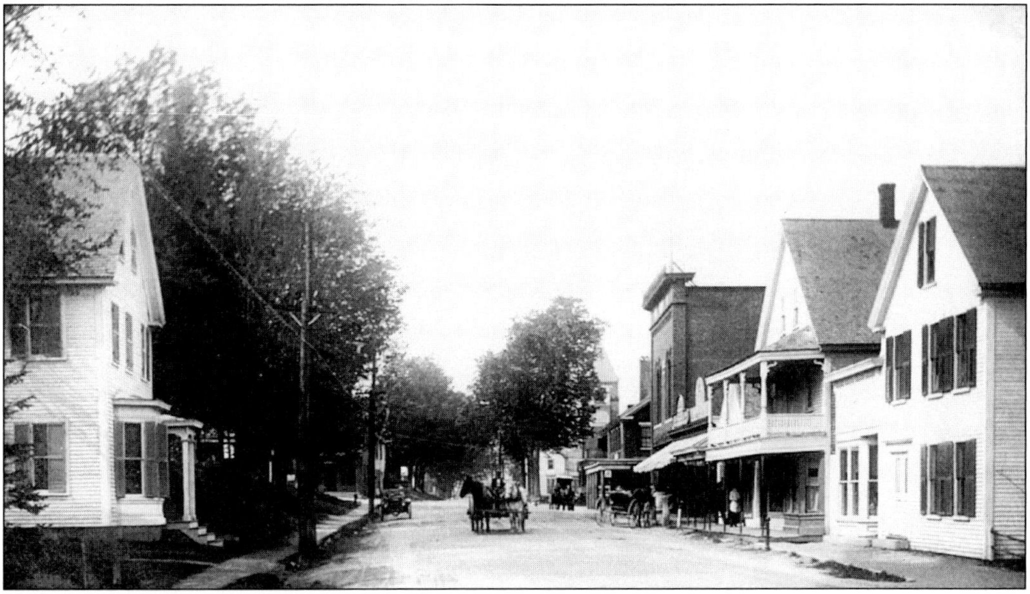

Epping is a pleasant little town in the valley of the Lamprey River, with old white houses built close together along elm-shaded streets. This Main Street photograph looking north was taken sometime between 1907 and 1911.

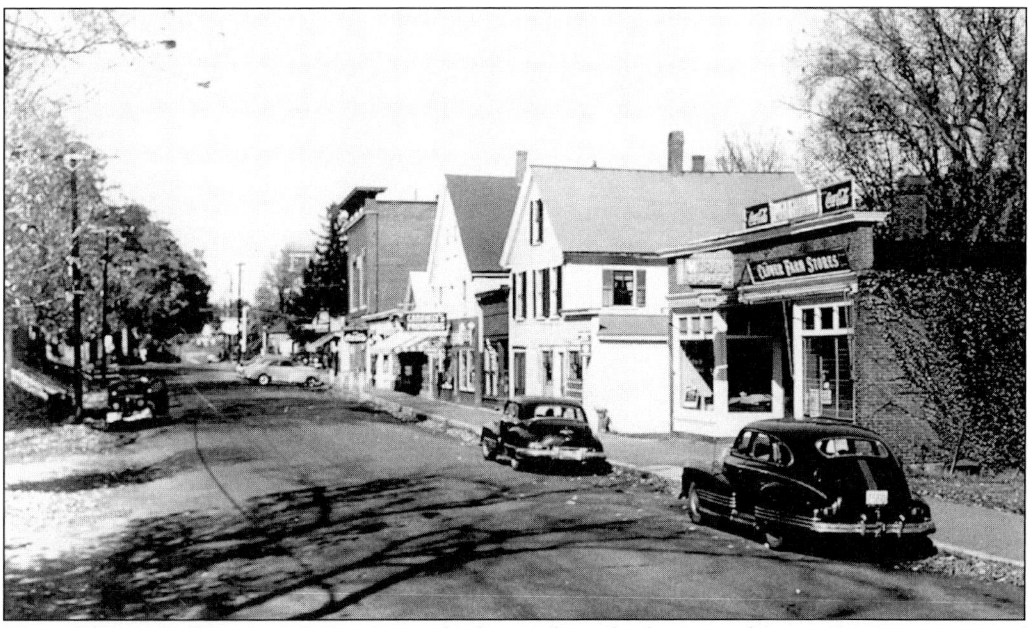

This 1945 view of Epping's Main Street looks north at the business district. Epping was one of the earliest settlements in New Hampshire. Originally a part of Exeter, it was not incorporated as a separate parish with town privileges until 1741. The name was taken from Epping, England, "a nice little town in Essex, seventeen miles from London, in the middle of Epping Forest," as Col. Joseph L. Chester wrote in 1876.

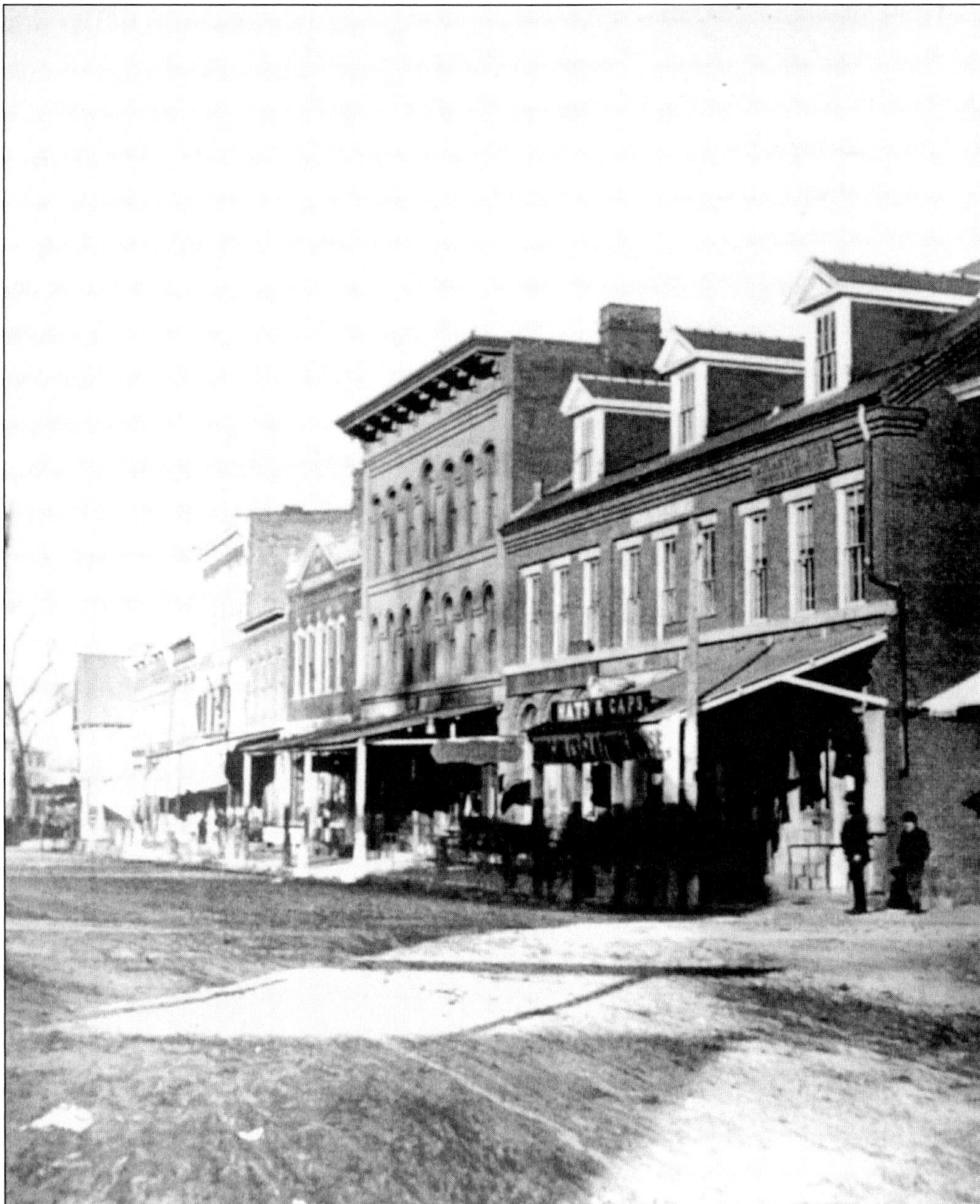

A frontier town, Exeter suffered during the French and Indian War. There was no general attack upon the town, but the citizens gained military experience in their fights with the Native Americans. Exeter's territory, which, according to the Native American agreement, covered about 400 square miles, was reduced to about 17 square miles when the towns of Newmarket (1727), Epping (1741), Brentwood (1742), Fremont (1764), and Newfields separated from it. In this view, looking west, is Water Street in Exeter *c.* 1875.

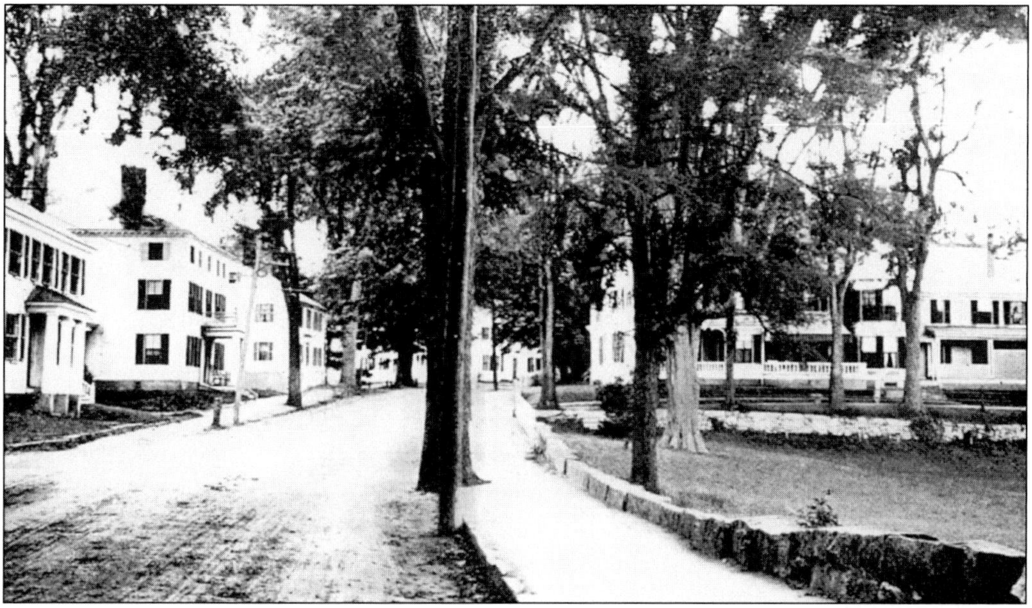

This *c.* 1910 photograph of Main Street in Exeter looks west from Academy Street (now Tan Lane). Exeter is a typical Colonial town settled among low, rolling hills and is the home of Phillips Exeter Academy. Winding elm-shaded streets, dignified white houses, and academy buildings give it a serenity in sharp contrast to the unrest in its history.

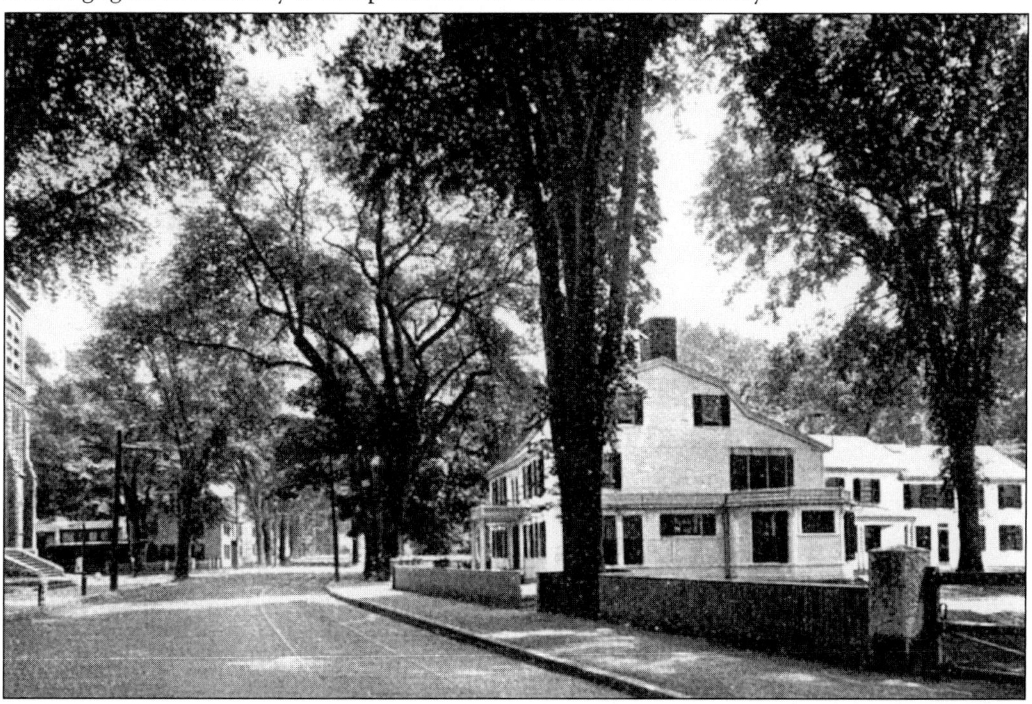

A major street through Exeter is Front Street, seen in this 1907 view. The Governor Bell House is on the right. Settled in 1638 and predated only by settlements at Dover and Portsmouth, Exeter sprang up by the falls of the Squamscott River. It grew around the personality of the Reverend John Wheelwright, a political and religious outcast from Puritanical Massachusetts.

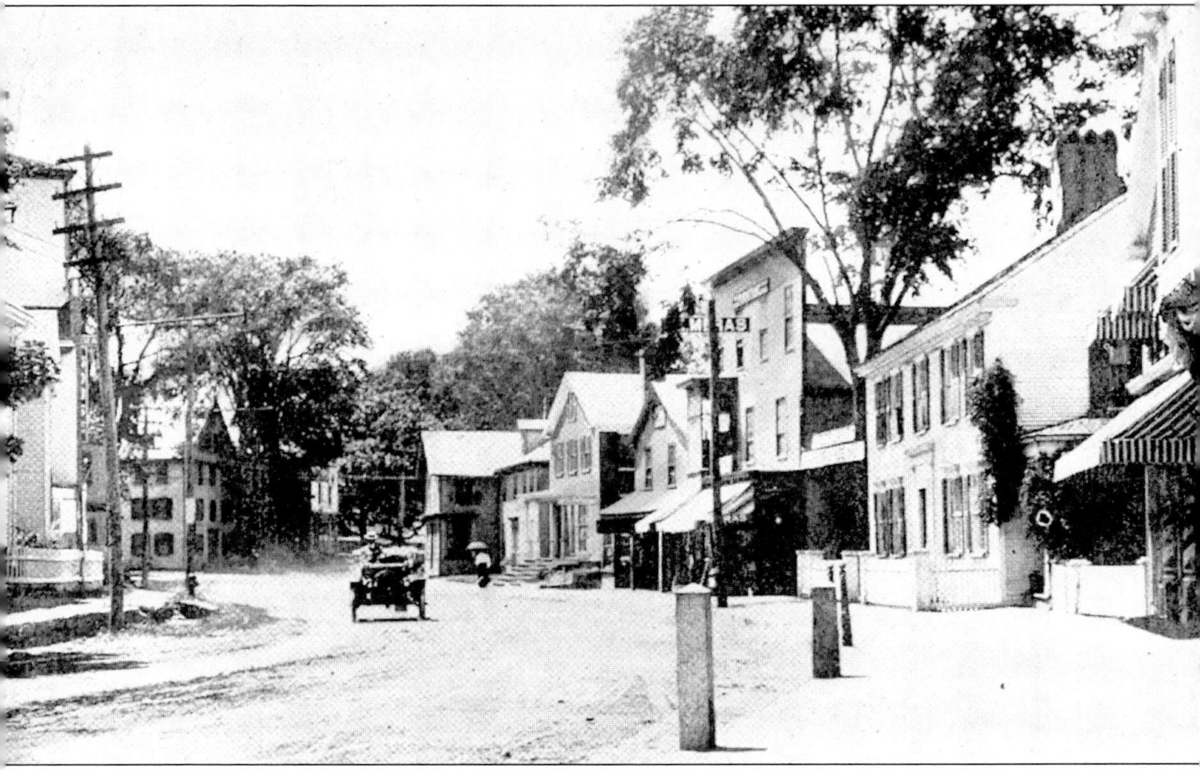

This is a view of the west end of Water Street in Exeter *c.* 1910. The opera house is on the left. In 1775, the capital was moved from Portsmouth to Exeter. The first provincial congress met in Exeter on July 21, 1774, and several sessions were held in Exeter the following year. On December 21, 1775, the first provincial congress "took up government" by making itself into a house of representatives. The congress adopted a written constitution on January 5, 1776. By this act, New Hampshire became an independent colony. Exeter was then the center of the state's civil, legislative, and military activities.

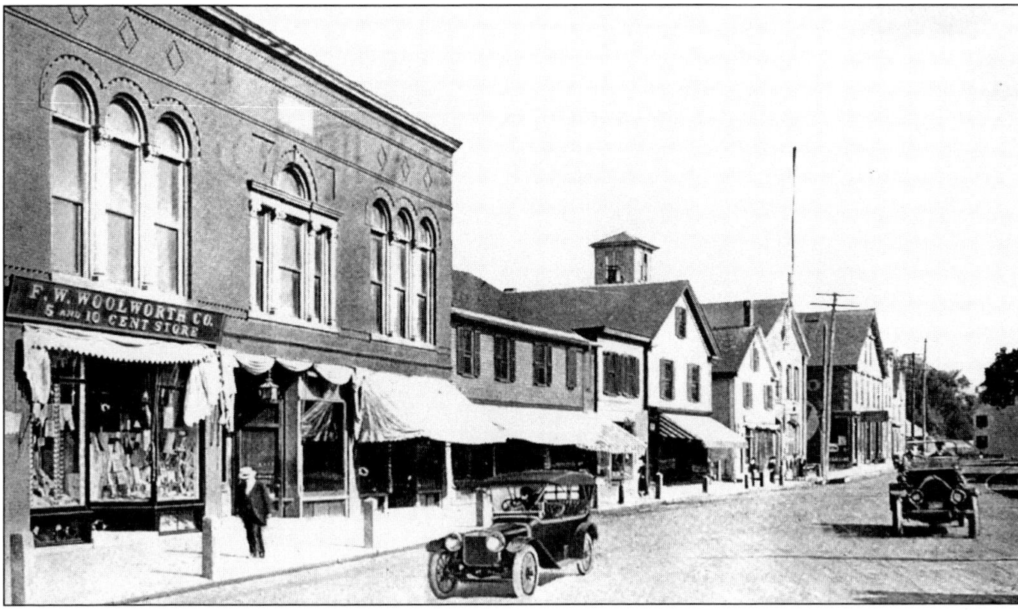

This *c.* 1912 view of Water Street in Exeter looks east. Woolworth's moved to a new building farther west along Water Street in 1915.

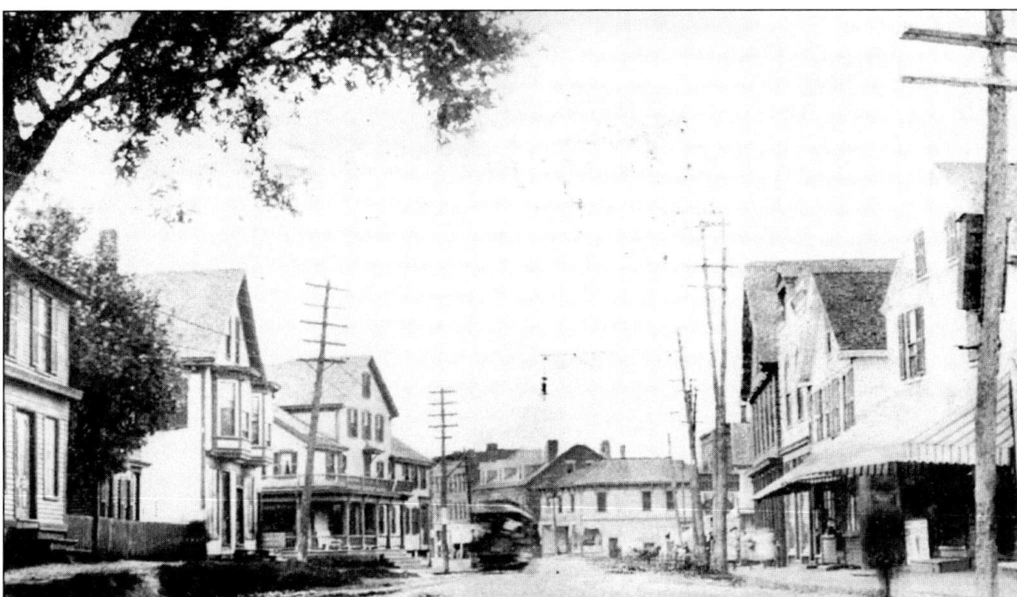

Trolley cars were once used in Exeter, as seen in this *c.* 1910 Water Street view, which looks west. During the early 1900s, Water Street west of the Great Bridge was very busy.

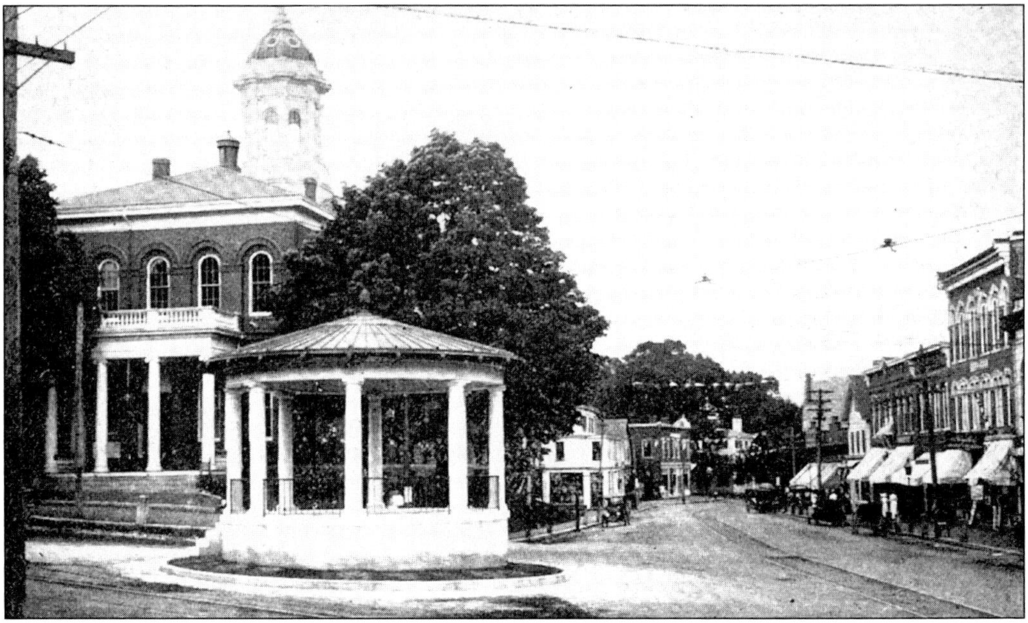

The town square at the intersection of Water and Front Streets in Exeter held the Swasey Bandstand Pavilion, dedicated in 1916. In January 1774, the town resolved that "we are ready on all necessary occasions to risk our lives and fortunes in defence of our rights and liberties." Two British ministers, Lords North and Bute, were burned in effigy before the jail.

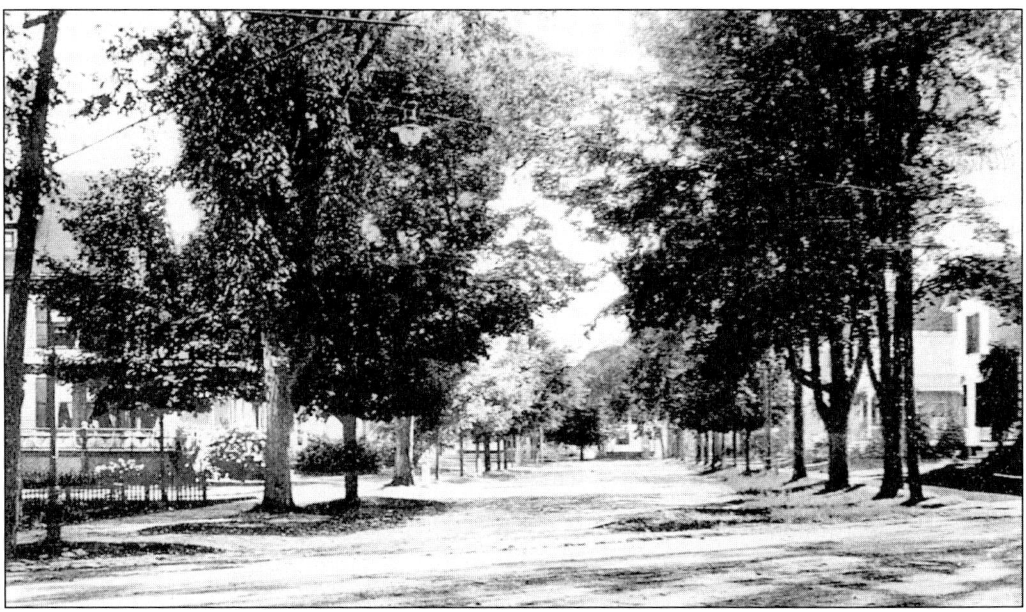

This is a view of Gill Street from Front Street in Exeter in 1909. It is a typical view of the more secluded residential neighborhoods in the larger towns and cities.

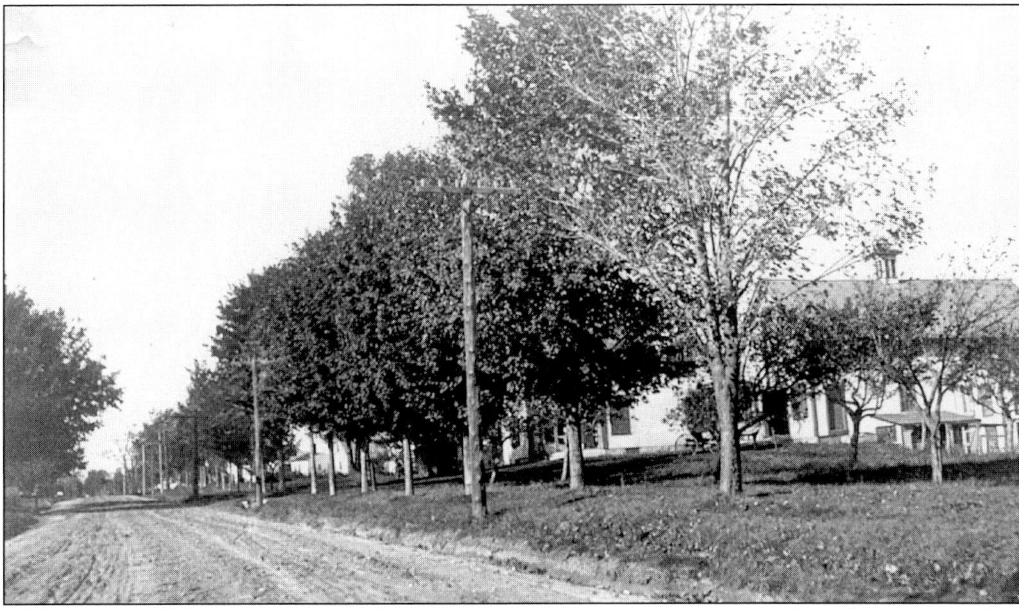

The residential section of Epsom is seen in this 1920s Main Street view. Note how the houses are set back from the street and the large trees are evenly spaced on the shoulder of the thoroughfare. Epsom derived its name from the English market town near London. There is no record of the first settlement, but there were several families here before it was incorporated in 1743.

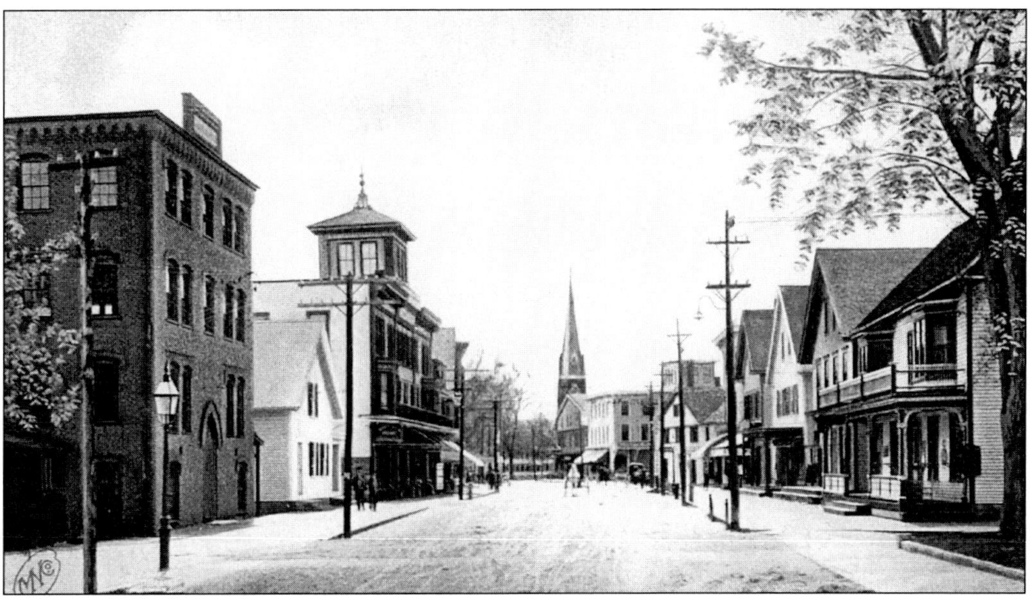

Farmington's Main Street and business district is seen in this 1908 view. Main Street, with its general store, town hall, church, and possible five-and-dime store, attracted many people to the village each weekend for their week's supplies. Farmington was credited as being a compact industrial town and was known for shoe manufacturing.

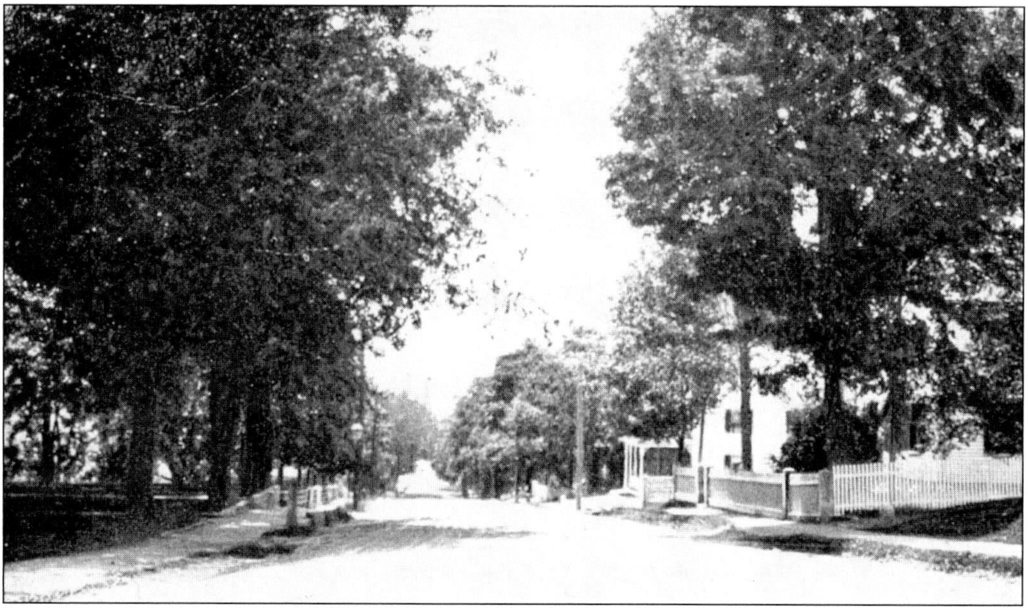

This view of Main Street looks south down the residential section of Farmington in 1908. The elm and maple trees greet visitors to the country homes. Formerly a part of Rochester, Farmington was incorporated in 1798. Jeremiah Jones Colbath (1812–1875), who changed his name to Henry Wilson on reaching manhood, was born here. He served as vice president of the United States from 1873 to 1875.

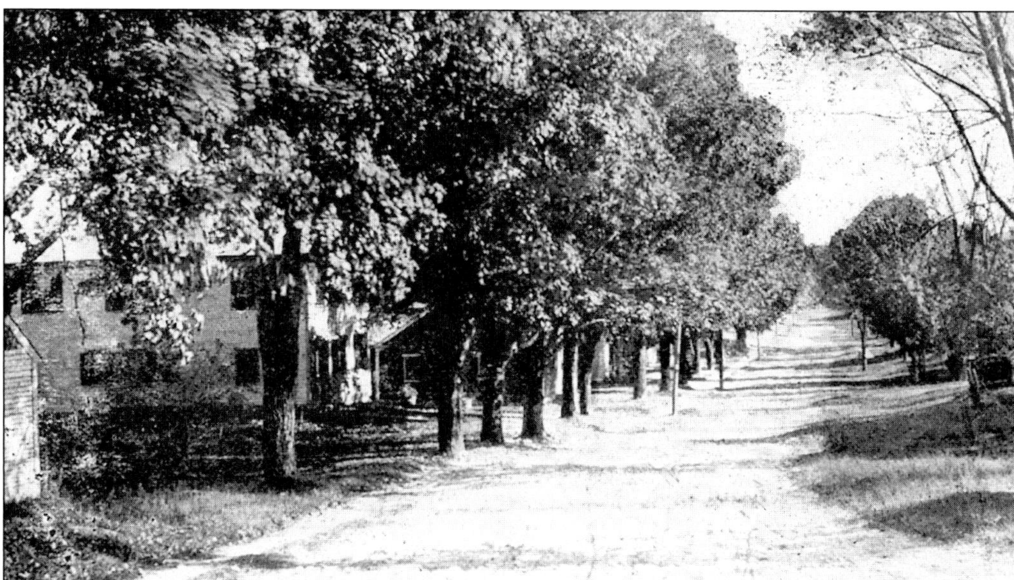

This view of Main Street in Francestown looks south and dates from the late 1800s. The dignity and repose of Main Street is shown through the many maple trees that frame the way. This quiet little hamlet was granted in 1752 and incorporated 20 years later. The name Francestown came from the first name of the wife of Governor Wentworth. The town was a part of New Boston for 21 years.

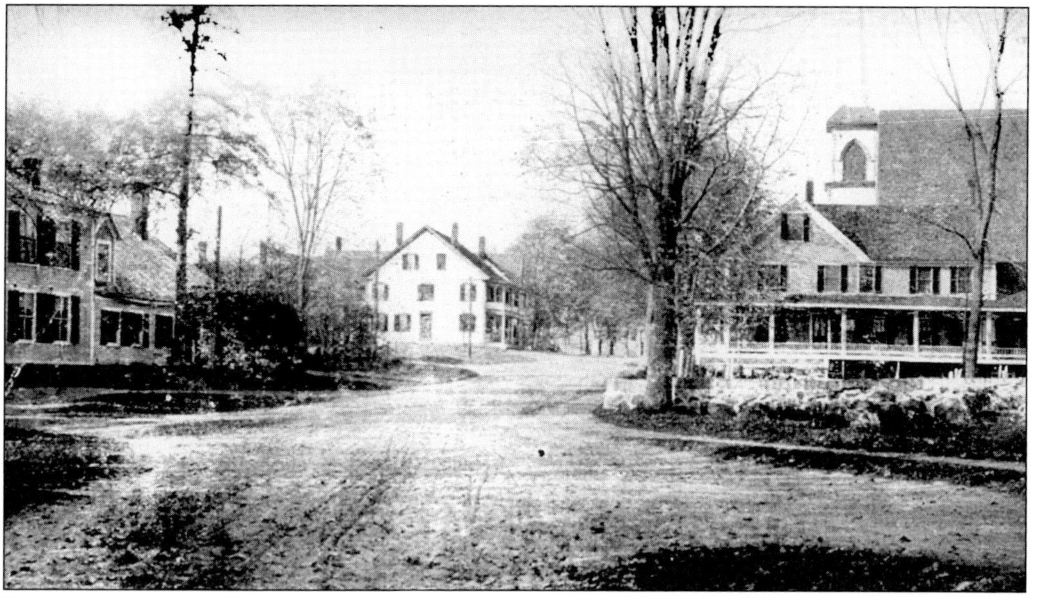

Seen is Main Street in Francestown in the early 20th century. The quiet village at a major intersection, with its numerous old houses around a tall-spired white church, warmly greets visitors.

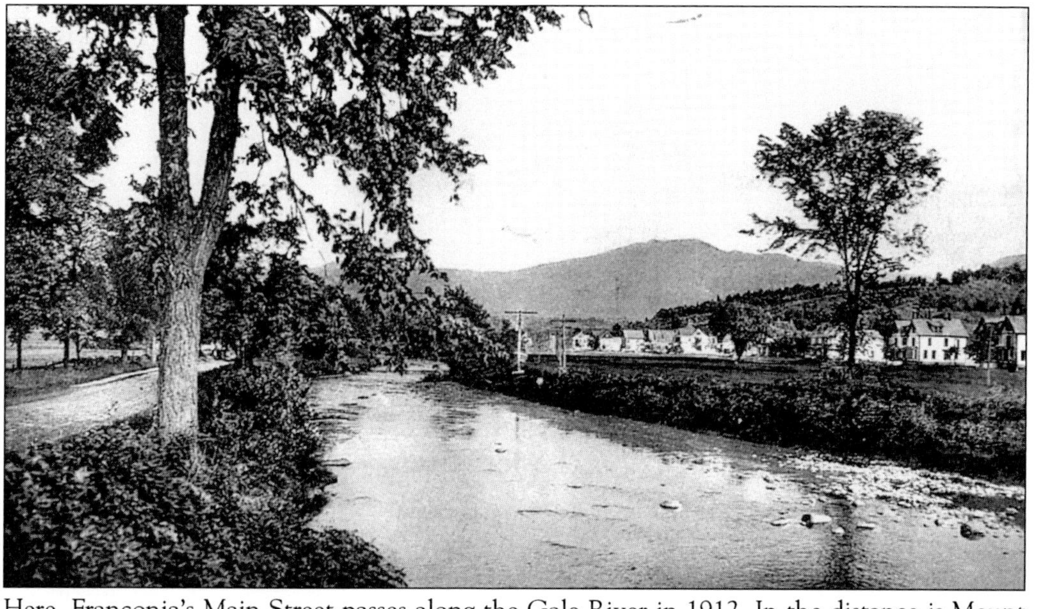

Here, Franconia's Main Street passes along the Gale River in 1912. In the distance is Mount Lafayette in the White Mountains. Franconia is a serene little village with a number of small cottagelike houses under fine trees. It is set in a great basin surrounded by hills that slope to towering mountains. The town was first granted in 1764 under the present name of Franconia, but no settlement was made in fulfillment of the terms; it was regranted in 1772 as Morristown. Litigation ensuing from these conflicting grants delayed settlement until 1774, when Capt. Artemas Knight and others came to this area. The town was incorporated in 1782 under its original name.

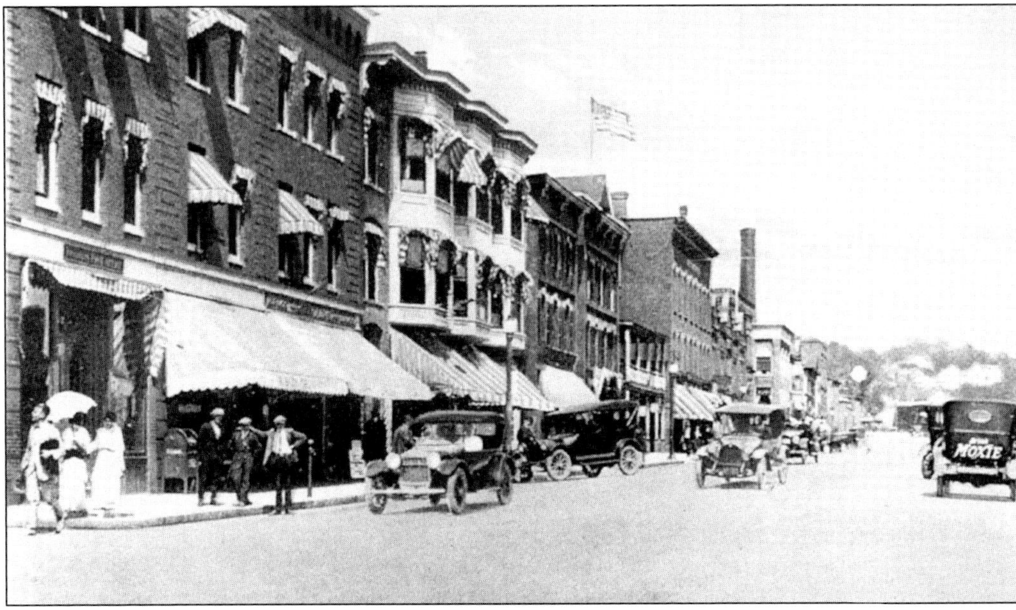

In this 1920s view, which looks east, is Franklin's Central Street. Franklin was considered the industrial center of the area. Franklin is situated at the junction where the turbulent Pemigewasset River and the mildly flowing Winnipesaukee River meet to form the Merrimack. Franklin's history closely parallels that of Salisbury, since it was part of that town until 1828, when it was incorporated as the town of Franklin, taking its name from Benjamin Franklin. In 1895, it was granted a city charter.

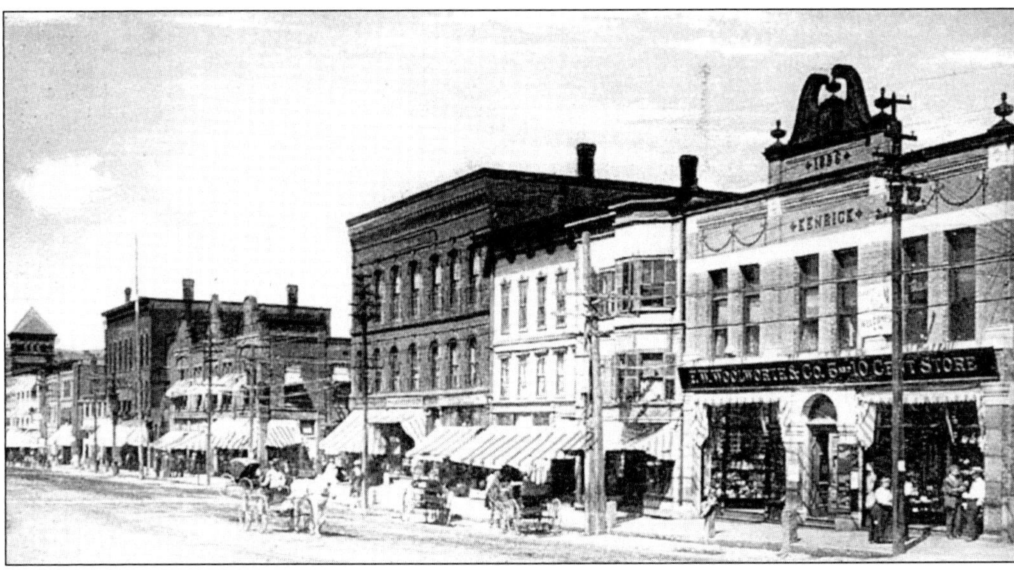

At first glance, Franklin's business section appears more than adequate for the local trade, but it is also the shopping district for a large summer population. Note the E.W. Woolworth five-and-ten store on the right in this 1921 view, looking west, of Central Street.

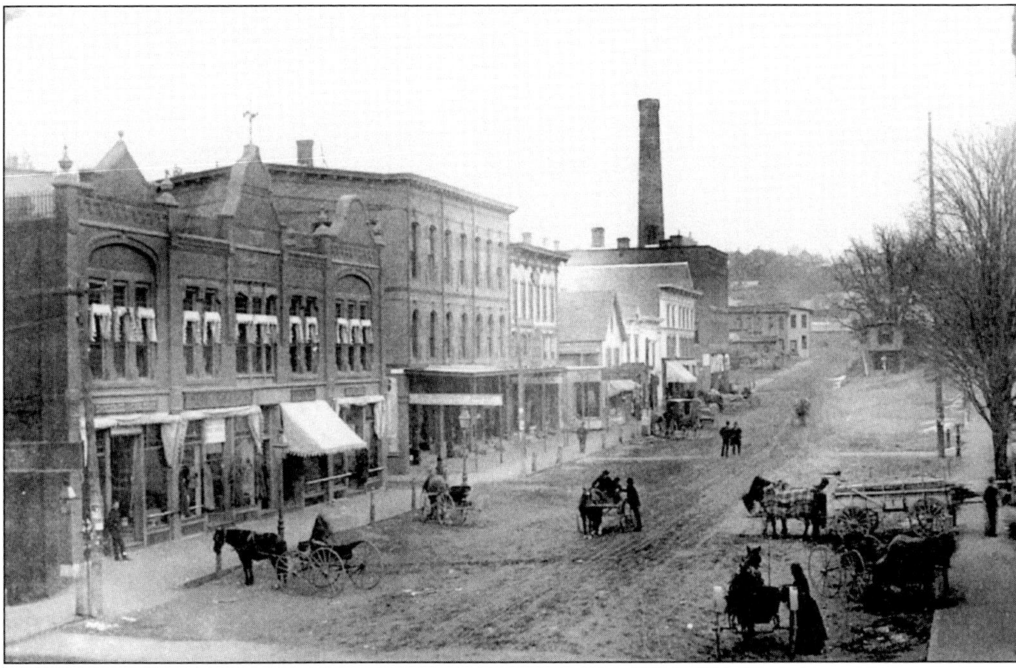

This is an early-1900s photograph of the business district of Franklin.

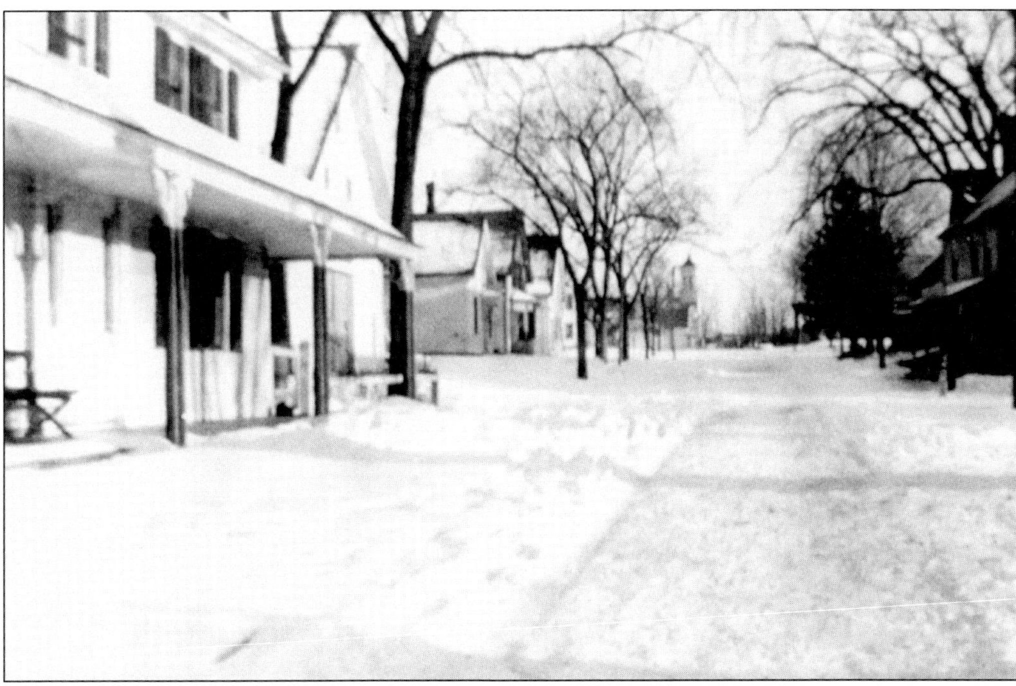

Fremont's Main Street is seen after a snowfall in this 1918 view looking east. This area became known as Liberty Square after a liberty pole raising on July 4, 1861. Fremont was the site of the first Civil War riot in New England, which occurred on the same day as the raising of the liberty pole.

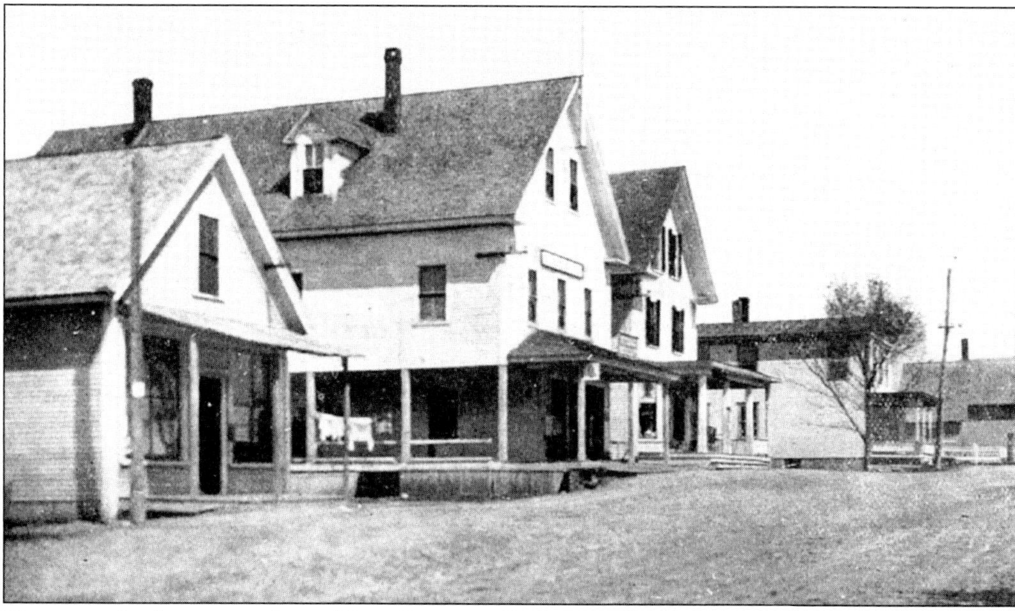

This view, looking east, shows Main Street in Fremont village *c.* 1909. The three buildings on the left were destroyed in the Great Fire of May 25, 1910. This photograph of the post office and the north side of Main Street was taken before the fire.

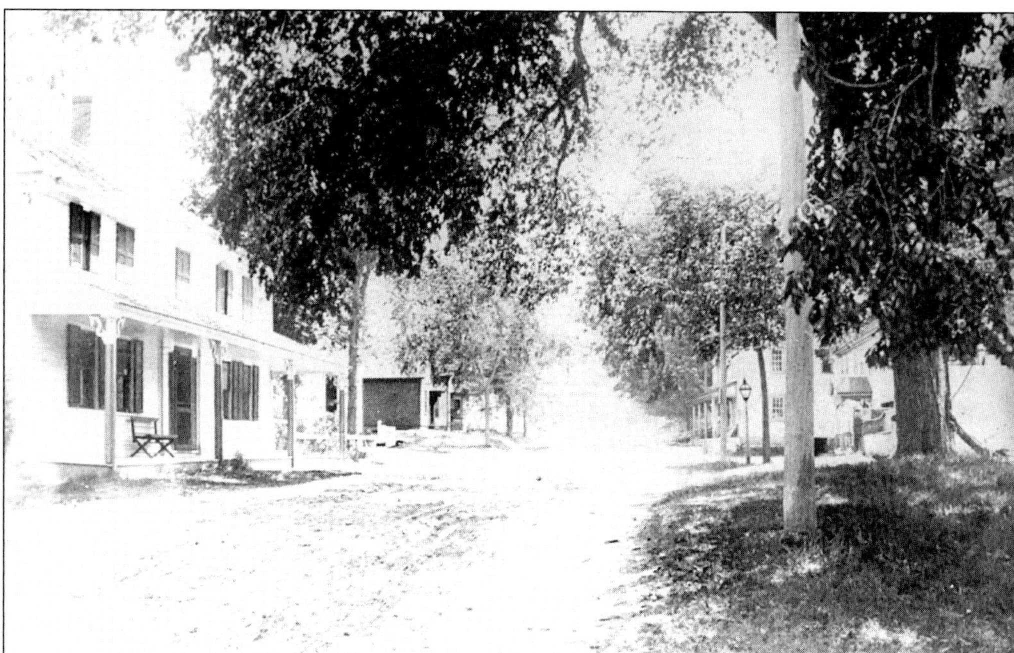

This area of Fremont, known as Liberty Square, was located in the business district of the town that was interchangeably known as Black Rocks Village, Poplin Rocks, Fremont Rocks, and Rocks Village to denote the location of a large rock outcropping that formerly stood near this ancient town center. In 1910, the outcropping was blasted to oblivion to make way for the new state highway. This *c.* 1907 view looks east.

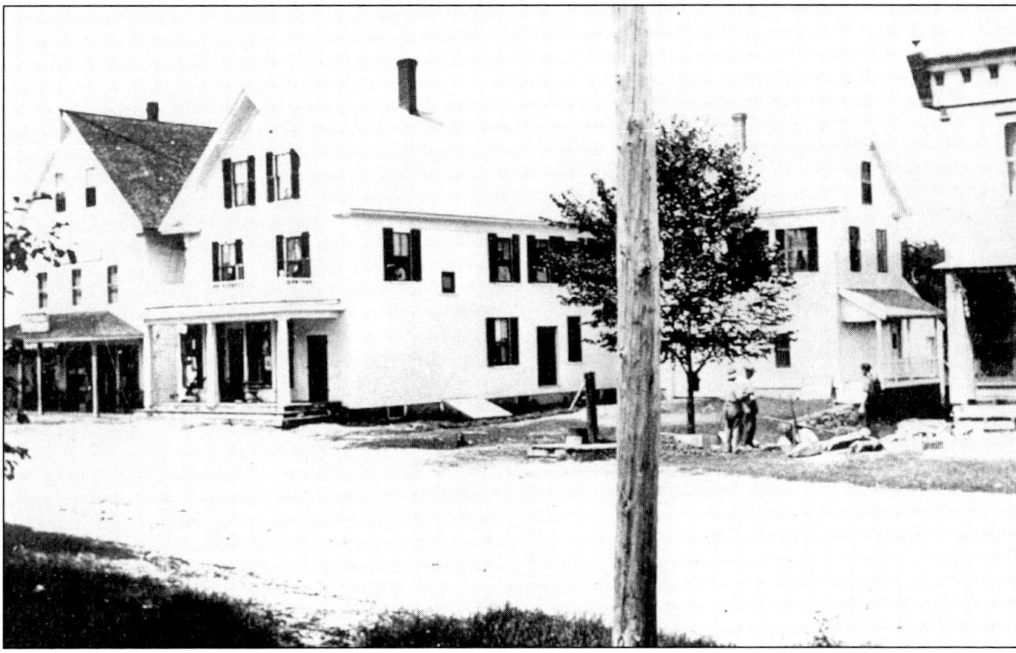

This is a *c*. 1905 photograph of Main Street in Fremont village. In 1742, a section of Exeter was cut off and incorporated under the name Brintwood, and later Brentwood. It was a very large territory.

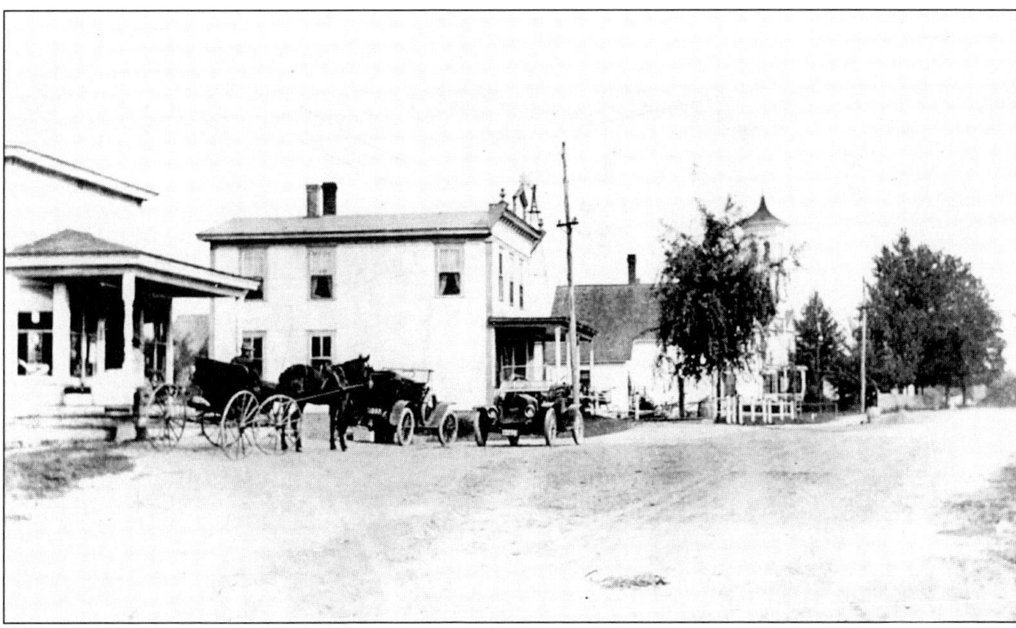

In 1764, a section about four miles square in the western part of Keensborough was incorporated as a separate township under the name of Poplin. In 1854, the name was changed to Fremont for John C. Fremont, the noted American West pathfinder and, in 1856, the first Republican candidate for president of the United States. This view of Main Street in Fremont village looks east *c*. 1912.

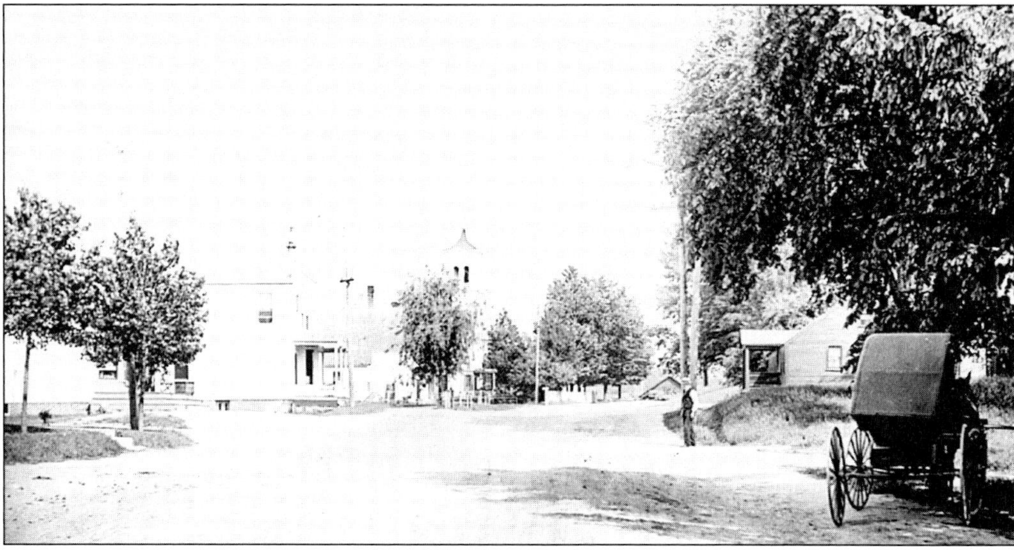

At one time, Fremont was a very prosperous shoe manufacturing center, producing 30,000 pairs annually; however, agricultural labor and barrel making were the principal occupations. This view of Main Street in Fremont village looks east *c.* 1912.

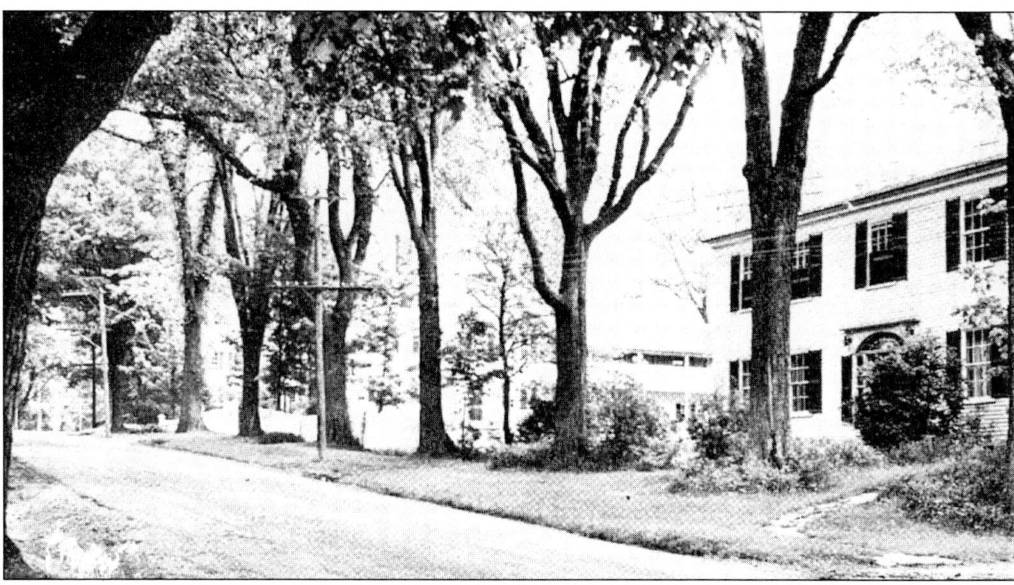

This photograph shows Province Road in Gilmanton in the 1920s. The stately trees provide the proper setting for one of the oldest highways and towns in the state. When the town was granted in 1727, taking the name of one of the grantees, it included parts of the present Gilford, Laconia, and Belmont. It was incorporated in 1859.

Three

Goffstown to Newport

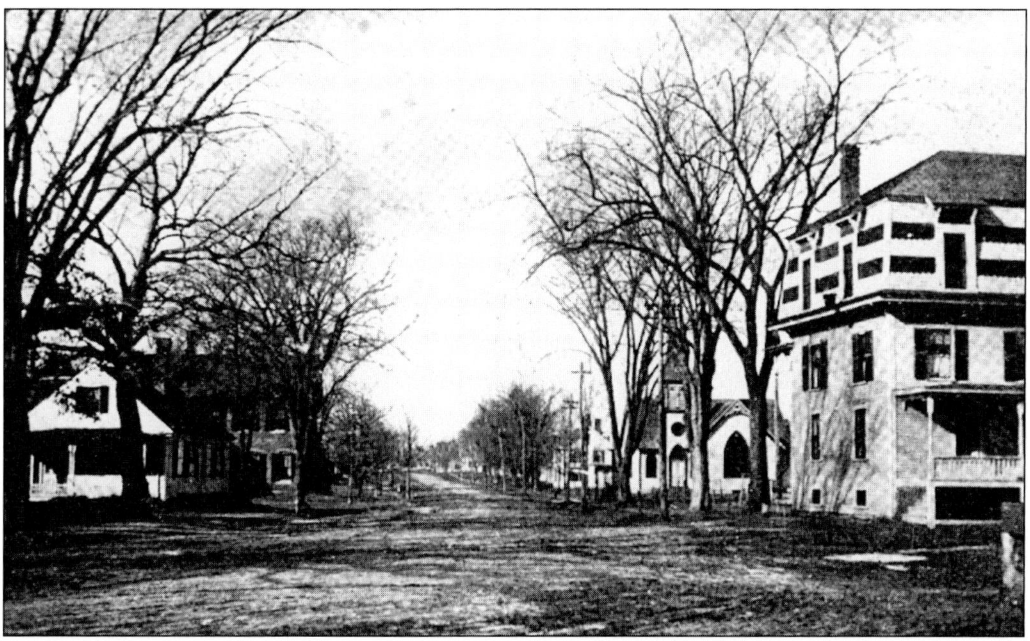

The quiet and attractive village of Goffstown lies along the winding S-shaped street seen in this 1907 view looking west. This is North Main Street. Originally granted as Narragansett No. 4, the town reverted to the Masonian proprietors, who regranted it with part of present Hooksett and Manchester to the Reverend Thomas Parker of Dracut, Massachusetts, and others. The town was incorporated as Goffstown in 1763. Goffstown is a member of the New Hampshire Main Street community.

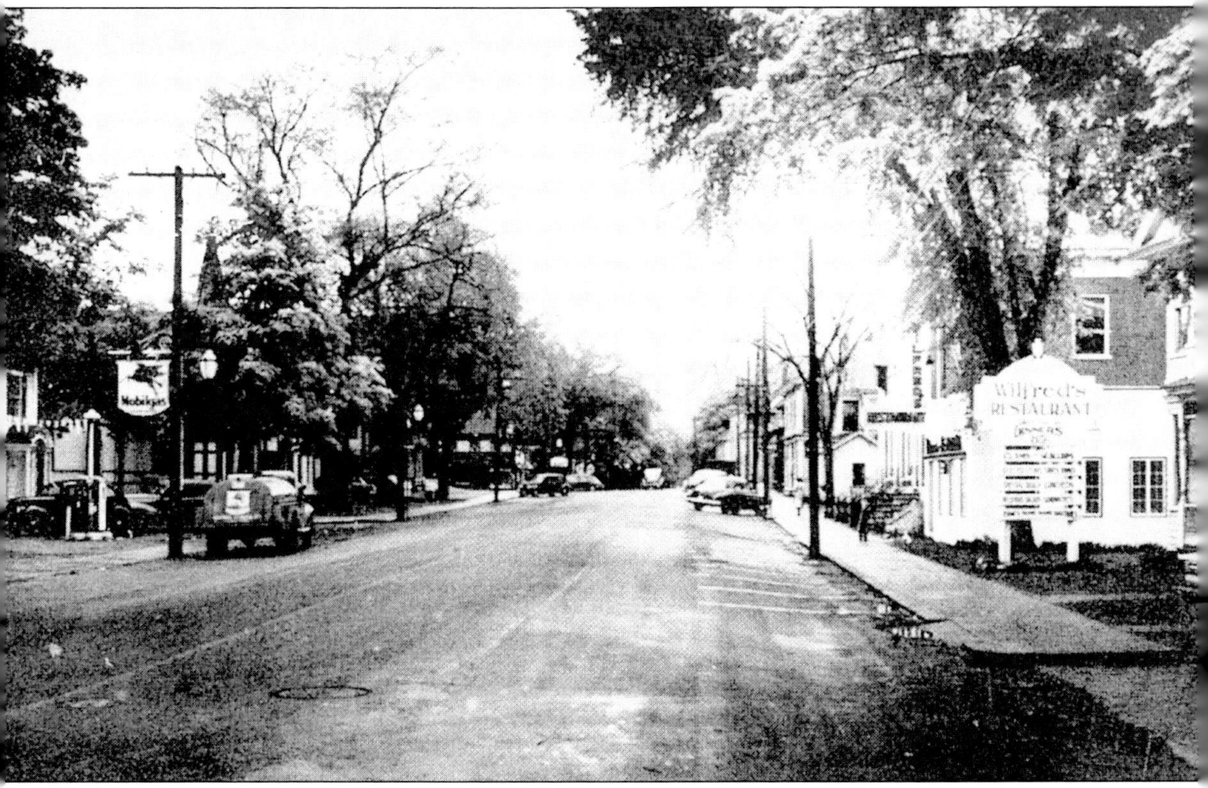

This view, looking south, shows Main Street in Gorham as seen in the late 1940s. This settlement lies in a sheltered valley at the juncture of the Androscoggin and Peabody Rivers. The busy Main Street indicated Gorham's importance as a commercial center, while its natural surroundings of towering summits made it a notable tourism center for all the northern mountains in the Presidential Range. The first grant was made to the neighboring town of Shelburne. In 1770, a grant was made of additional territory known as the Shelburne Addition. This addition included the site of the present town of Gorham, incorporated in 1836. The first permanent settlement was made *c.* 1805 by Stephen Messer of Andover, Massachusetts, but most of the first settlers were Maine Yankee stock.

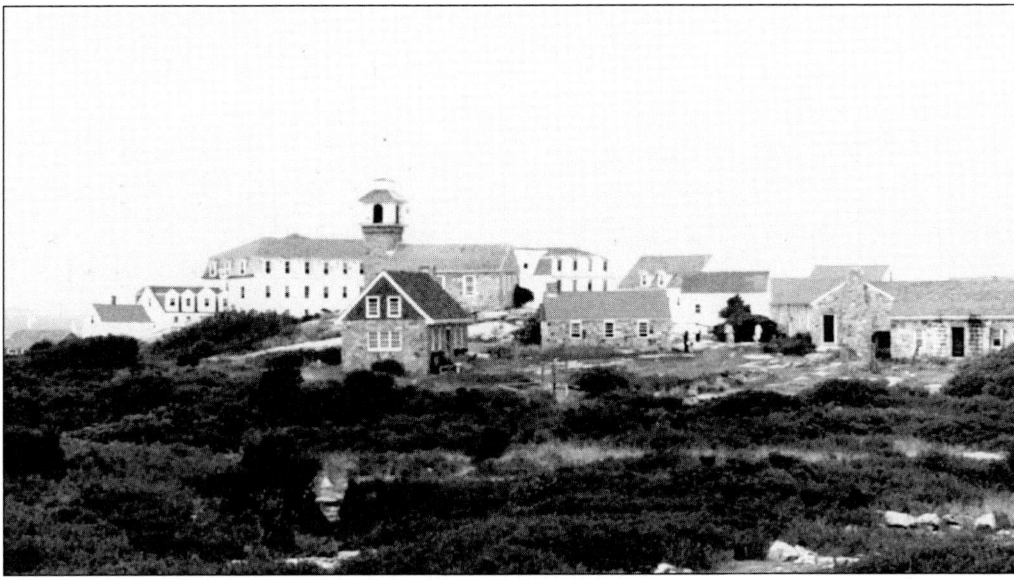

This is Gosport village on the northern end of Star Island. Though it does not have a Main Street, there are handsomely clustered houses in the village and a tiny church crowning the highest rock. Gosport was incorporated as a New Hampshire town in 1705. The charter was rescinded in 1876, and four of the nine islands that make up the Isles of Shoals and that belonged to New Hampshire were annexed to Rye. The other five islands belong to Maine.

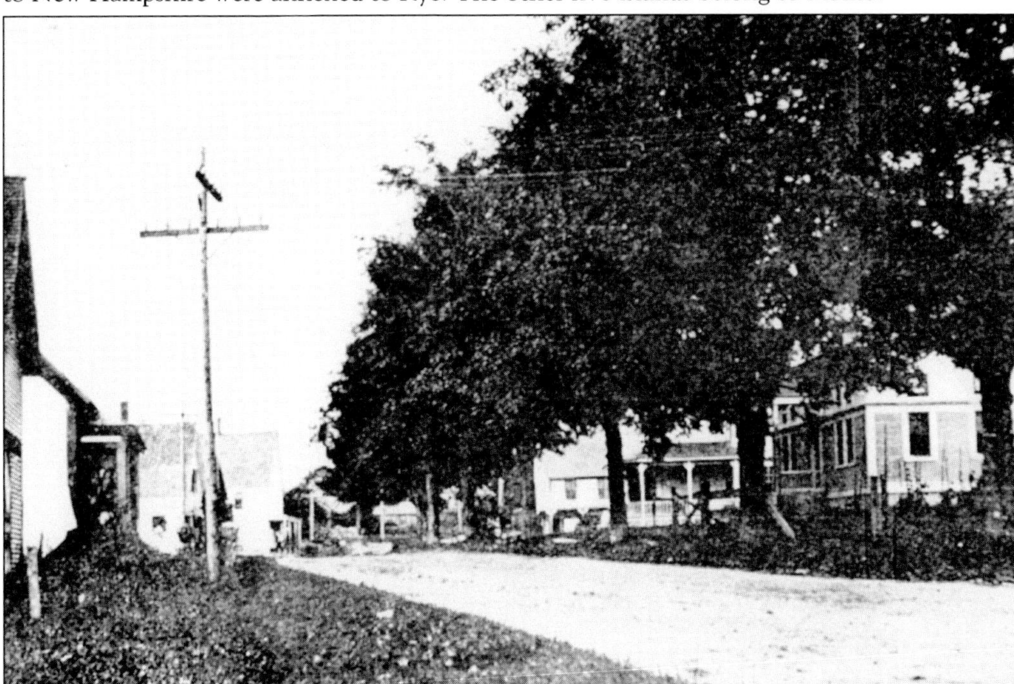

This is a view of Main Street in Grantham in 1908. Large shady trees grace the business districts, as they do in so many small towns in New Hampshire. Grantham was granted in 1761 and incorporated in 1816 under its present name. Grantham was one of the townships in New Hampshire that voted to join Vermont in 1788.

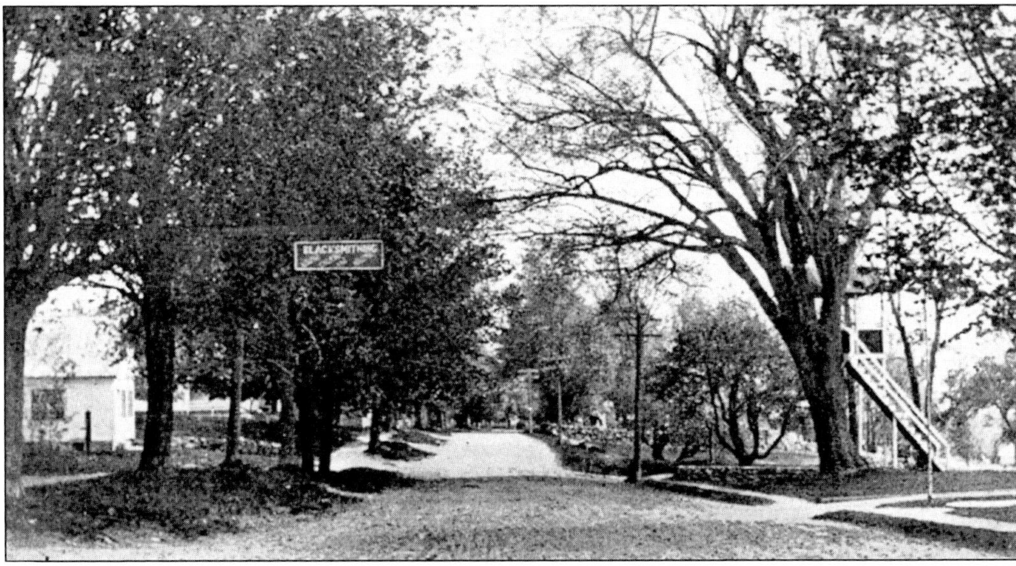

The attractive long-street village of Hampstead was originally a part of Amesbury and Haverhill, Massachusetts, and was known as Timber Lane by the settlers in 1721. In 1749, the town was granted by Governor Wentworth with the name of a London suburb. This view of Main Street was taken in the early 1900s.

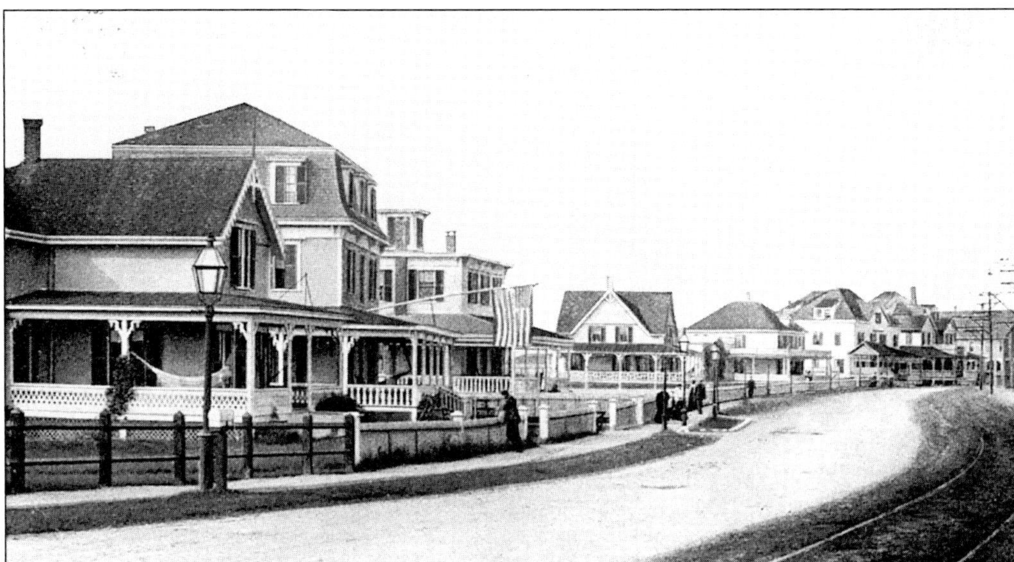

Ocean Avenue is a major thoroughfare in Hampton Beach and is seen in this 1909 view. Hampton was originally an outpost of the Massachusetts Bay Colony, which maintained a blockhouse here in 1635 against the numerous attacks by Native Americans. It became one of New Hampshire's four original towns and the mother of many of the smaller surrounding towns.

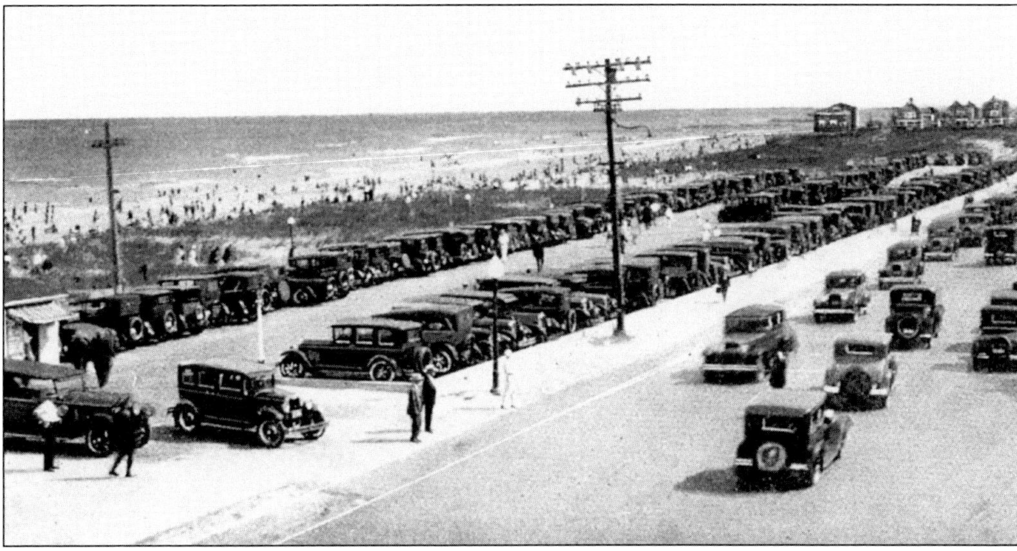

This view of Ocean Avenue at Hampton Beach looks south and dates from the 1930s. Note the parking lot at the beach full of the vehicles of summer bathers. In 1638, settlers in Exeter purchased this territory from the sachem Wehanownowit. They promptly changed the Native American name of Winnicummet (meaning "beautiful place in the pines") to Hampton at the incorporation of the town in 1639. This ocean resort has now welcomed thousands of tourists and bathers each year.

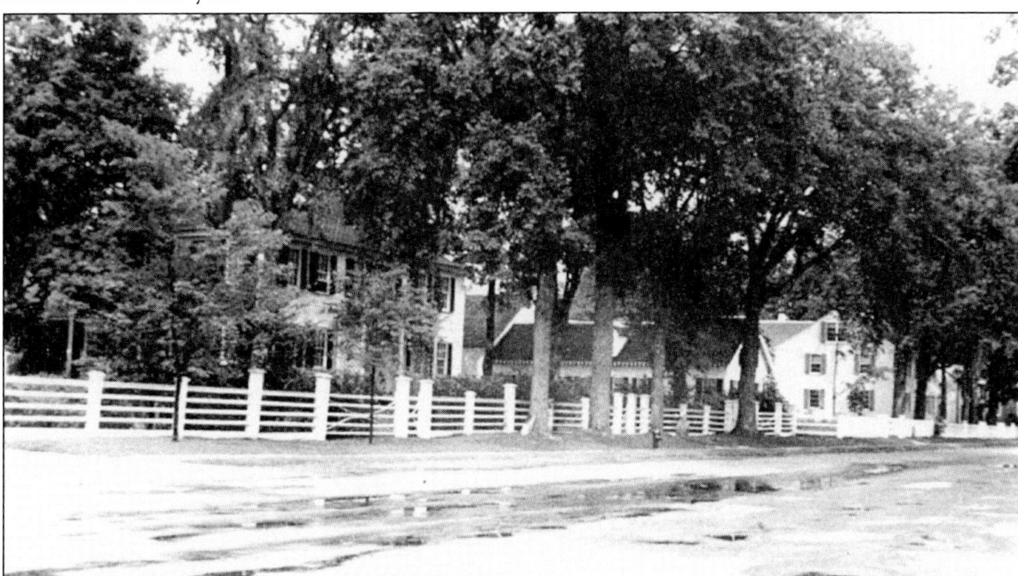

Seen is the village Main Street in Hancock in 1953. Many stately homes along Main Streets in New Hampshire were framed by the typical New England white fence. John Grimes first settled in Hancock in 1764, but there were not enough settlers to warrant incorporation until 1779. The town then took the name of John Hancock, who, as president of the Continental Congress, was the first to place his signature on the Declaration of Independence. Hancock was once a manufacturing center, and for some time, nearly one-half of all the cotton manufactured in the state was made here.

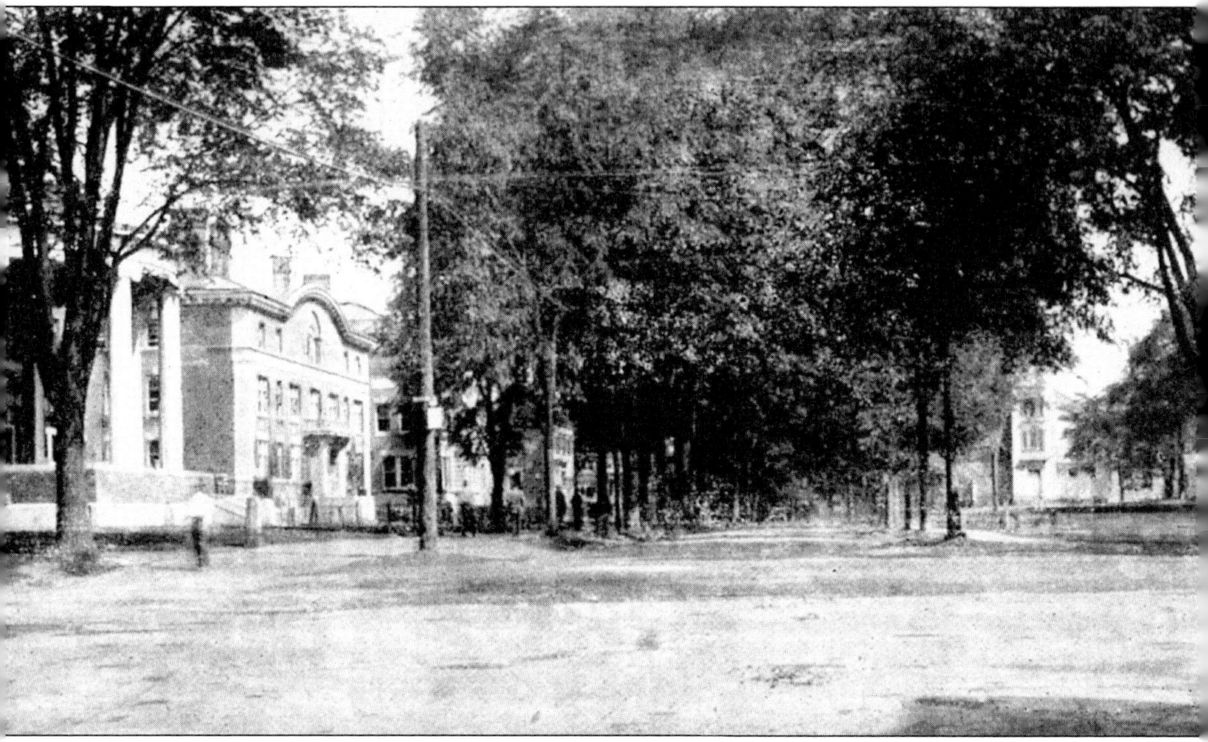

This view of North Main Street in Hanover dates from the early 1900s. Hanover, situated on a plateau above and half a mile back from the Connecticut River, is surrounded on three sides by hills that rise gradually to a culmination in Moose Mountain. Hanover is the seat of Dartmouth College, New Hampshire's oldest educational institution. Dartmouth College occupies a preeminent position among American colleges as one of the few remaining champions of liberal arts education. Before Dartmouth College, however, there was a little settlement here on this high land above the Connecticut River. The town of Hanover, a tract of 22,400 acres, chartered by Gov. Benning Wentworth on July 4, 1761, was not settled until the spring of 1765.

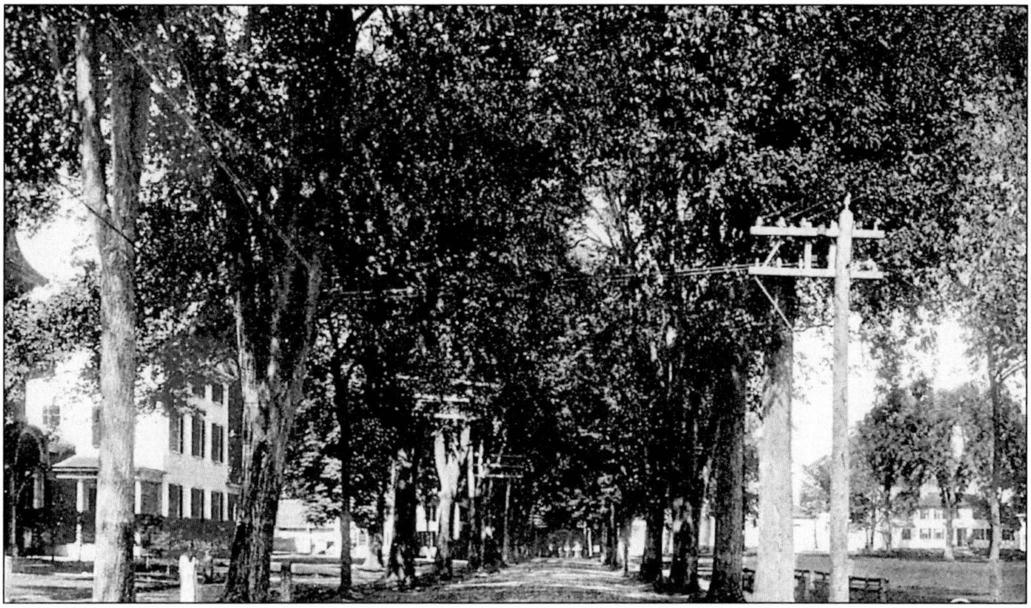

This residential street scene from Hanover shows Crosby Hall on the left *c.* the mid-1900s. The center of the town is tastefully framed by shade trees, and everywhere about it are impressive buildings, from the dignified, white Colonial group of the earlier days to the graceful white tower of the library and the fine row of Georgian structures. Everywhere there is a feeling of harmony.

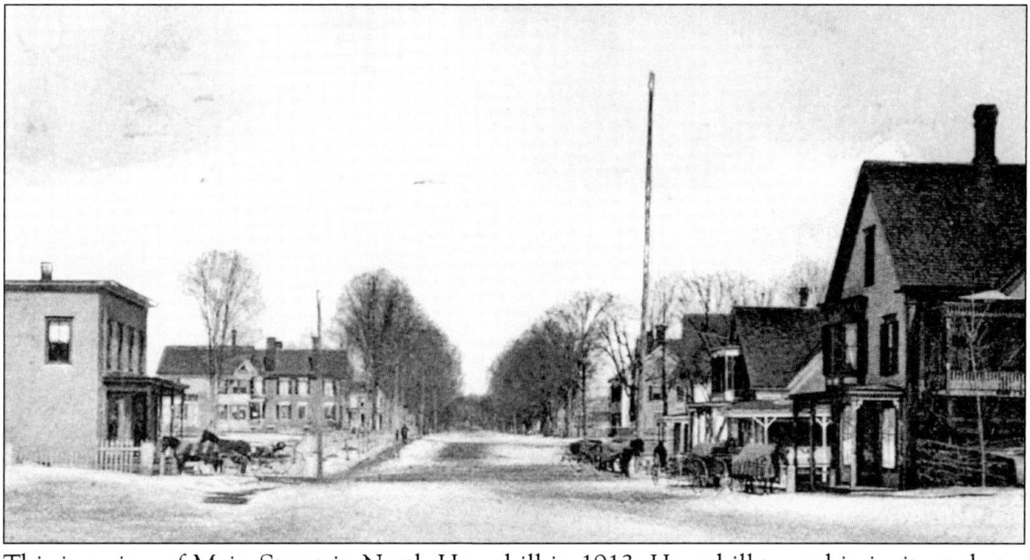

This is a view of Main Street in North Haverhill in 1913. Haverhill township is situated at a sufficient height above the Connecticut River to give a broad outlook for many miles over the valley and distant hills in Vermont. From Main Street, the ground slopes gradually toward the river and the wide farmland around the Great Ox-Bow in the river, which the Indians found long before the European settlers arrived. The town was named for Haverhill, Massachusetts, from which many of the early settlers came. The charter for the town was granted in 1763. Haverhill was the site of four forts, but no trace of them remain.

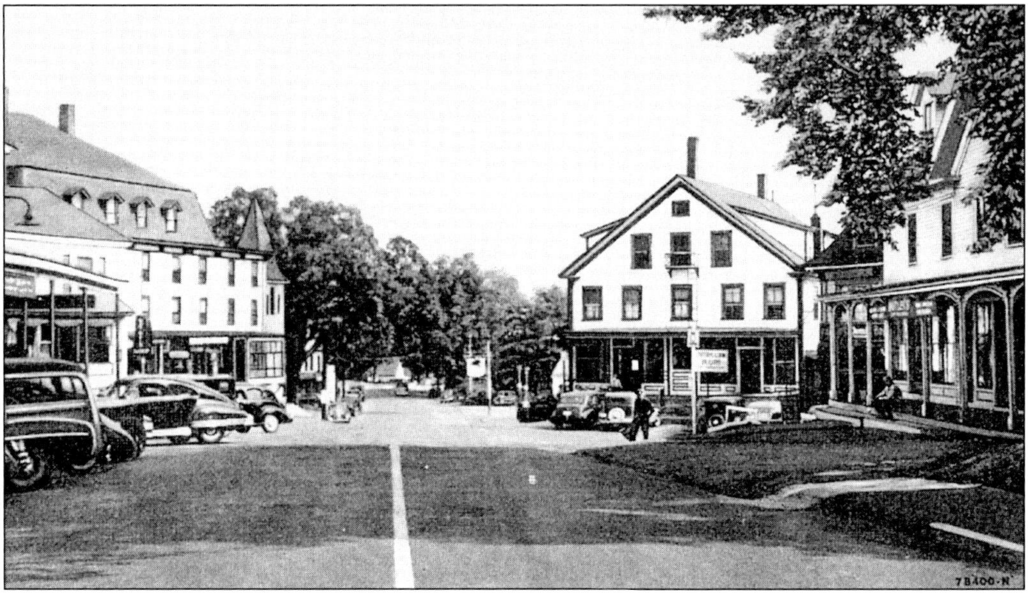

Hillsboro's Main Street at Central Square is seen in the 1940s. The village Main Street is gracefully softened by tall maples that line the thoroughfare. Its houses and stores are on high land above the Contoocook River, which once furnished power to the mills. The town was incorporated in 1772. Hillsboro is presently a member of the New Hampshire Main Street community.

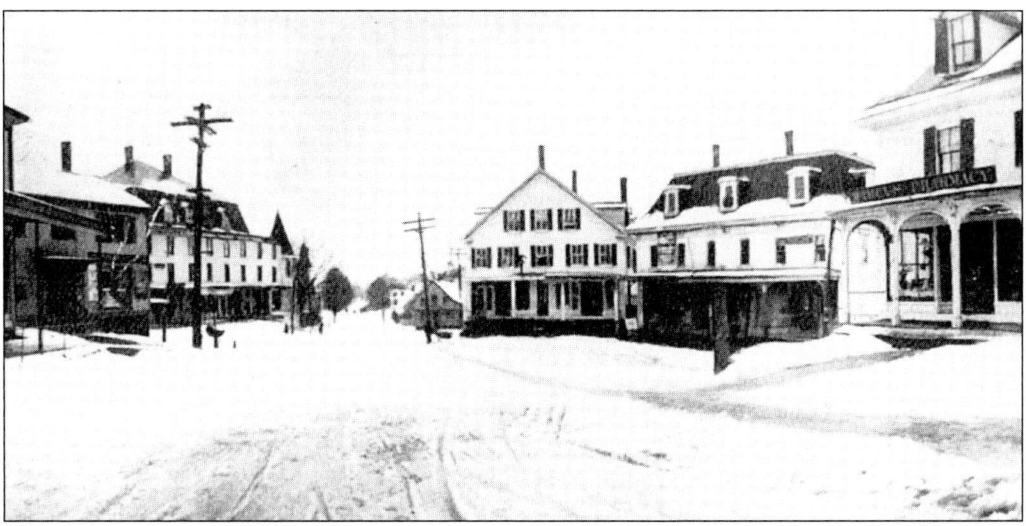

This view of the square in Hillsboro Bridge was taken in the winter of 1907. On January 18, 1742, the first boy, John McColley, was born in the settlement, in a log hut erected where Marcy's Block stood. In May of the same year, the first girl, Elizabeth Gibson, was born in a hut on the settlement's main road. When they reached maturity, Colonel Hill offered them 100 acres of land if they would marry and settle in the new town. They accepted his offer.

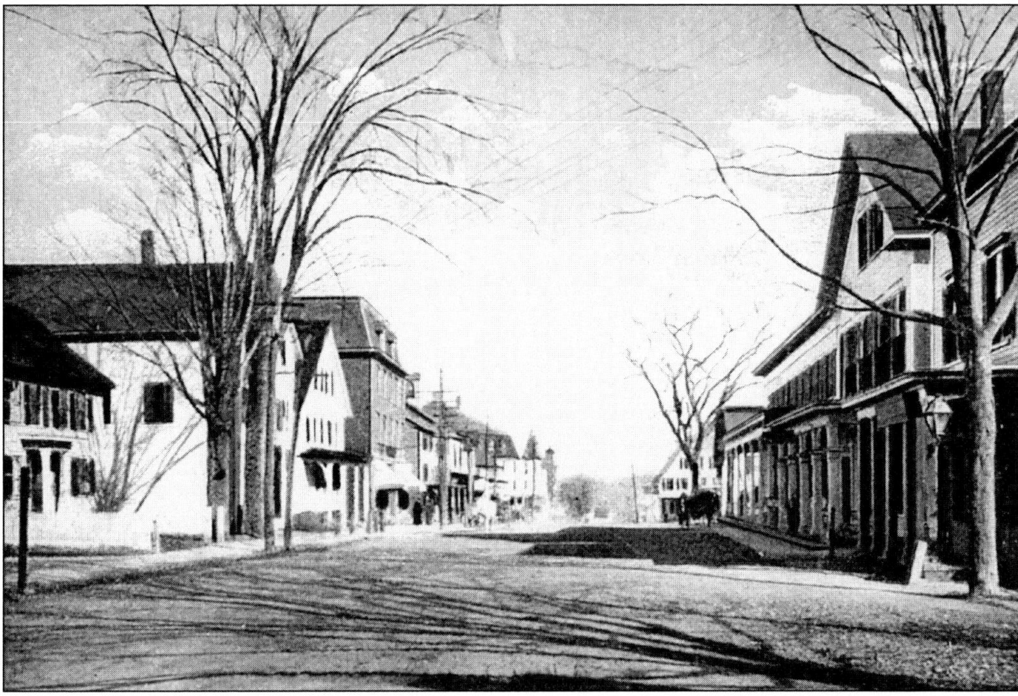

This is a view of Main Street in Hillsboro Bridge in the late 1800s. The great bridge across the Contoocook is a successor to the first built in 1799, which was a marvel of engineering. Its memory was perpetuated in the name Hillsboro Bridge, which was formerly used for the village.

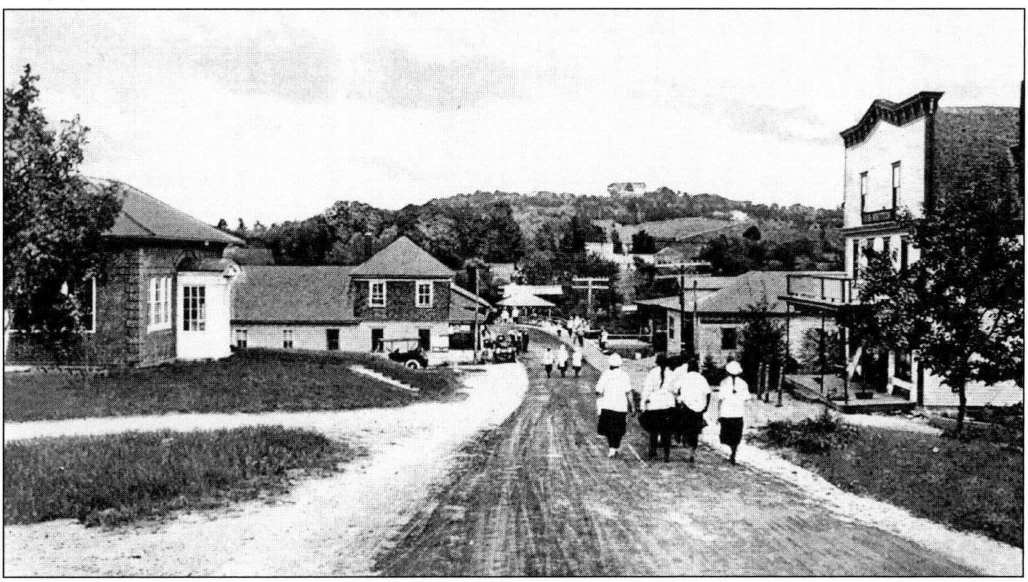

The Holderness Main Street is seen in this view, which looks south toward the bridge in the early 1900s. The town library is on the left, and Sheppard Hill is in the distant center. This summer resort, located on a promontory between Squam Lake and Little Squam Lake, has become a thriving summer resort with more of the semblance of an English village than any other town in the state. The original town grant of six square miles on the Pemigewasset River was made by Gov. Benning Wentworth in 1751.

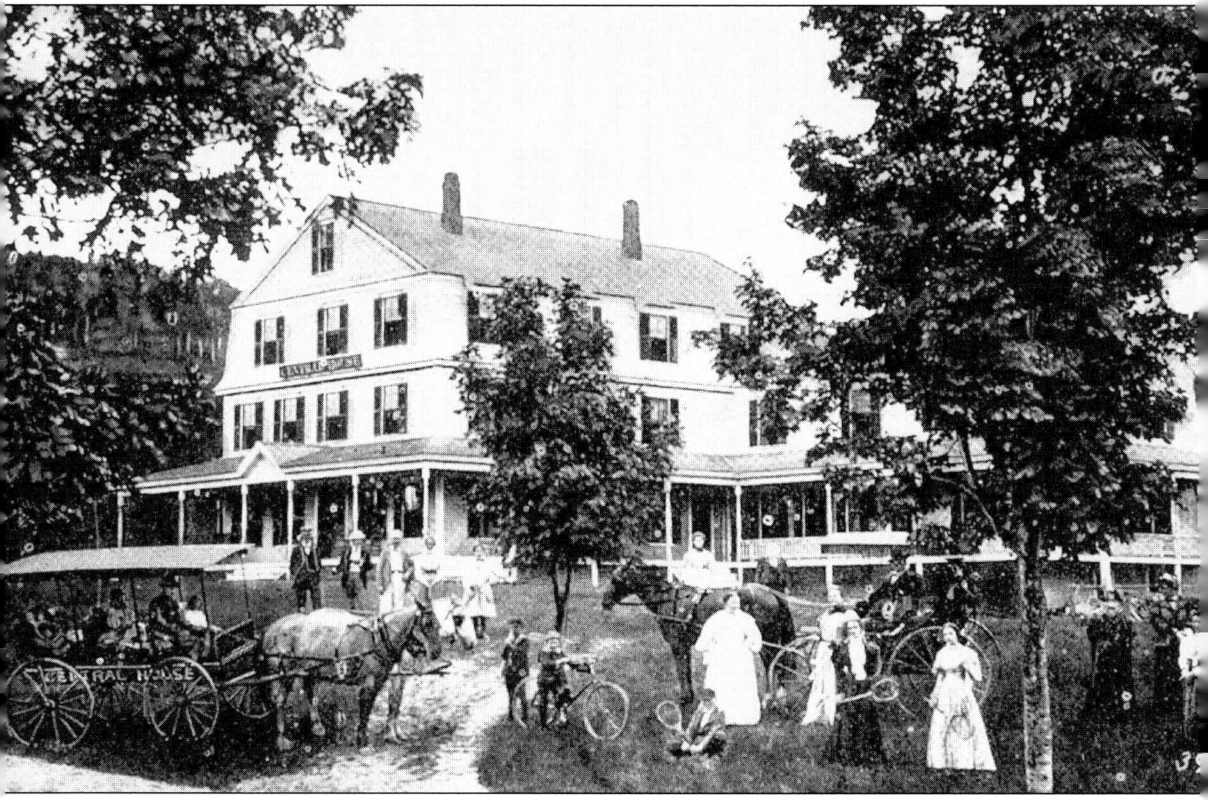

This is a *c.* 1895 view of the Central House on North Main Street in Holderness. At the turn of the century, many fine inns, hotels, and boardinghouses were established throughout the White Mountains and the Lakes Region of the state. These hotels, like the Central House, thrived during the summer months when the city people came to vacation in the region for the entire season. In 1887, the inn advertised that it had a capacity for 60 guests and that it cost $2.50 daily and from $9 to $15 weekly. In 1967, this fine old house was sold to the Squam Lakes Science Center.

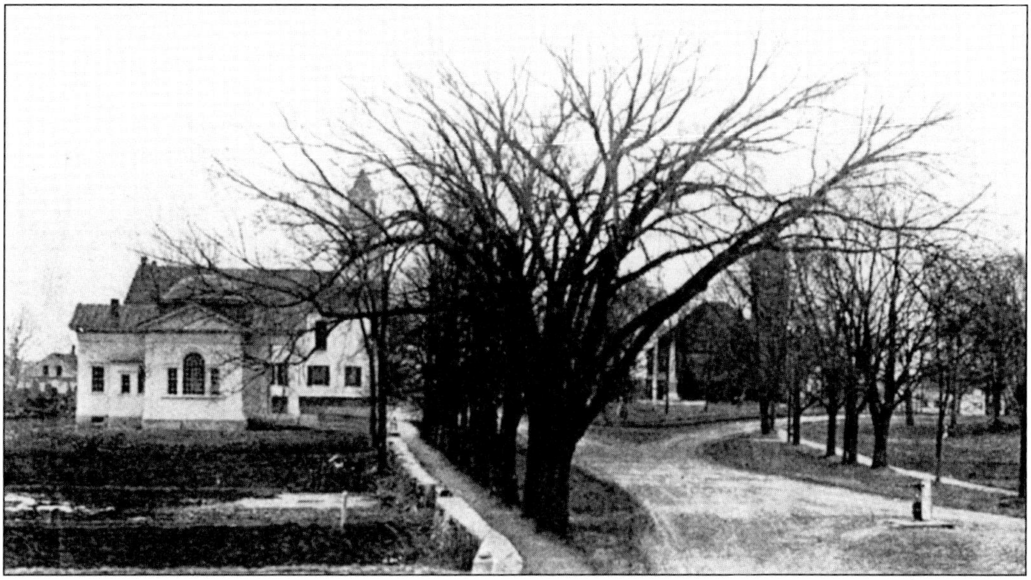

An attractive rural village, Hollis is graced with fine churches and white houses set at wide intervals along Main Street. Originally a part of Dunstable, it was set off as West Dunstable in 1739 and incorporated in 1746, taking the name of Holles in honor of the family name of the Duke of Newcastle, a close friend of Gov. John Wentworth. After the Revolution, the spelling was changed to Hollis to perpetuate the name of Thomas Hollis, a benefactor of Harvard College. This view of Main Street looks east from Cranford Inn in the early 1900s.

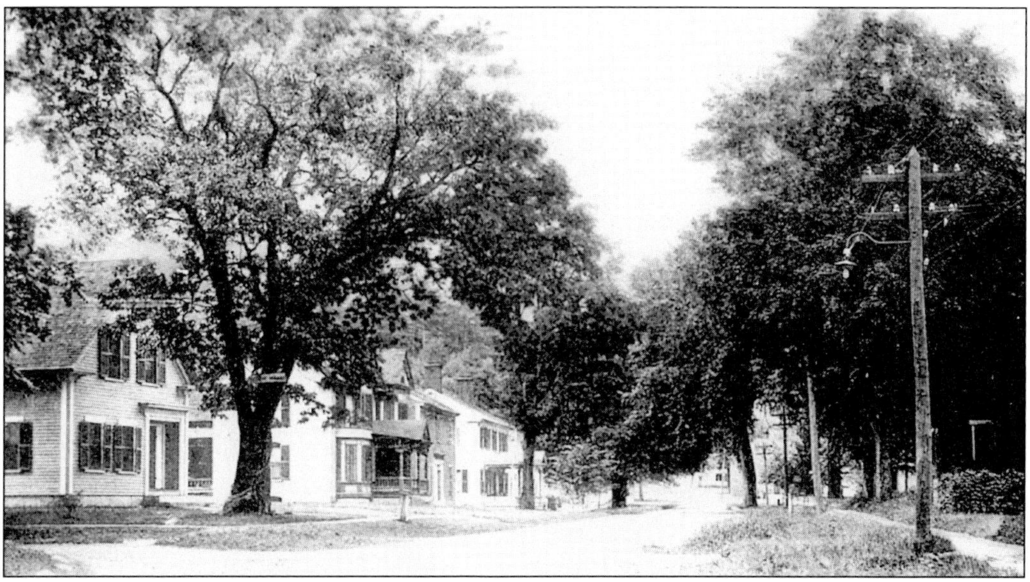

This is a view of Main Street in Hooksett dating from 1907. This pleasant reclusion of the combined houses and shade trees provides a soft tone of late summer. In October 1719, about 80 persons from Hampton and Portsmouth associated for the purpose of obtaining a grant of a township in "Chestnut Country." The first settlement in the territory that now comprises the town was probably made sometime shortly after 1745. The town was detached from Chester on the east side of the Merrimack, and Goffstown and Dunbarton on the west side, and incorporated as a separate town in 1822.

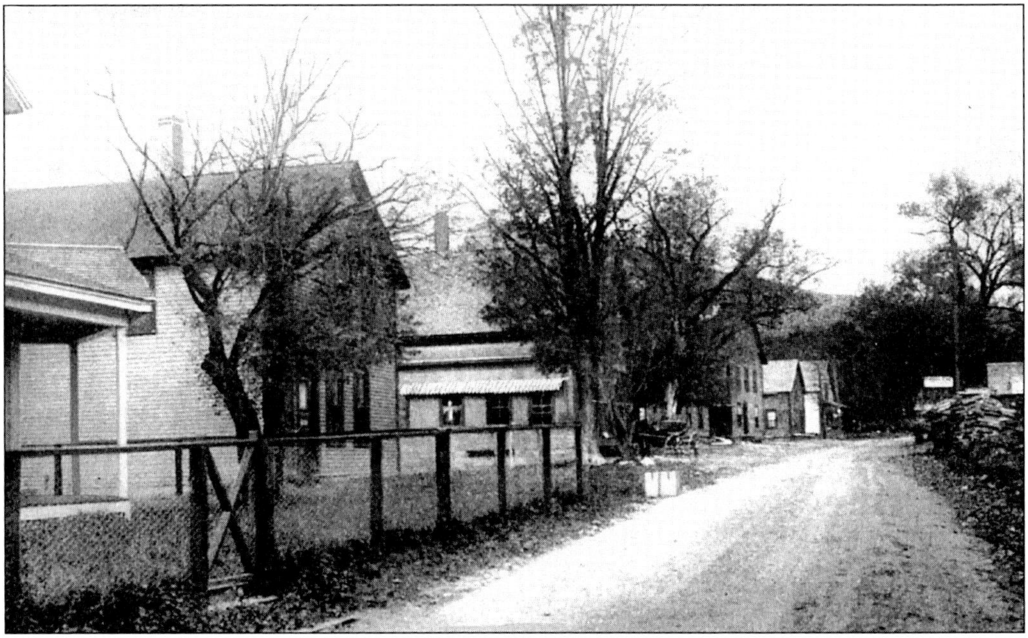

The small hamlet of Johnson is located in Franconia Notch. This view of Main Street in Johnson looks north in the early 1900s.

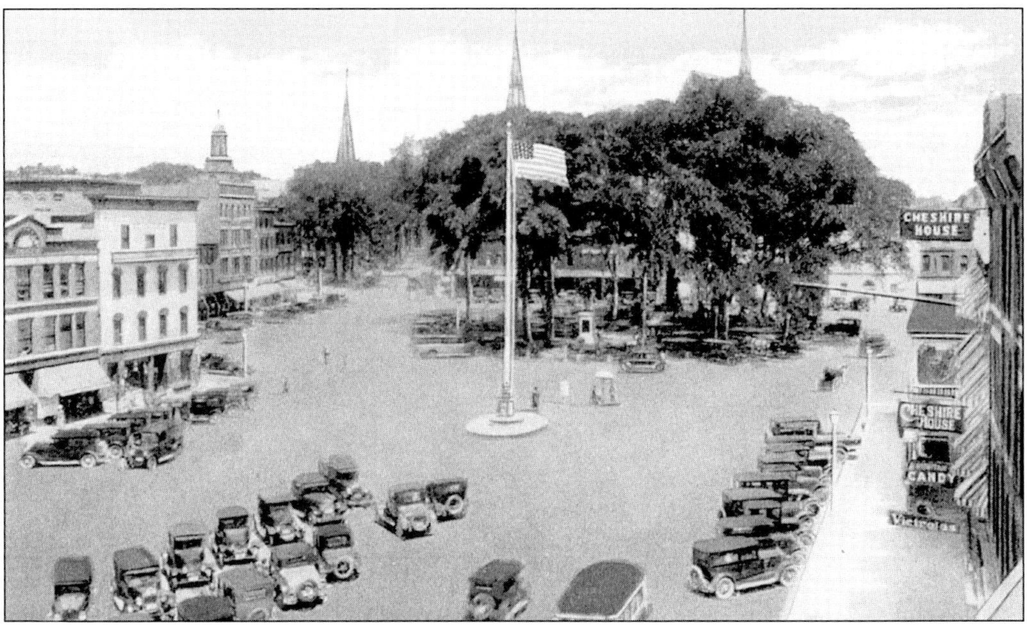

Seen is Keene's Main Street and Central Square in 1927. The first permanent settlement was in 1750, and three years later, a new charter named the town in honor of Sir Benjamin Keene, a friend of Gov. Benning Wentworth and an English diplomat in high repute at the time. Keene lost territory to Sullivan in 1787 and 1794 and to Roxbury in 1812. In 1812, however, territory was annexed from Swanzey.

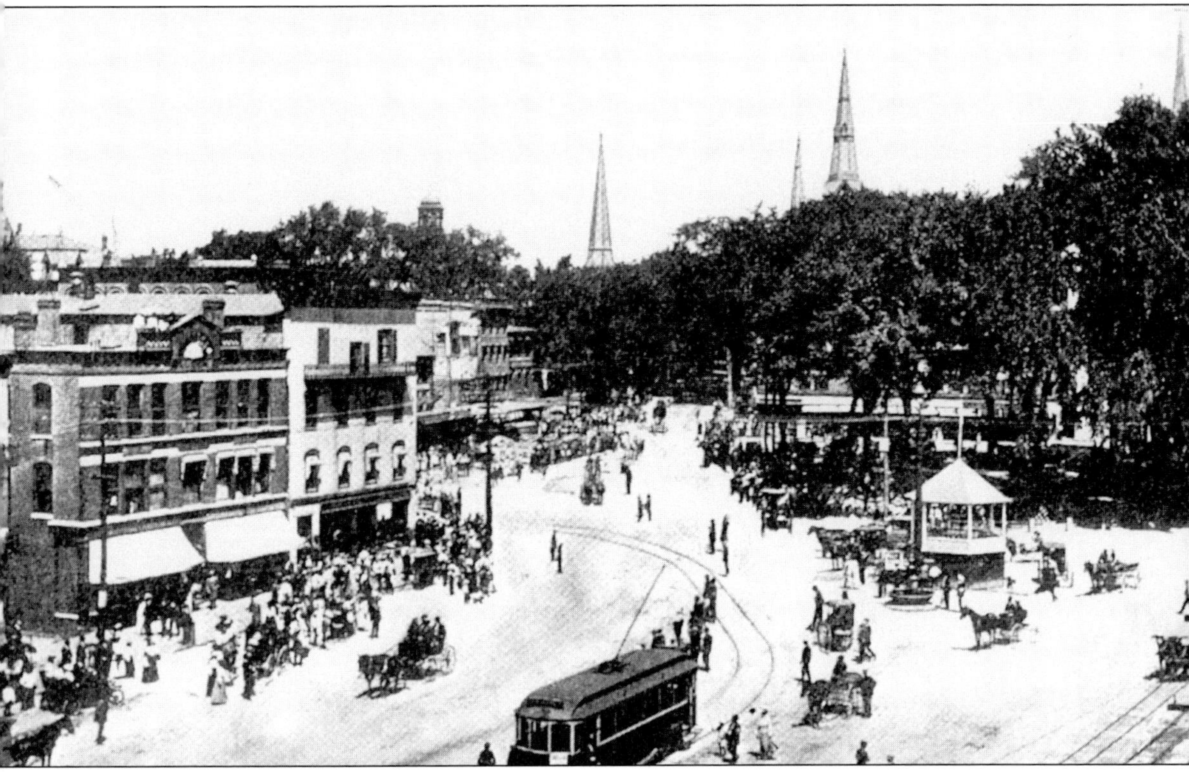

This is a late-19th-century view of Main Street and Central Square in Keene, a lively commercial city spread out on a level terrain bordered by low hills in the bed of a primeval lake. Central Square, dominated by the spire of the First Church, is the business hub of the city. This territory was granted in 1733 by the Massachusetts Bay Colony and named Upper Ashuelot. The first log cabin was built by Nathan Blake in the summer of 1736. The next year, about 40 men and their families came to the settlement. At a meeting held early that year, when the lots were being assigned, plans were made to leave a wide space for the main street by having each property holder move his claim to the rear of the lot. This act was responsible for the unusually wide Main Street of this city.

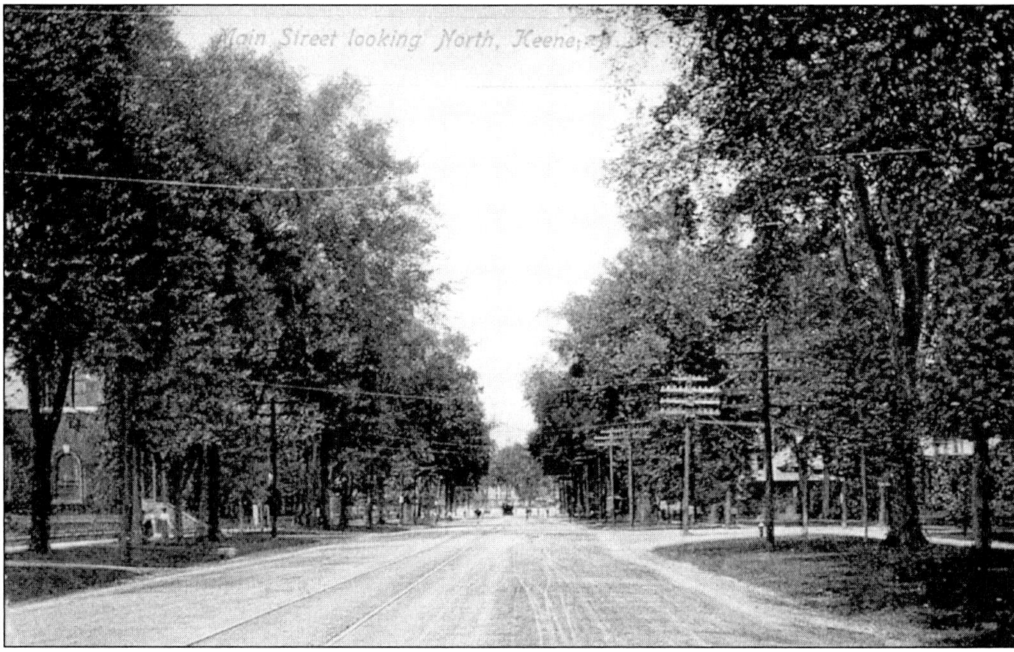

Keene's Main Street is seen in this 1907 view looking north. Large elms shade the city's 50 miles of streets. Keene is a city of homes, a high percentage of them privately owned, one-family houses. Around the western edge of the city winds the Ashuelot River, with many mills along its banks, while through the center runs Beaver Brook. Keene is the seat of Keene State College, an educational institution affiliated with the University System of New Hampshire.

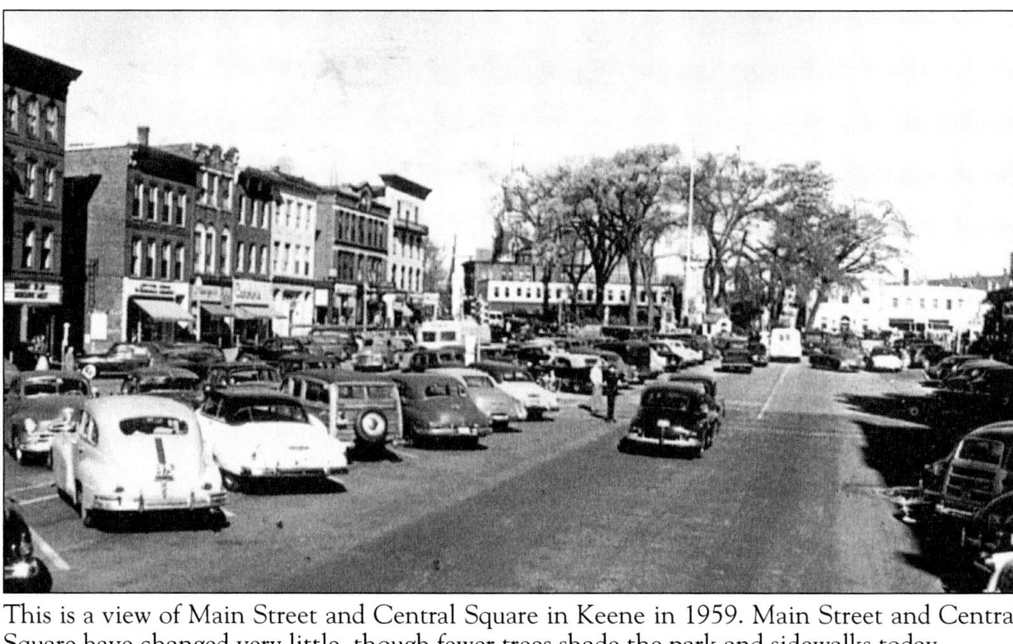

This is a view of Main Street and Central Square in Keene in 1959. Main Street and Central Square have changed very little, though fewer trees shade the park and sidewalks today.

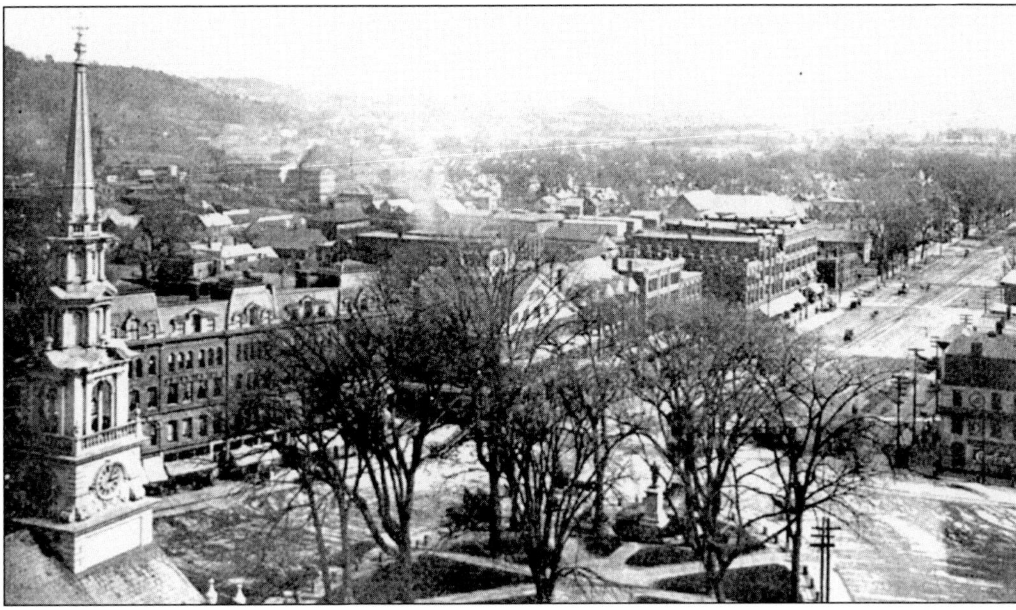

This bird's-eye view of Central Square and Main Street dates from 1927. This view of Keene looks southeast down the wide street. On the far left is the spire of the Congregational church.

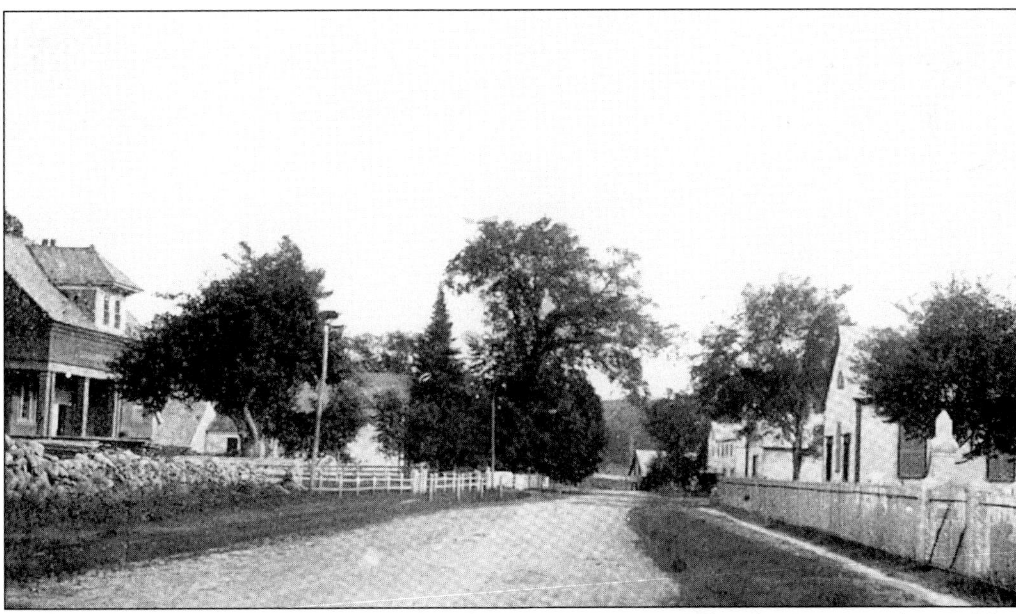

Kensington was one of 27 towns granted in what is now New Hampshire by Gov. Jonathan Belcher of Massachusetts in the 1730s. The town was named after Baron Kensington, who once owned the famous Kensington Palace in London. Kensington separated from Hampton in 1737. This c. 1910 view shows the town's Main Street.

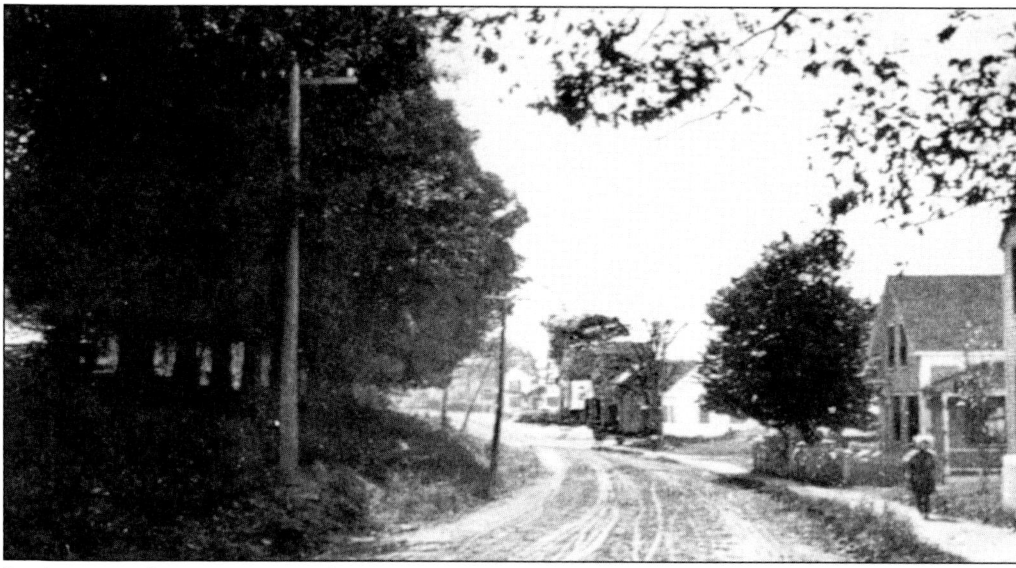

Looking east from Brown Academy *c.* 1910, this view shows Main Street in East Kingston. This settlement would appear to be a scattered village lying between two ponds in what was a part of the original Hampton grant. East Kingston separated from Kingston in 1738.

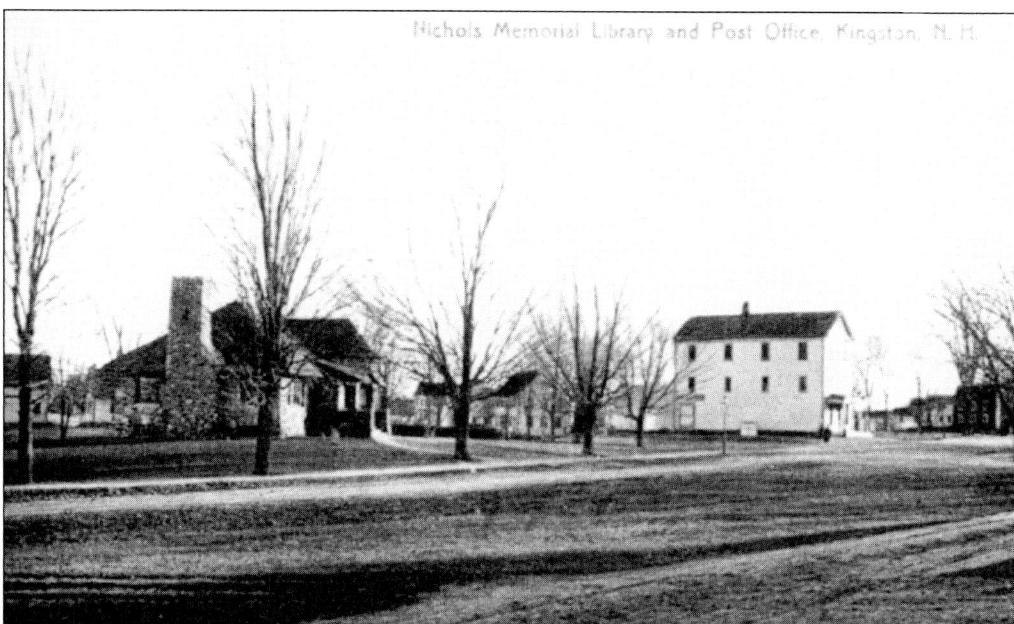

This view of Main Street in Kingston looks south *c.* 1910. Pictured is the Nichols Memorial Library and the post office. Kingston's open farmland and stately houses depict the modest income of farmers in New Hampshire. Kingston was set off and granted in 1694 to James Prescott and others; until 1800, the name was spelled "King's town." The large original grant was made smaller by the separation of East Kingston in 1738, Sandown in 1756, and Danville in 1760.

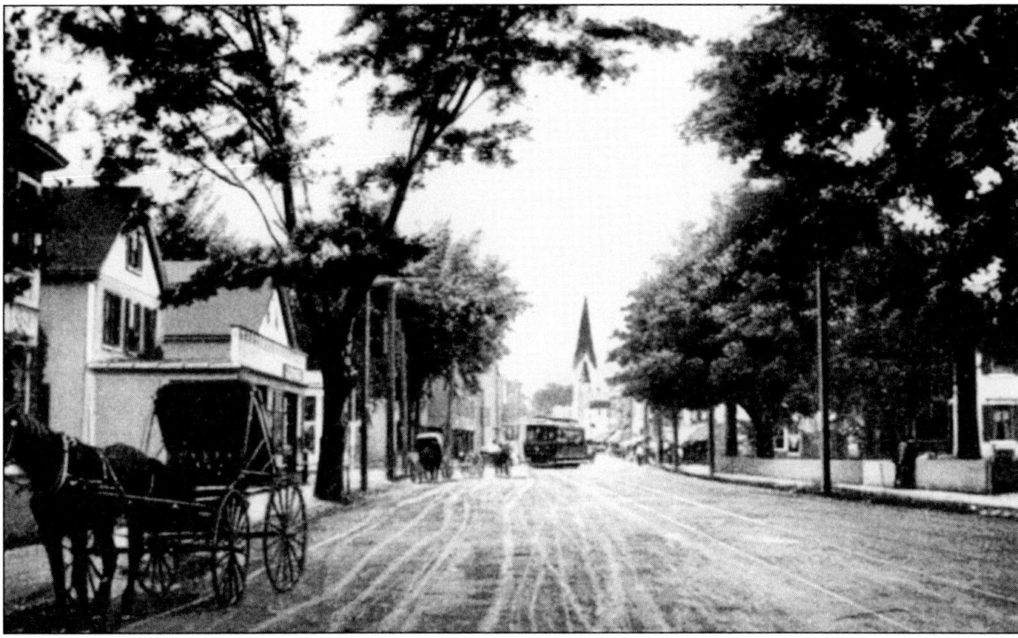

Laconia is a compact city of houses and business establishments lining the slow-moving but clear waters of the Winnipesaukee River. Main Street is one long thoroughfare passing through Laconia from the northeast to the southwest. In 1768, the north and west sides of the Winnipesaukee were chartered by the governor and council as a part of Meredith. This section was known as Meredith Bridge until 1855, when it separated from Meredith and became known as Laconia. This 1908 view of Main Street in Laconia looks north.

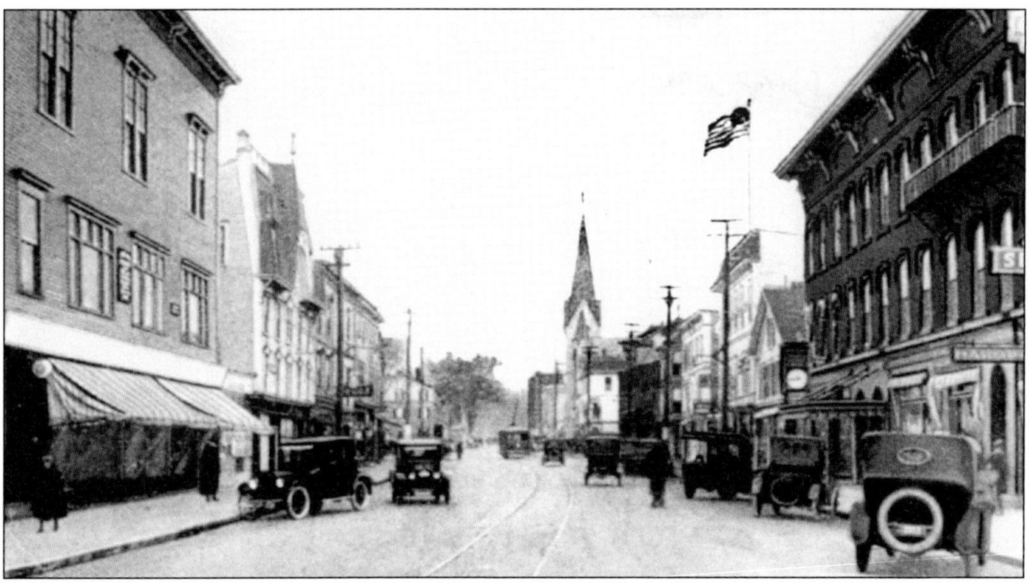

Main Street and shorter streets to its right and left constitute the business section of Laconia, which remained a town until 1893, when it received its city charter. The Honorable Charles A. Busiel, who later was elected governor of New Hampshire, was its first mayor. This view of Laconia's Main Street was taken in the late 1920s and looks north. Laconia is a member of the New Hampshire Main Street community.

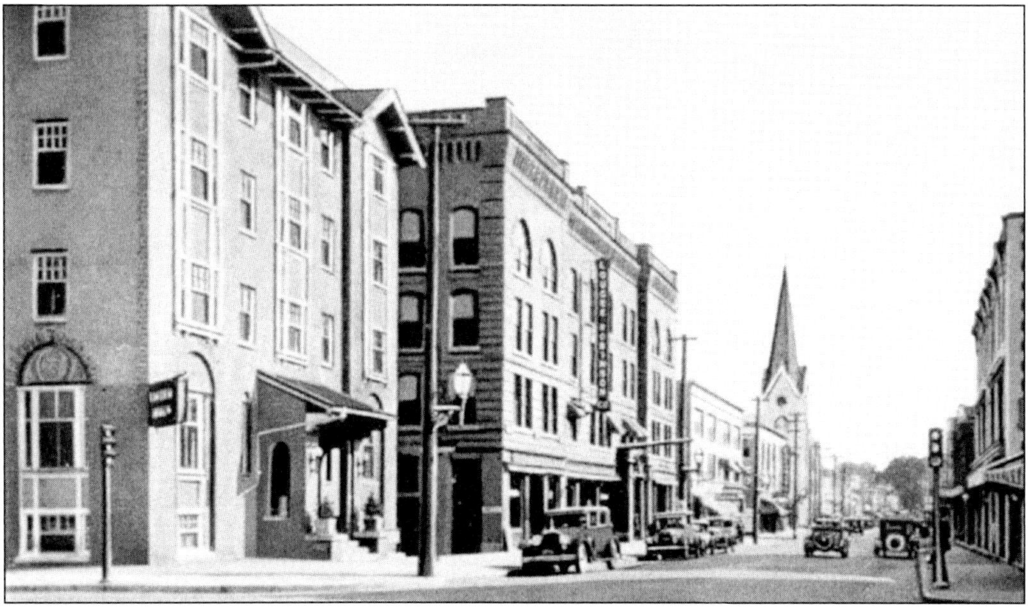

This view, looking south from Depot Square in Laconia, shows Main Street in the 1930s. On the left is Laconia Tavern, a landmark in Laconia. Numerous streets branch out from the business district and lead to the residential section. Laconia carries an air of prosperity, which is reflected in the business sections spread throughout the city.

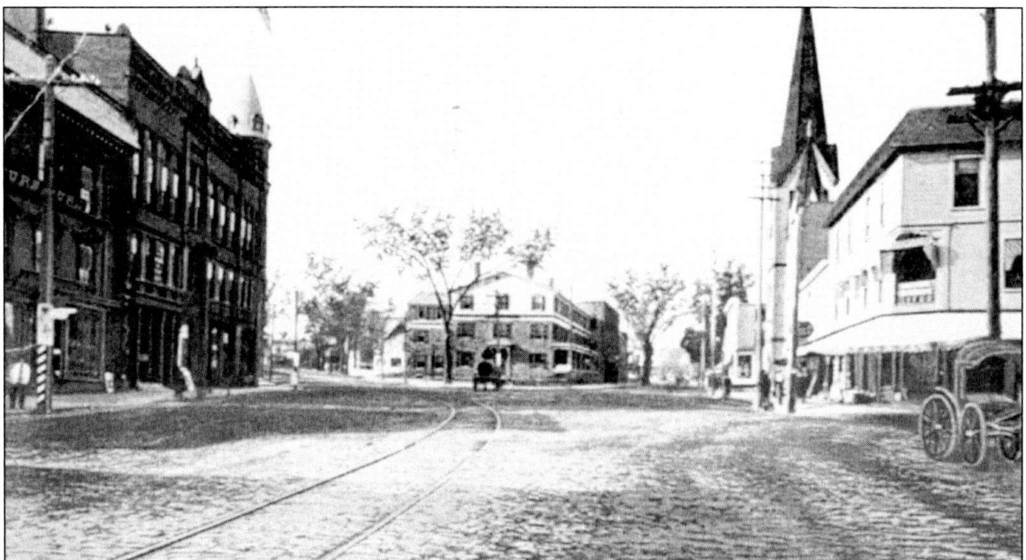

Seen is Laconia's Bank Square in 1911. Laconia was first visited by the European settlers in 1652, when Gov. John Endicott of the Massachusetts Bay Colony sent four men, Capt. Simon Willard, Edward Johnson, Jonathan Ince, and John Sherman, to survey and lay claim to the surrounding region. Following the Merrimack and Winnipesaukee Rivers, they made their way through present Laconia as far as the "weirs," and there on a large rock chiseled the governor's initials as well as their own with the date, August 1652, to mark the northern boundary of the Massachusetts Bay Colony.

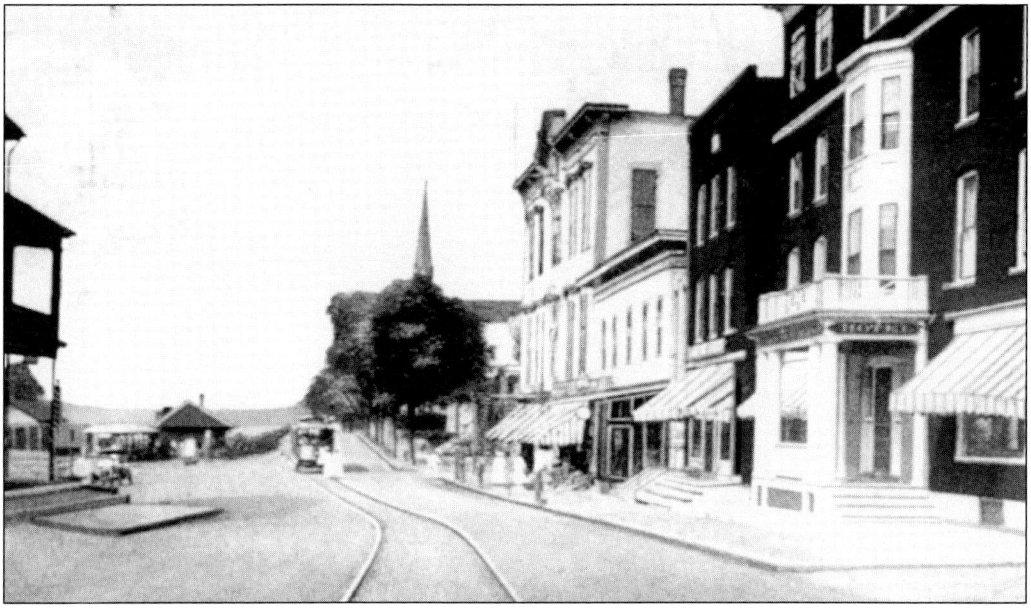

Lakeport, a section of Laconia, is located at the lower end of Lake Paugus, named for a Native American chieftain. Lakeport is built partly on flat land and partly on low hills. This is a view of Union Avenue in Lakeport in 1923.

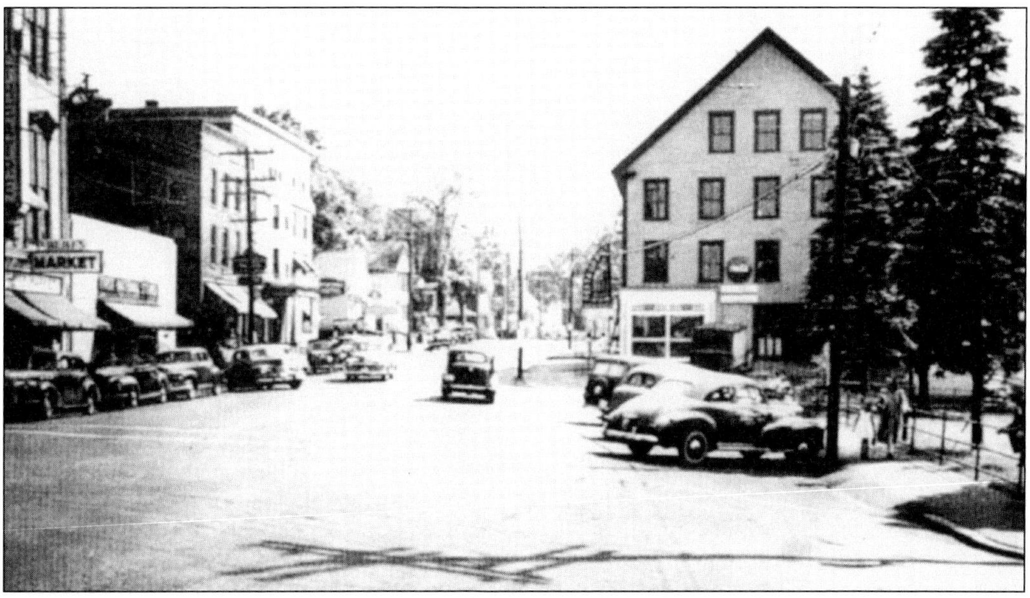

For many years, this busy intersection was known as Lake Village and was a village unto itself. This view of "the Square" looks southwest on Union Avenue in Lakeport in the 1940s.

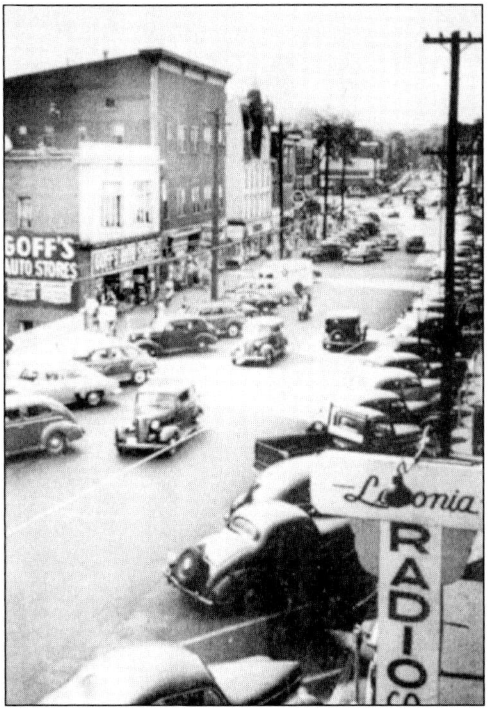

This view of Laconia's Main Street looks north in the 1940s. The automobile changed the face of the city with the additions of parking meters and painted lines in the street.

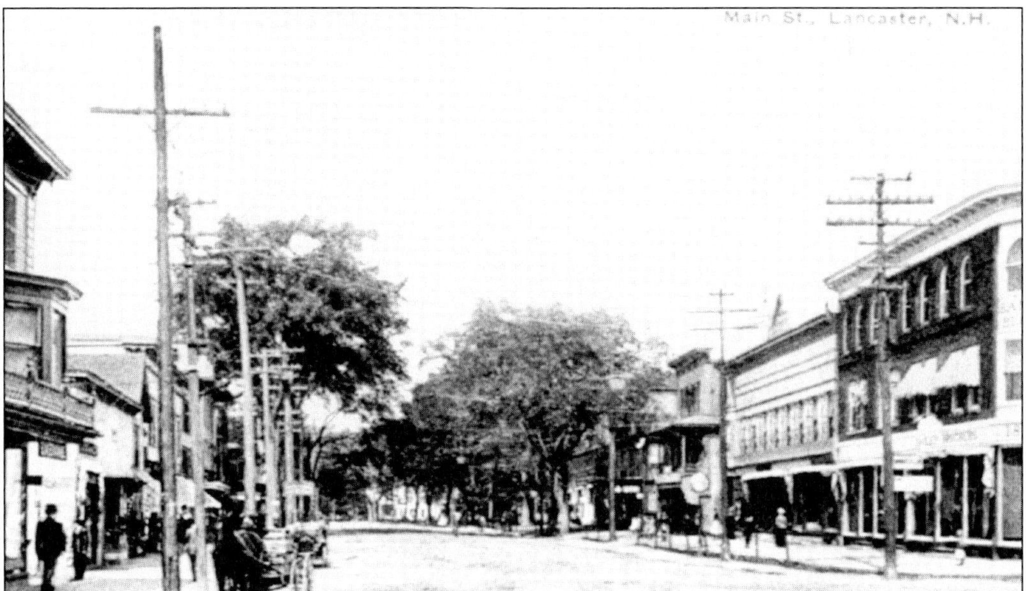

Seen in 1915, Lancaster's Main Street, an impressively wide street with many rare old houses sufficiently spaced to enhance their beauty, gives the community a distinguished appearance. Lancaster is located in a fine intervale at the confluence of the Connecticut and Israel Rivers, the latter passing through the center of the village. Bordered by low hills, the town is in the midst of mountains with blue silhouettes rising above the skyline. Lancaster is an important trading center for a large area in both Coos and Grafton Counties. Lancaster's charter was granted in July 1763.

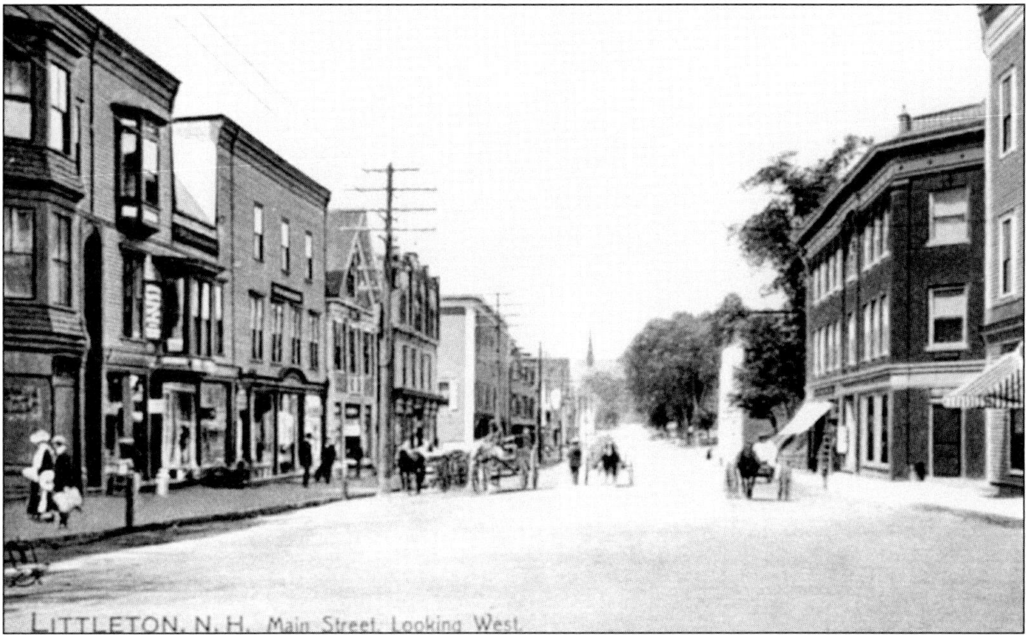

This is a view of Main Street looking west in Littleton in the late 1800s. Main Street is the principal business thoroughfare of the town. In the summertime, teams of tourists staying at mountain resorts come to Littleton's Main Street; they seem to justly consider Littleton the business section of the mountains. The stores are equal to any found in the larger places in the state.

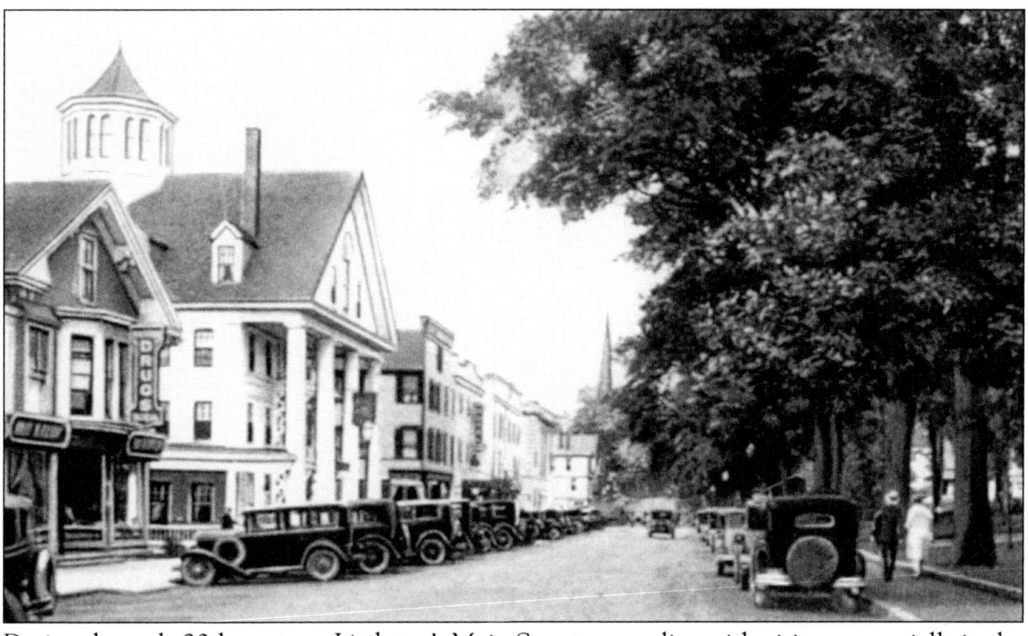

During the early 20th century, Littleton's Main Street came alive with visitors, especially in the summer. Littleton's location on western edge of the White Mountain area is its chief claim to scenic beauty. On the left is the famous Thayer's Hotel, a grand hotel in the city. This view of Main Street looks west in the 1930s.

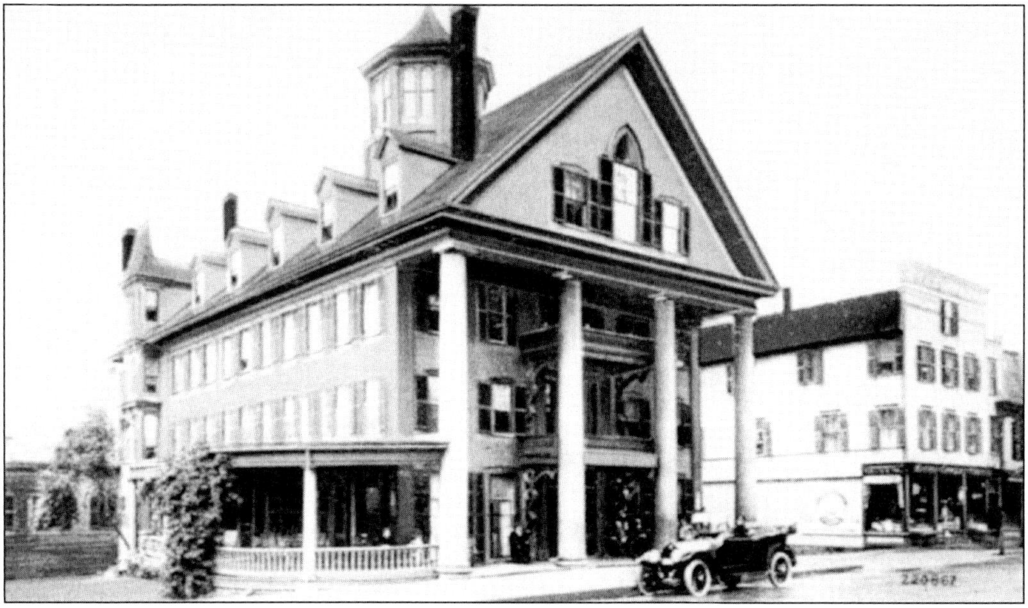

Thayer's Hotel, in the center of the business district in Littleton, is seen here in the 1920s. This hotel was established as the White Mountain House in 1850. Thayer's Hotel has long been considered an institution in Littleton.

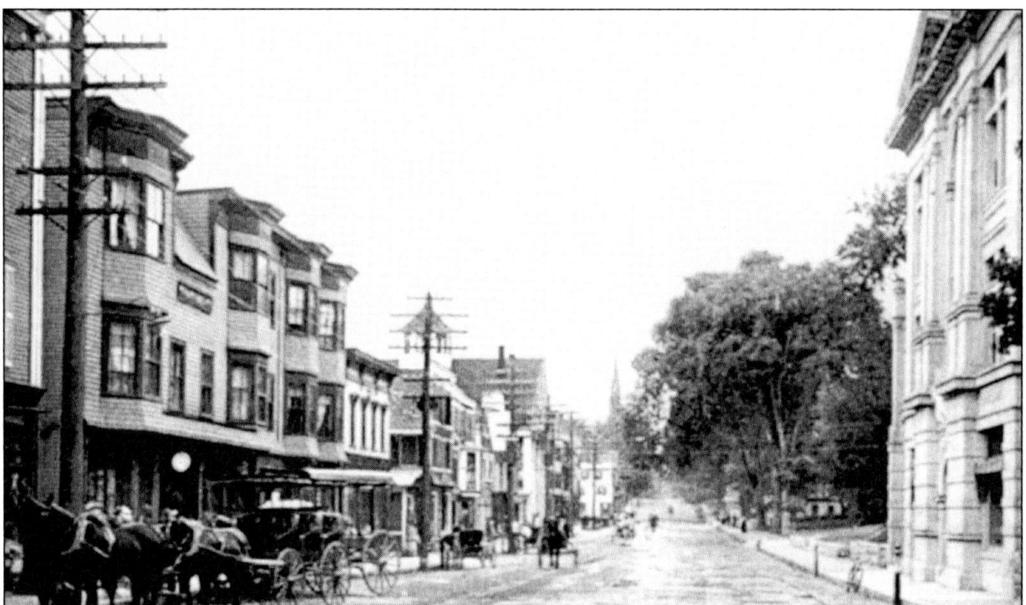

This view of Main Street looks west to the business district of Littleton in 1908. The Ammonoosuc River, which runs through the town and has a drop of 235 feet, has done much for the development of the area as a major trade center in the White Mountains. Littleton is a member of the New Hampshire Main Street community.

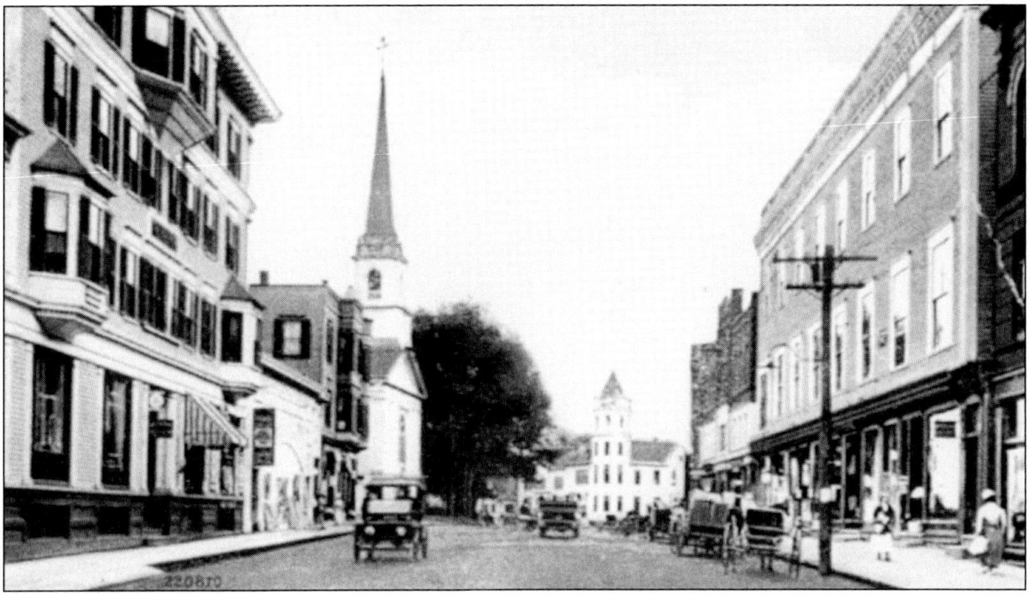

Littleton was first granted under the name of Chiswick, after an old English parish, in 1764, but the terms of this grant were not completely fulfilled and the charter was revoked. The town was regranted in 1770 under the name of Apthorp, in honor of a friend of Governor Wentworth. The town of Apthorp, including the major part of what is Dalton, was divided in 1784 into two townships by the two men who owned most of the land, Moses Little and Tristram Dalton, and the two towns were named for them. Littleton was incorporated in 1784. This view of Main Street looks east from the post office in 1917.

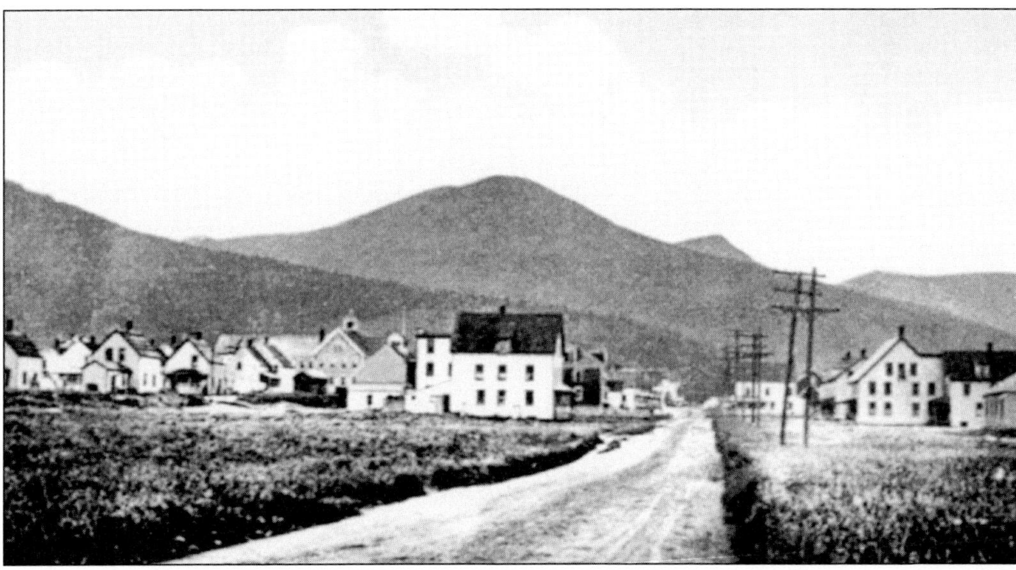

This view of Main Street looks east at the village of Lincoln in the early 1900s. The middle branch of the Pemigewasset River flows southward through the central part of the town, making this an ideal setting for the lumber trade. The town was granted on January 31, 1764, to James Avery and others; however, as late as 1791, Lincoln had only 22 settlers and very few farms. Lincoln became a loggers' haven during the late 1880s through the 1920s.

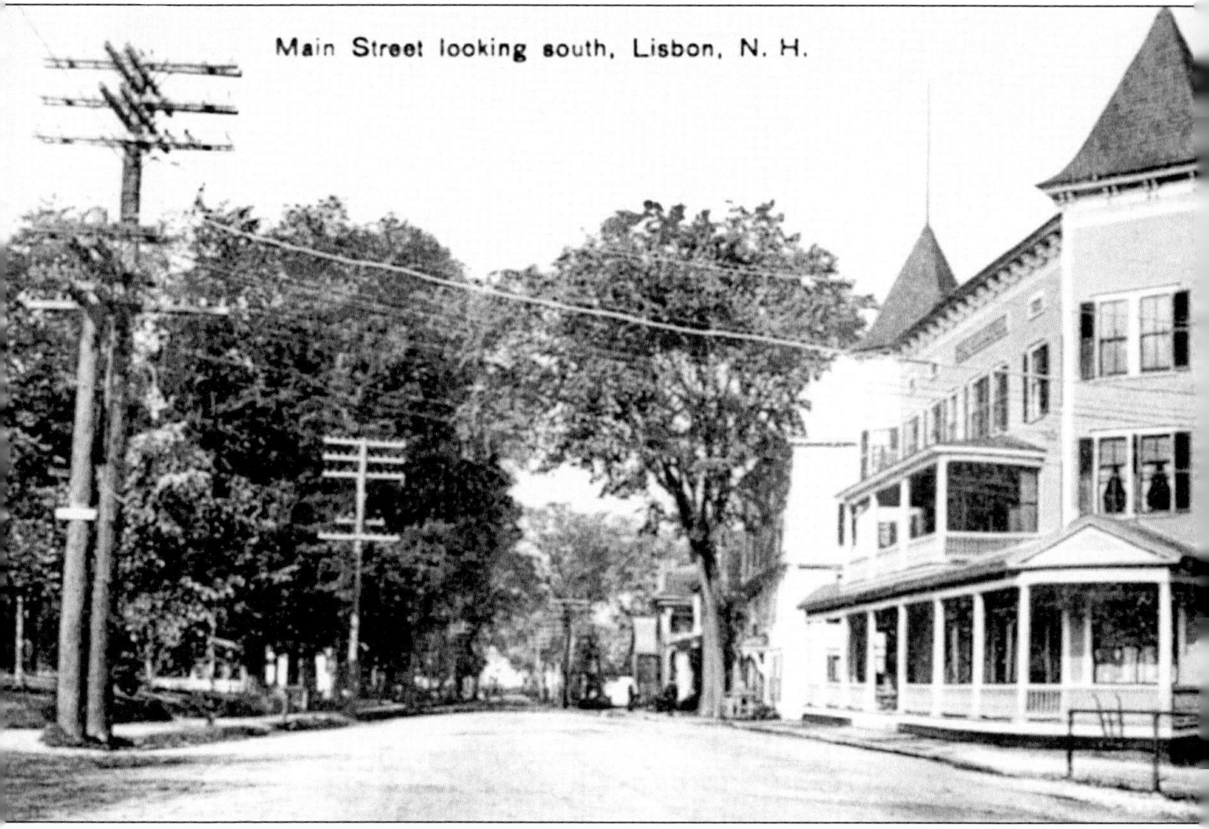

Lisbon is located on both banks of the Ammonoosuc River, which falls quite rapidly between sharp hills that crowd close to the river's edge. Its streets are lined with huge shade trees through which many fine homes can be glimpsed on the surrounding hills. Lisbon was first granted under the name of Concord in 1763, and as Chiswick the following year. Through failure of grantees to fulfill the conditions, it was again incorporated as Gunthwaite in 1768. This name was soon dropped, and it was called Concord again until 1824, when it became known as Lisbon; the reason for the change is not known. Lisbon was among the 35 New Hampshire towns that, in 1778, nearly succeeded in joining the independent Republic of Vermont or in becoming a separate state. Seen in this early-1900s view, which looks south, is Main Street in Lisbon.

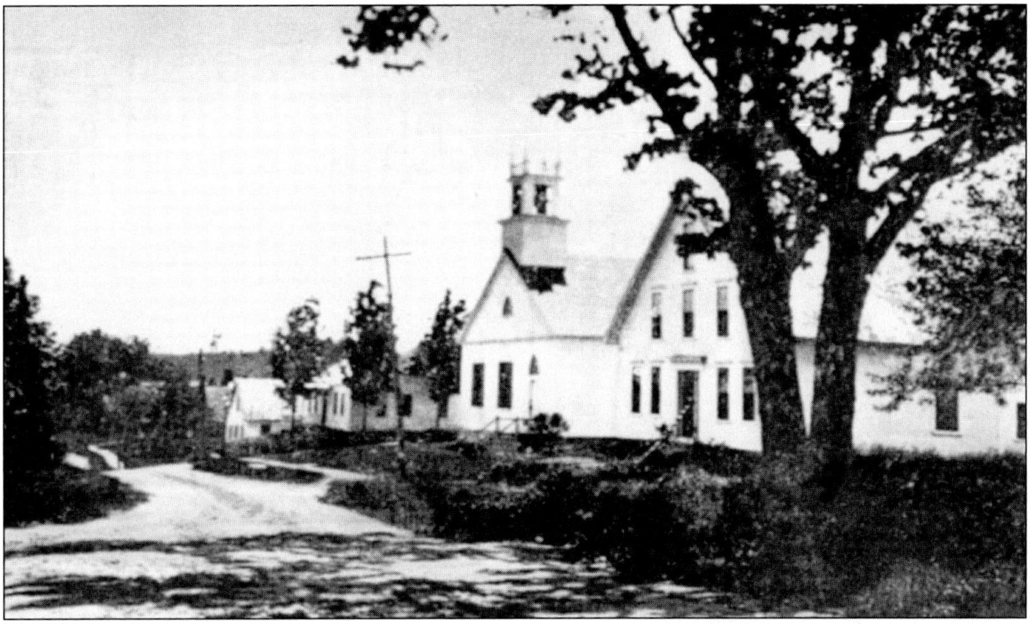

The Free Baptist Church in Lochmere is seen in this late-1800s Main Street view. The township of Tilton includes the town of Lochmere. Its name is taken from the Scottish word "loch" (lake) and "mere," an old English word for sea.

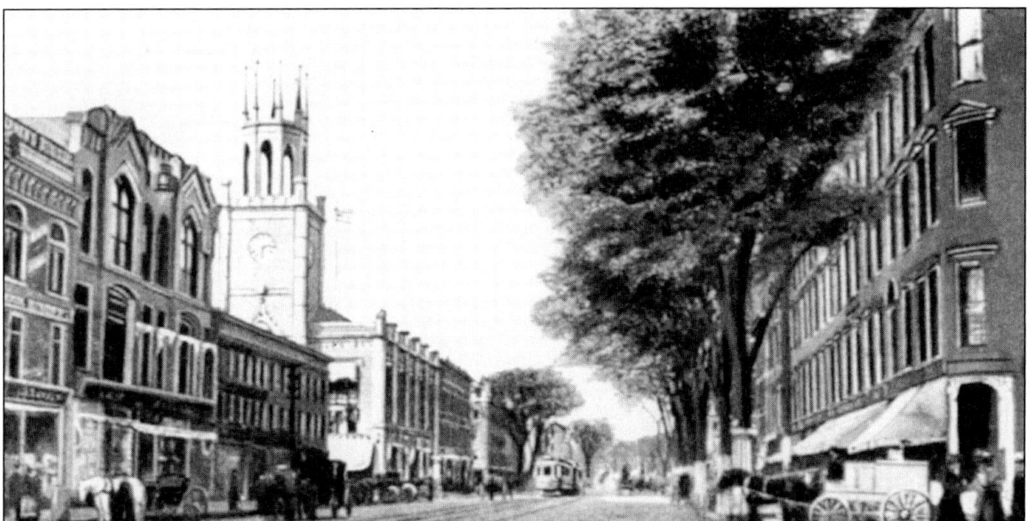

Elm Street, the major thoroughfare in Manchester, is seen in this late-1800s view, which looks north. It was not until 1636 that European settlers sent out by Governor Winthrop explored the Merrimack valley. Until 1703, the region around the falls was visited only by hunters, fishers, and trappers. The first settlement within the present city limits was made in 1722 by John Goffe Jr., Edward Lingfield, and Benjamin Kidder, who came from the Massachusetts Bay Colony and established themselves on Cohas Nook at the falls in the southern part of the city, which bears Goffe's name.

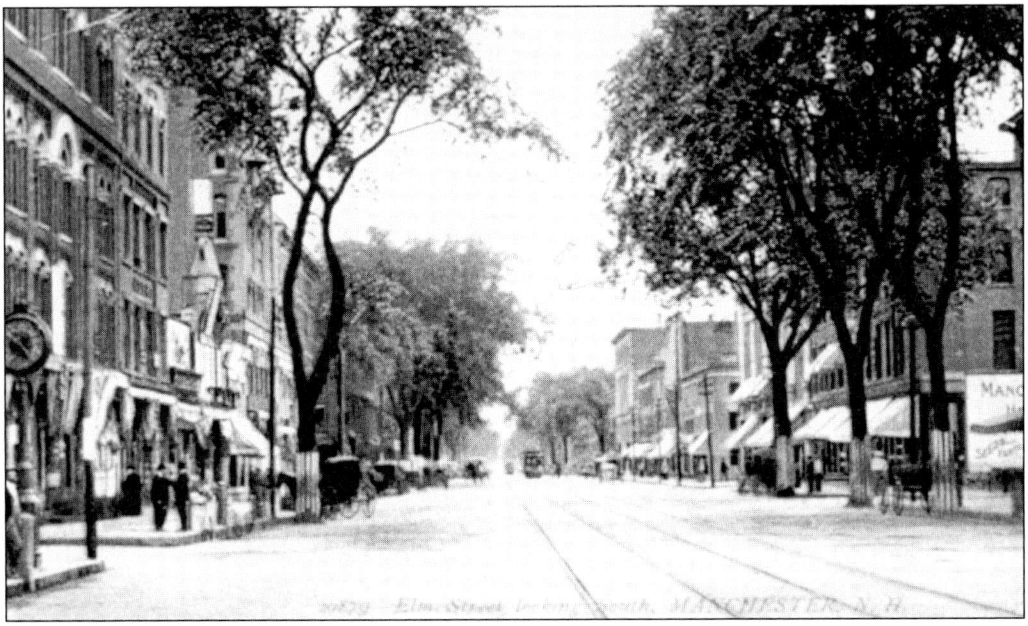

This is a southerly view of Elm Street in Manchester in the late 1800s. Elm Street is one of the handsomest thoroughfares in New England. It is 100 feet wide and three miles long, with spacious sidewalks and roadways and major banks, insurance buildings, and other large businesses located along it. The street was named for a row of elm trees originally planted in the center of the roadway.

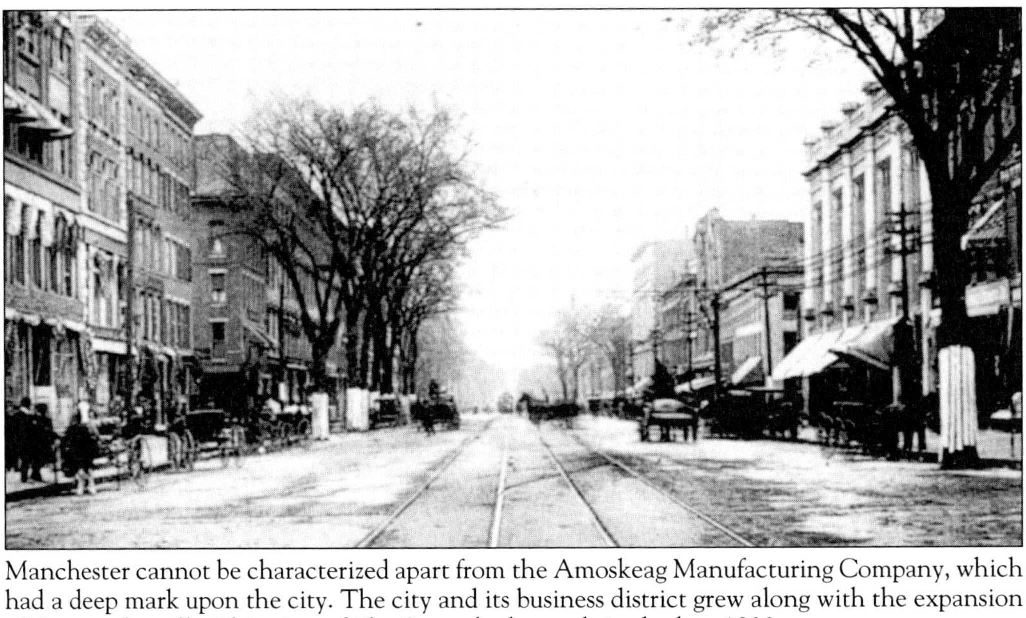

Manchester cannot be characterized apart from the Amoskeag Manufacturing Company, which had a deep mark upon the city. The city and its business district grew along with the expansion of the textile mills. This view of Elm Street looks south in the late 1800s.

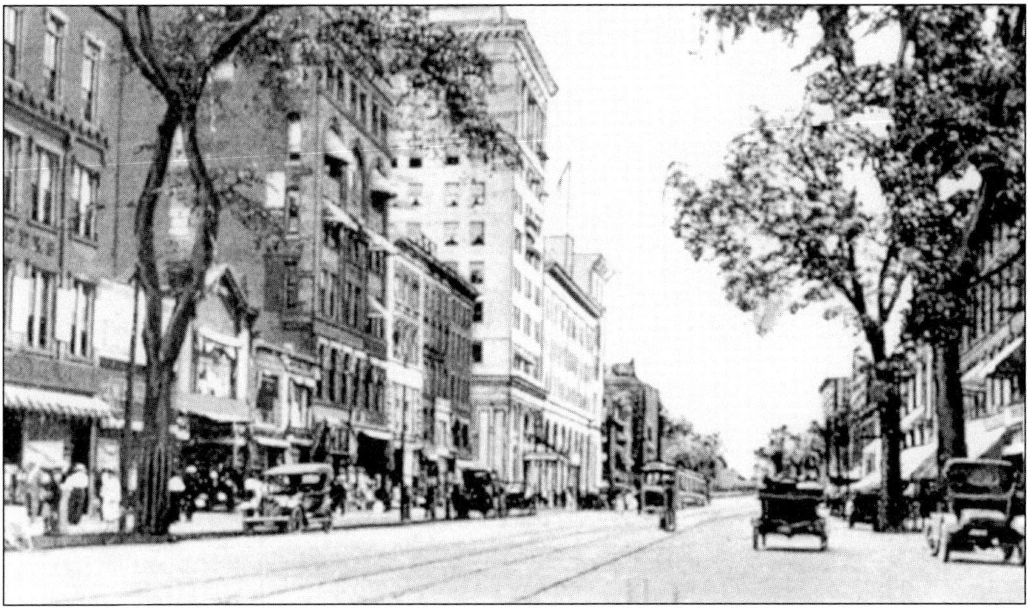

In 1924, the face of Manchester was changing and the automobile was soon replacing all prior transportation, including the street railway company. The prosperity of the city continued until the 1920s, when the shrinking markets and foreign competition affected the cotton industry as a whole. Workers resisted efforts to force their low wages still lower, and the business of the city's textile company dwindled. From 1922 to 1935, the textile industry had its ups and downs, and it eventually closed it doors and filed a voluntary petition of bankruptcy. However, this had little impact upon the thriving Elm Street.

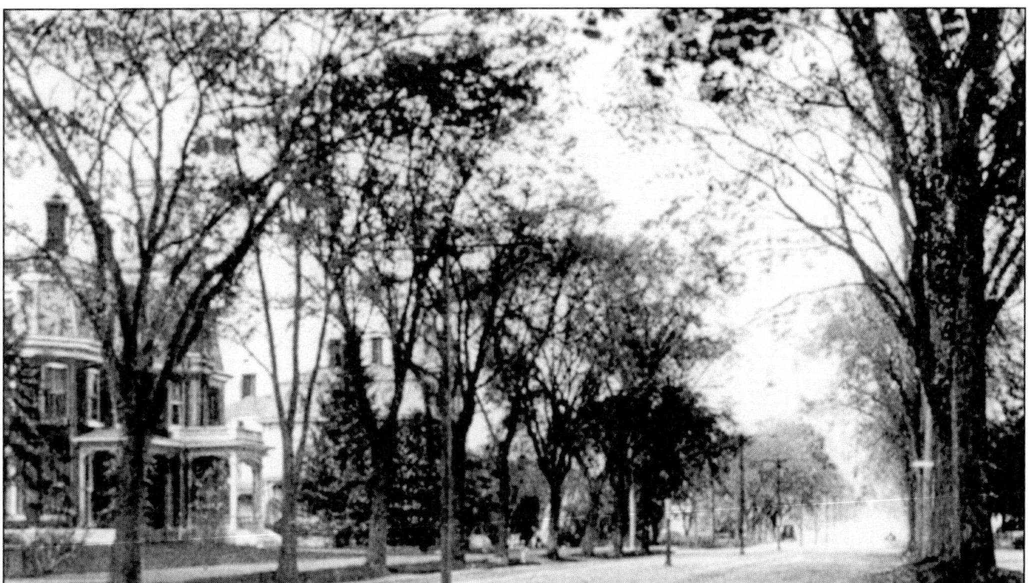

The northern residential district of Elm Street retained its elegance even during the difficult years of the 20th century. This view of Elm Street looking north dates from 1915.

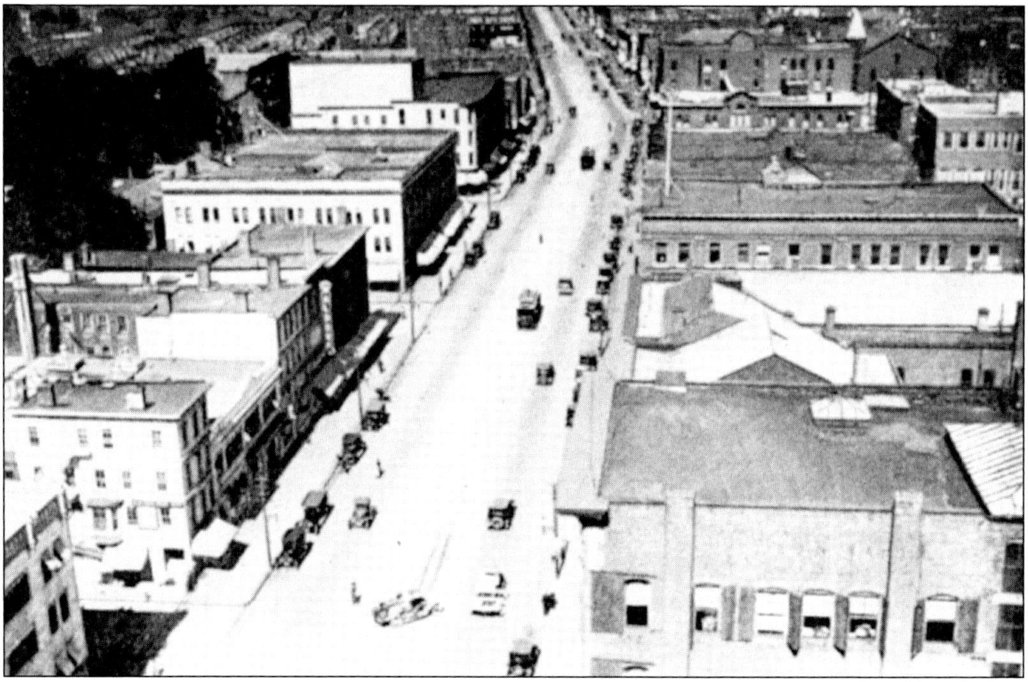

As seen in this 1927 view of Elm Street, Manchester changed considerably with the loss of the shading elm trees along the side of the street and the paving of the roads to accommodate the automobile.

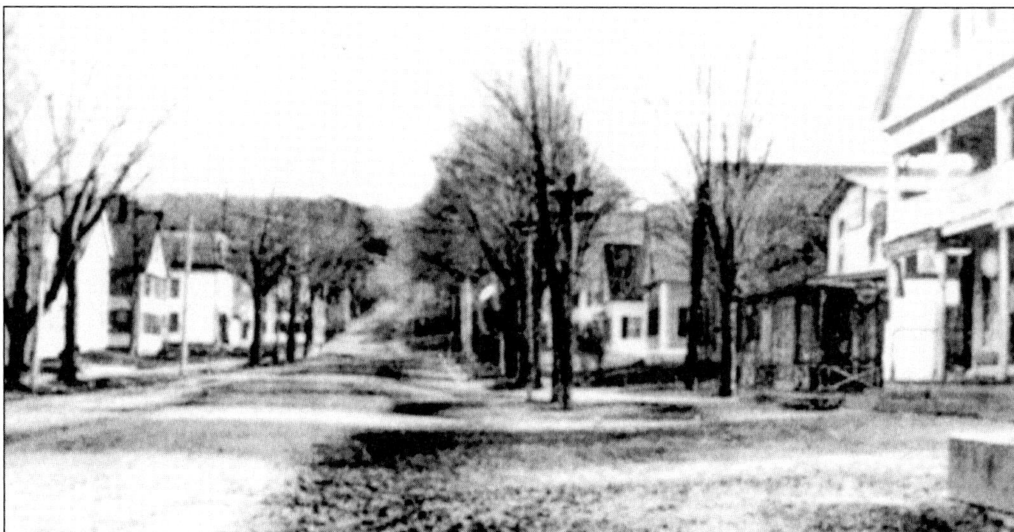

This is a view of Main Street in Marlborough looking south in the late 1800s. From the center of the business district, you can see the wide Main Street with its closely knitted white houses. When the town of Marlborough, then Monadnock No. 5, was granted in 1752, there was a wide difference of opinion regarding what the new town's name should be. Oxford, Salisbury, Worcester, and Marlborough were suggested, but New Marlborough was finally decided upon because many of the early settlers had come from Marlborough, Massachusetts. The town was incorporated in 1775.

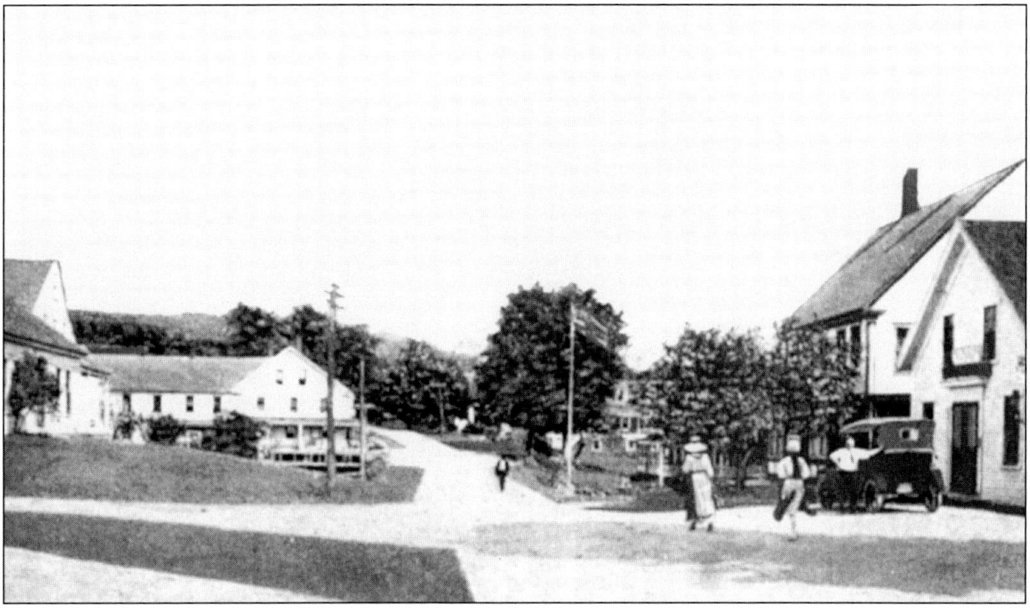

Seen are the post office and general store on Main Street in Melvin village in 1931. The beauty of this location on the east side of Lake Winnipesaukee is unsurpassed, with the massive Ossipee Mountains as a background and the waters of Tuftonborough Bay in the foreground.

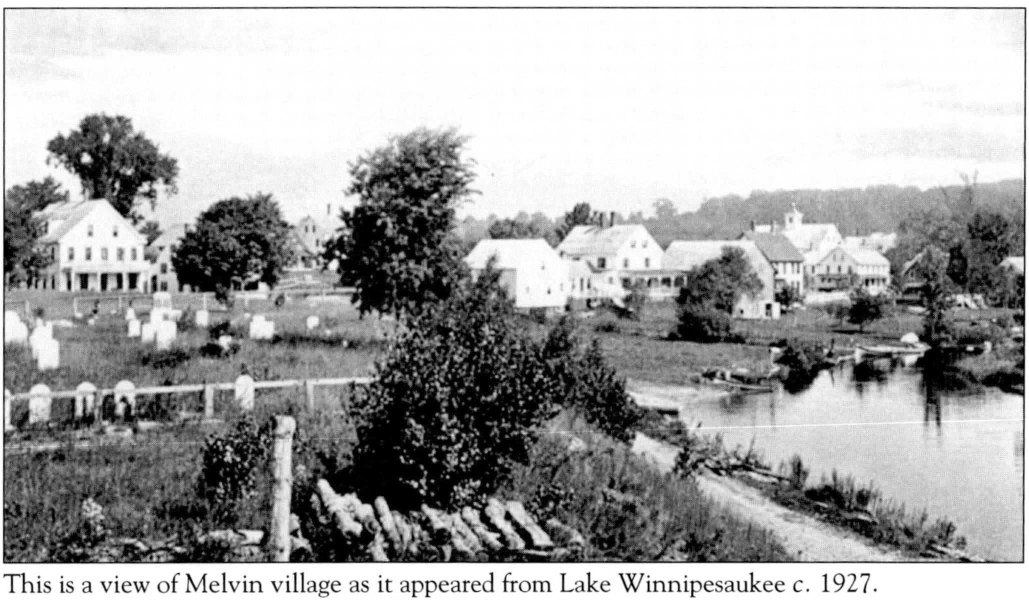

This is a view of Melvin village as it appeared from Lake Winnipesaukee *c.* 1927.

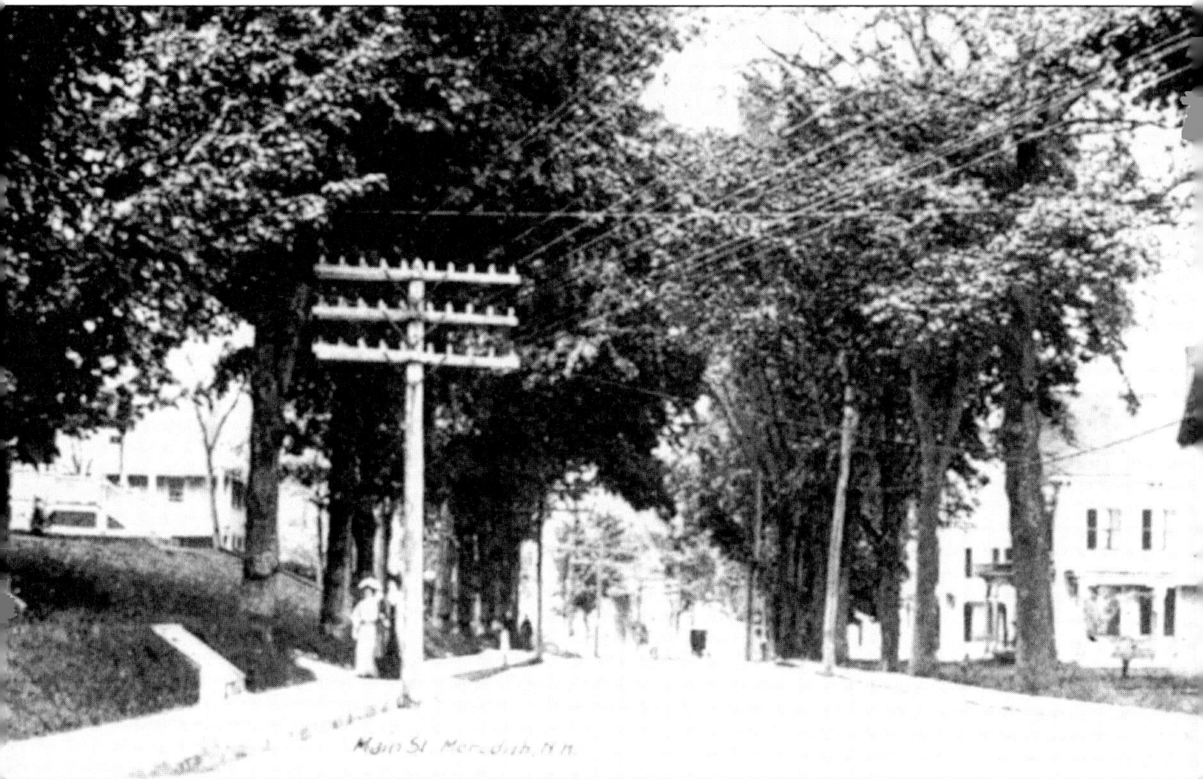

Like so many of the main streets in New Hampshire, Meredith's Main Street is majestically framed with many elm and maple trees. Most of these houses remain in the landscape of the community. The village of Meredith is located in a hollow between one arm of Lake Winnipesaukee and Lake Waukewan. It is largely residential and dependent on tourism. Meredith has no common about which to group its public buildings, like that of Plymouth, because the early proprietors laid out the original village some miles south of the present location, on the Parade Road, where they also laid out a common of six acres. This view of South Main Street in Meredith looks northeast and dates from 1910.

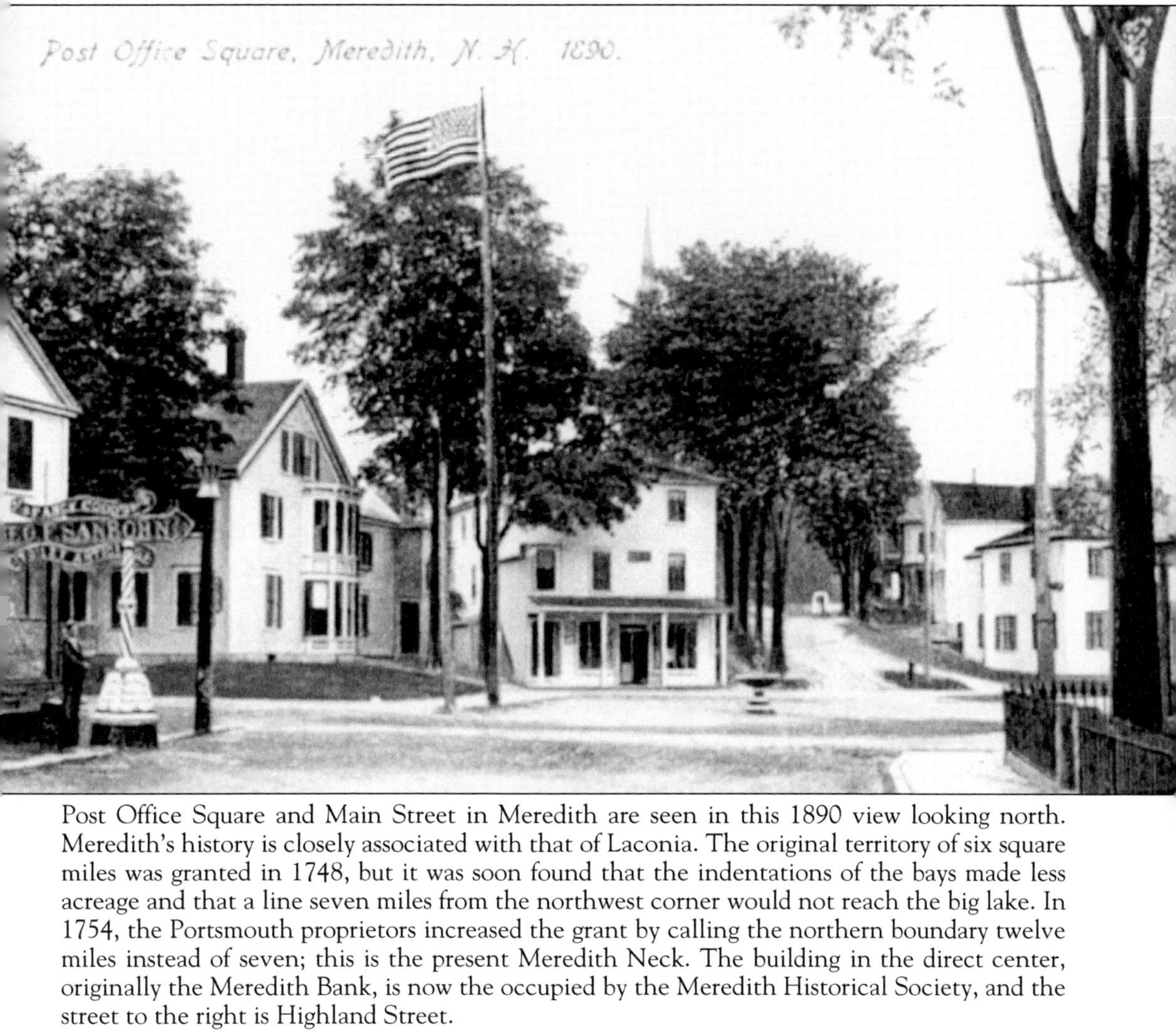

Post Office Square and Main Street in Meredith are seen in this 1890 view looking north. Meredith's history is closely associated with that of Laconia. The original territory of six square miles was granted in 1748, but it was soon found that the indentations of the bays made less acreage and that a line seven miles from the northwest corner would not reach the big lake. In 1754, the Portsmouth proprietors increased the grant by calling the northern boundary twelve miles instead of seven; this is the present Meredith Neck. The building in the direct center, originally the Meredith Bank, is now the occupied by the Meredith Historical Society, and the street to the right is Highland Street.

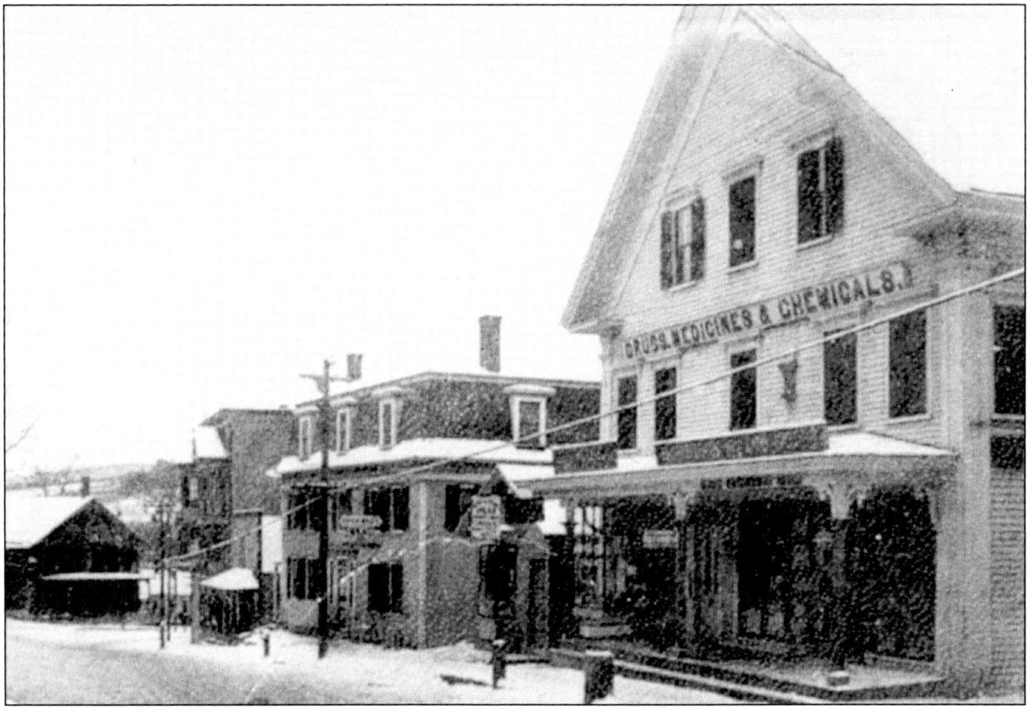

This view of Main Street in Meredith looks northeast in 1910. From Post Office Square, Main Street runs down the hill to the present intersection of Routes 25 and 3. The building on the left was a boardinghouse, later the Meredith Village Bank, and later the municipal building. The town was originally known as Palmer's Town, Second Township, New Salem, and was finally incorporated under its present name in 1768.

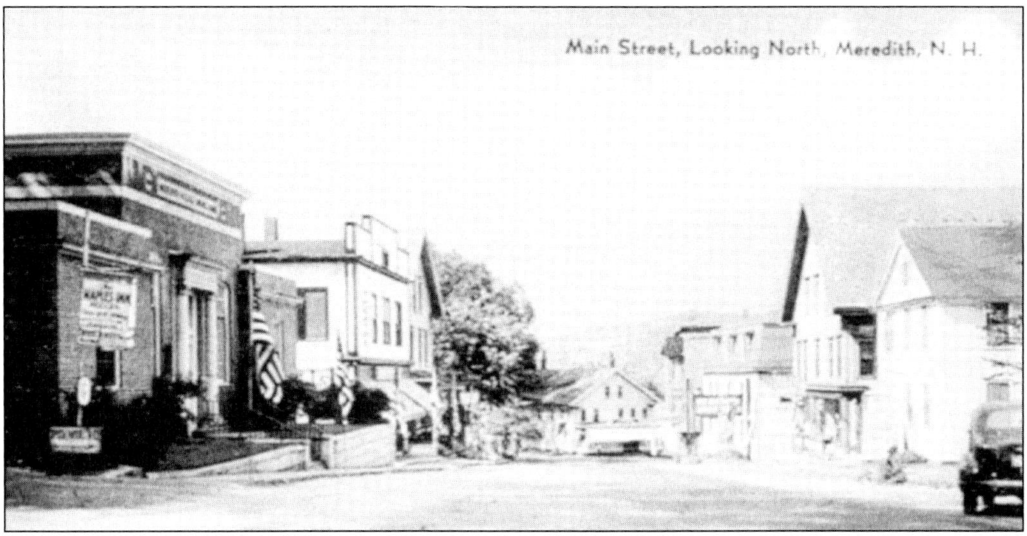

The municipal building is on the left in this view, looking north, of Meredith's Main Street in the 1940s. In 1768, the north and west sides of the Winnipesaukee River were chartered by the governor and council as a part of Meredith (Meredith Bridge). In July 1855, the land known as Meredith Bridge broke from Meredith and the town of Laconia was established. In July 1873, a part of Meredith was annexed to Center Harbor.

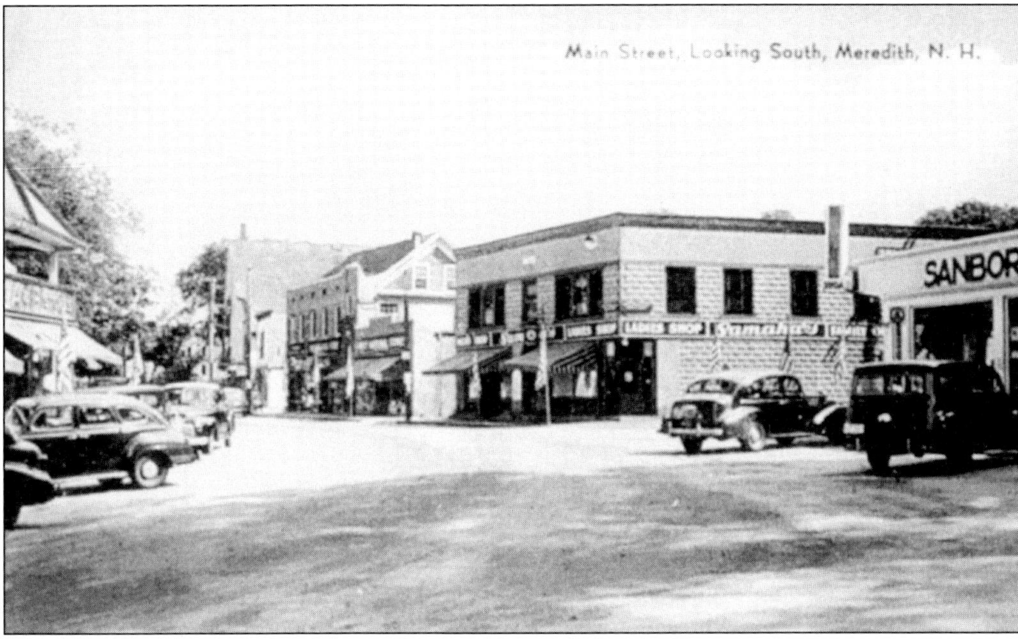

This 1940s view of Meredith's Main Street looks south. Meredith is a very prosperous four-season resort town today. Meredith is a member of the New Hampshire Main Street community.

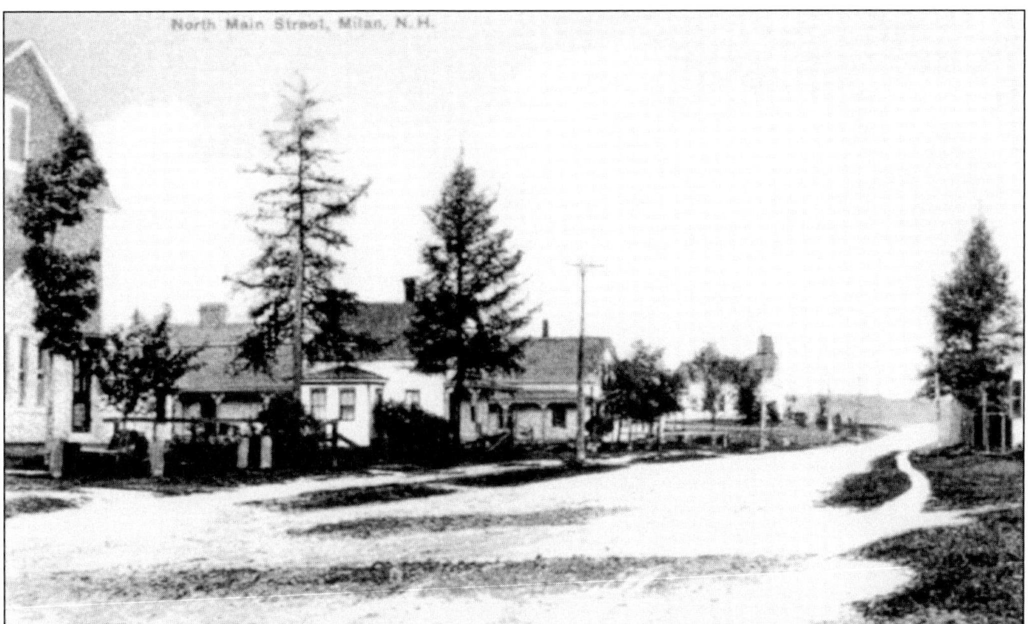

North Main Street in Milan is seen in this early-1900s view. The village, located in the open space of North Main Street, contains a close cluster of buildings, including the general store and church. Originally granted in 1771, the township was incorporated in 1824.

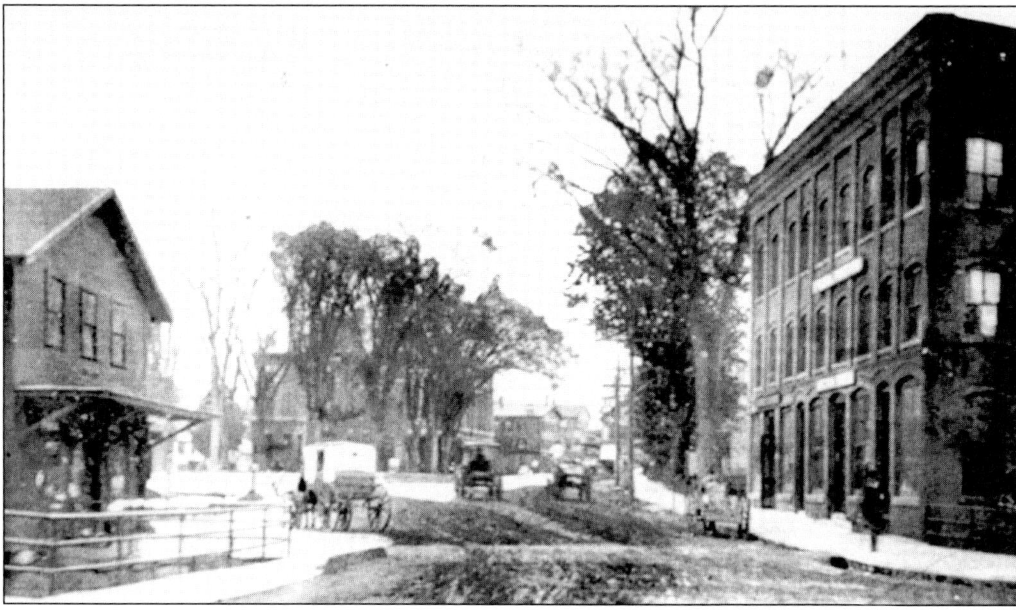

The Old Gristmill Store on the square in Milford is seen here in 1909. Milford is divided into two sections by the Souhegan River and holds a pleasing balance between industry and tourism. The river meanders into the village from the west through overhanging trees. Mills once lined the eastern bank, taking their power from the stream. Early in its history, a gristmill was built near the Native American ford in the river. The town's name came from the mill and the ford.

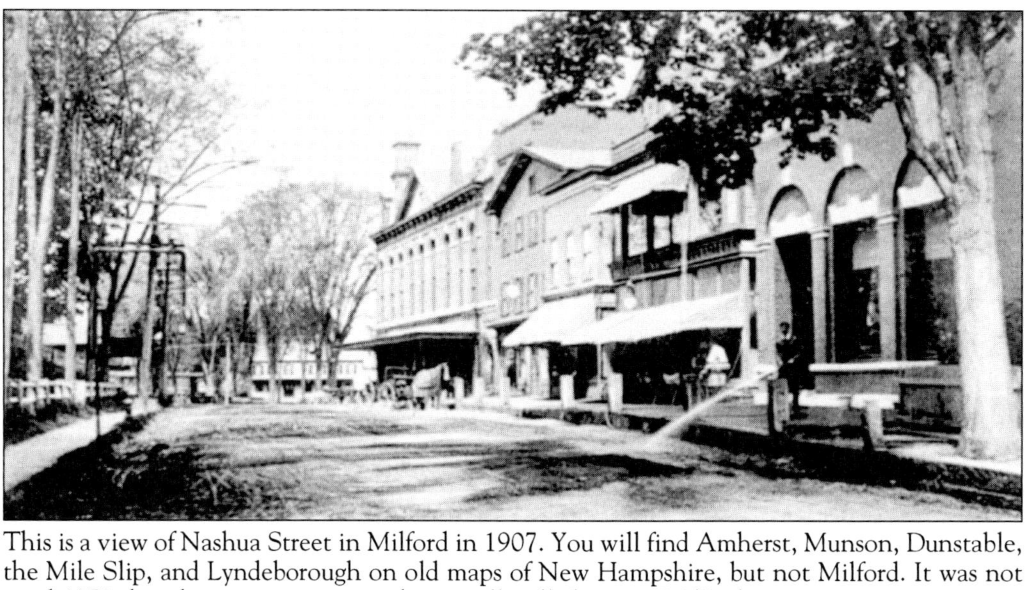

This is a view of Nashua Street in Milford in 1907. You will find Amherst, Munson, Dunstable, the Mile Slip, and Lyndeborough on old maps of New Hampshire, but not Milford. It was not until 1873 that the towns came together to officially become Milford.

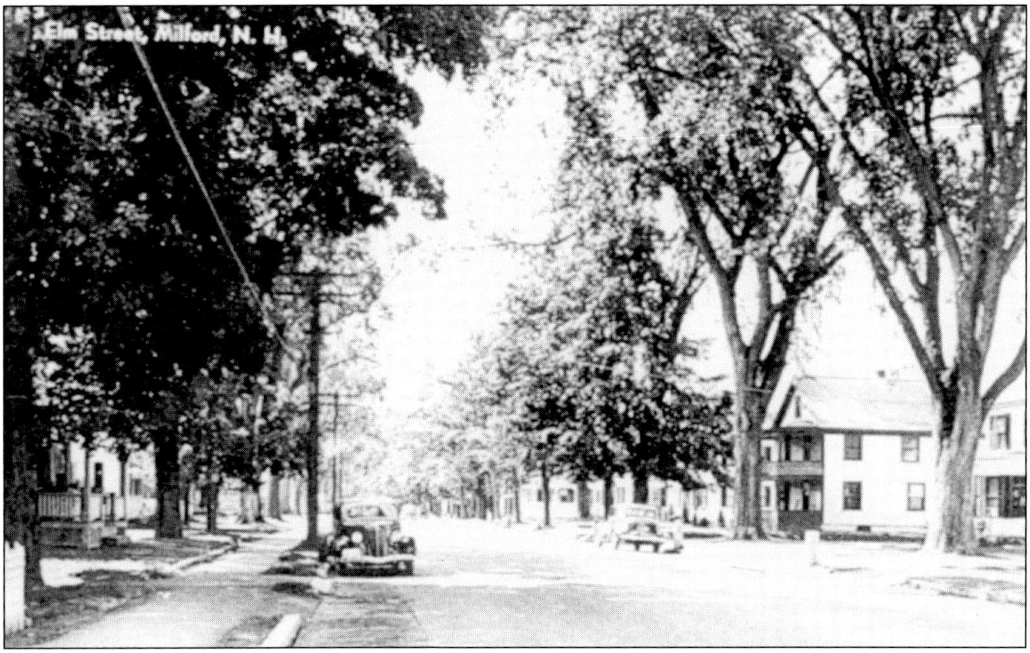

This view of Elm Street in the 1940s offers an excellent look at Milton's residential community. Fifty years before the incorporation of the town in 1794, settlers had made their way to this pleasant intervale. Milford is a member of the New Hampshire Main Street community.

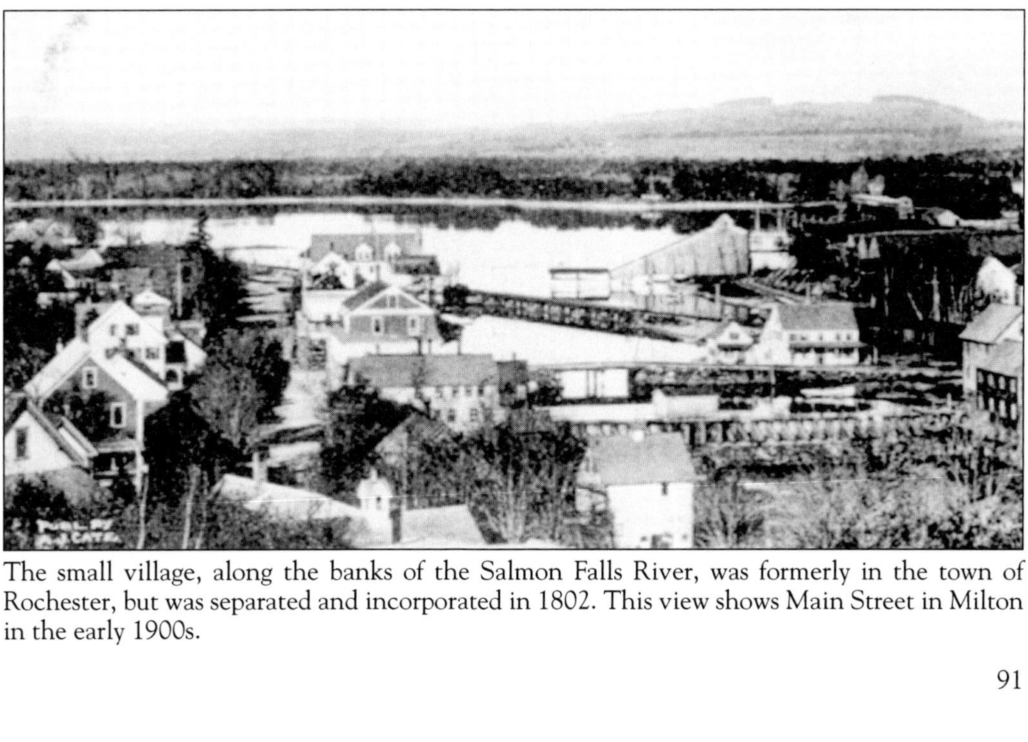

The small village, along the banks of the Salmon Falls River, was formerly in the town of Rochester, but was separated and incorporated in 1802. This view shows Main Street in Milton in the early 1900s.

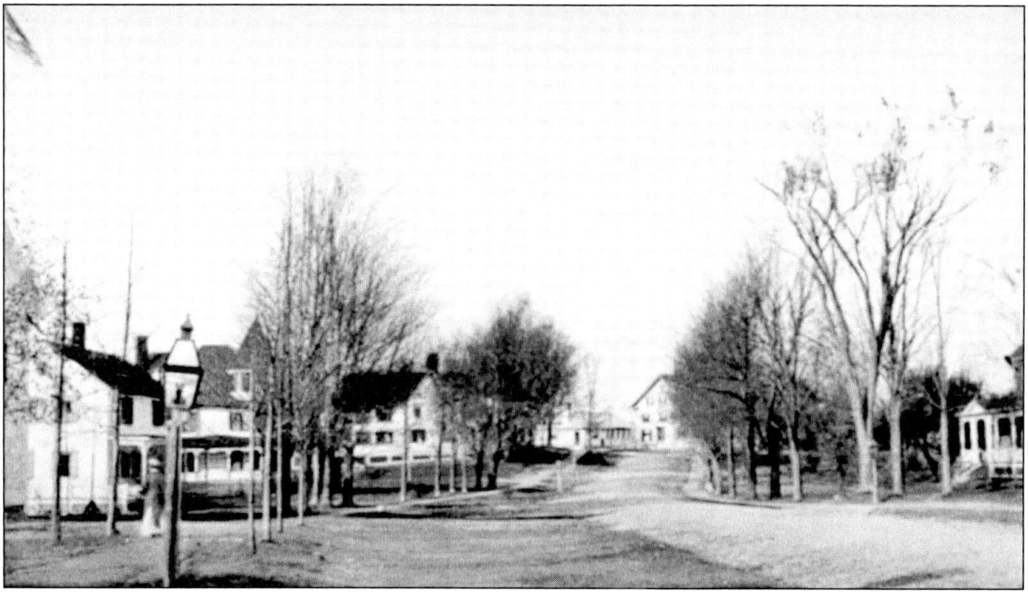

This 1910 view of Main Street in Mount Vernon looks north from the town hall. Perched on the summit of a steep hill, Mount Vernon is a popular summer residence. The town may be considered a suburb to Milford, for there is no business district of any size.

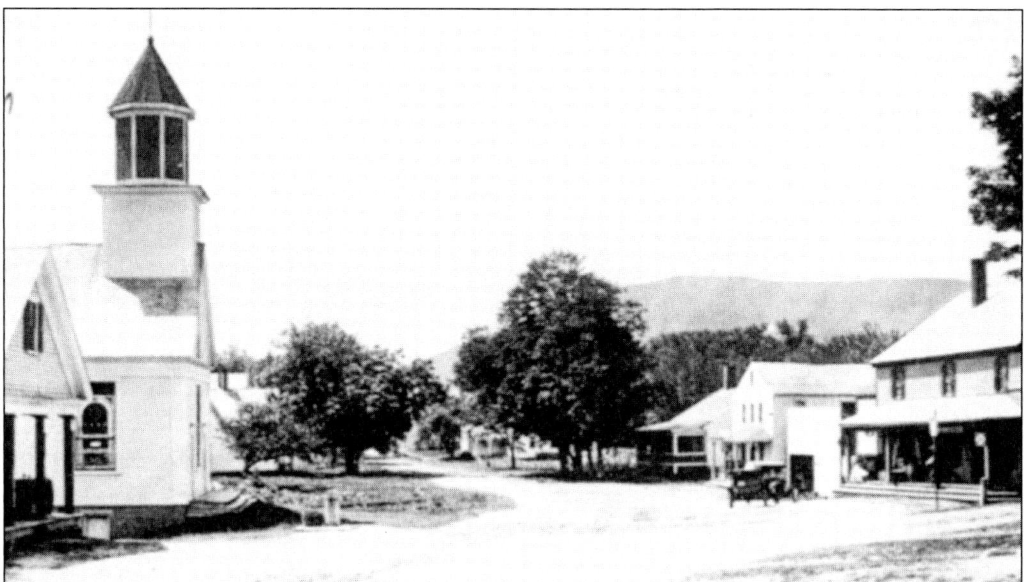

The community church is on the left and the Olde Country Store is on the right in this view, looking west, of Main Street in Moultonboro in the early 1900s. This resort settlement on Lake Winnipesaukee, accommodating many summer homes and seasonal camps, was incorporated in 1777.

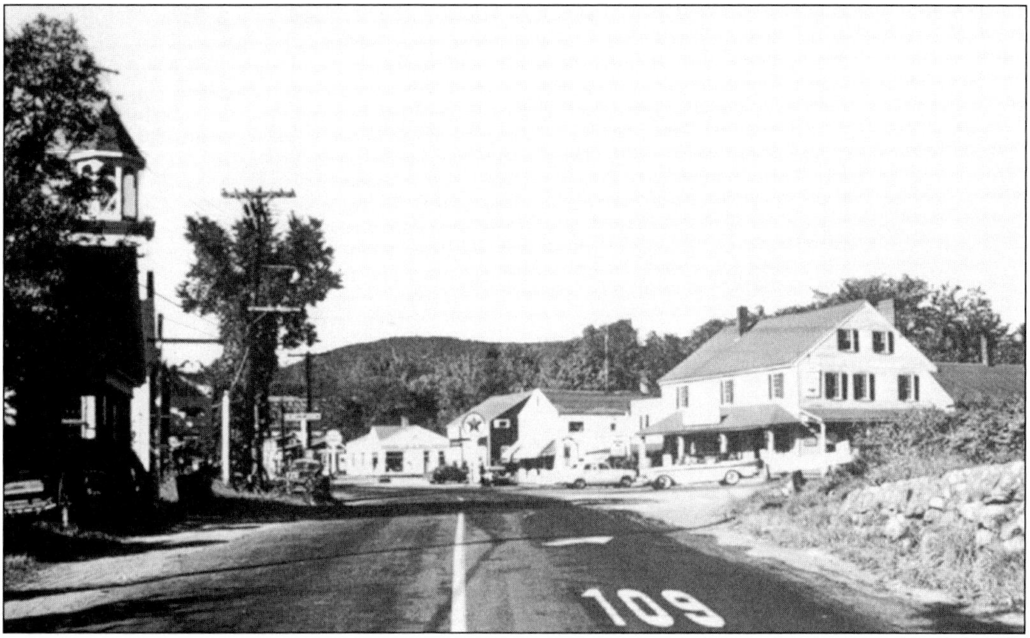

Another view shows Main Street at the Four Corners in Moultonboro, *c.* the 1990s. Here is located the Olde Country Store. Moultonboro was granted in 1763 by the Masonian proprietors to a group headed by Col. Jonathan Moulton, whose name was given to the settlement.

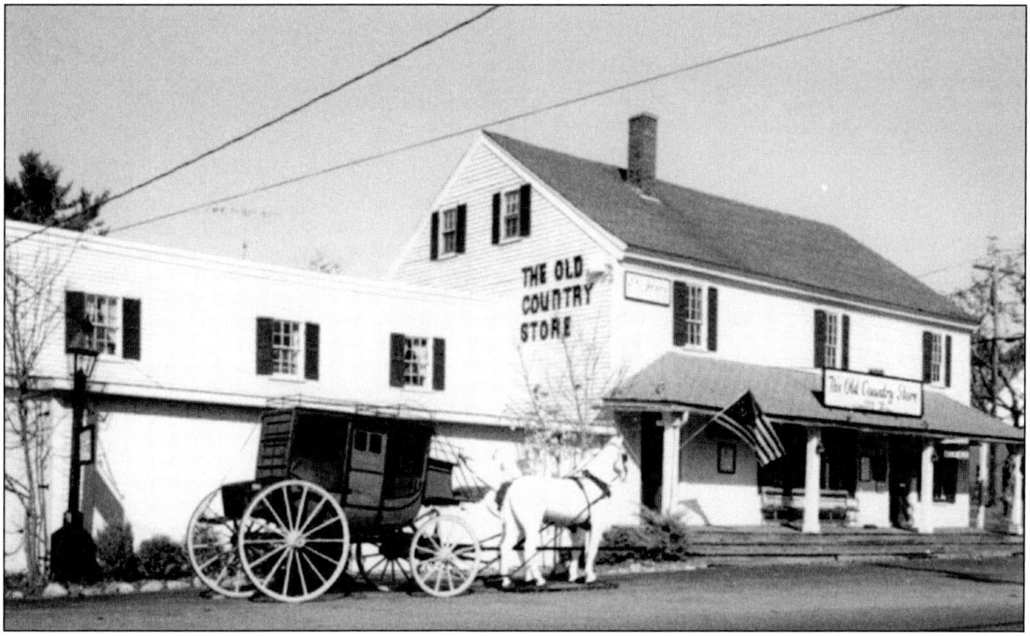

This is a view of the Olde Country Store at the Four Corners in Moultonboro in 1980. Since 1781, this active country store has served as a social and political center of the community. Once a tavern, the Olde Country Store was used as a stagecoach stop to the Conways. This durable structure is listed on the National Register of Historic Places. The former stagecoach stop now houses an original Concord Coach. Operated with turn-of-the-century store fixtures, its wares include cheddar cheese aged on the premises, pickles, penny candy, and hard-to-find items.

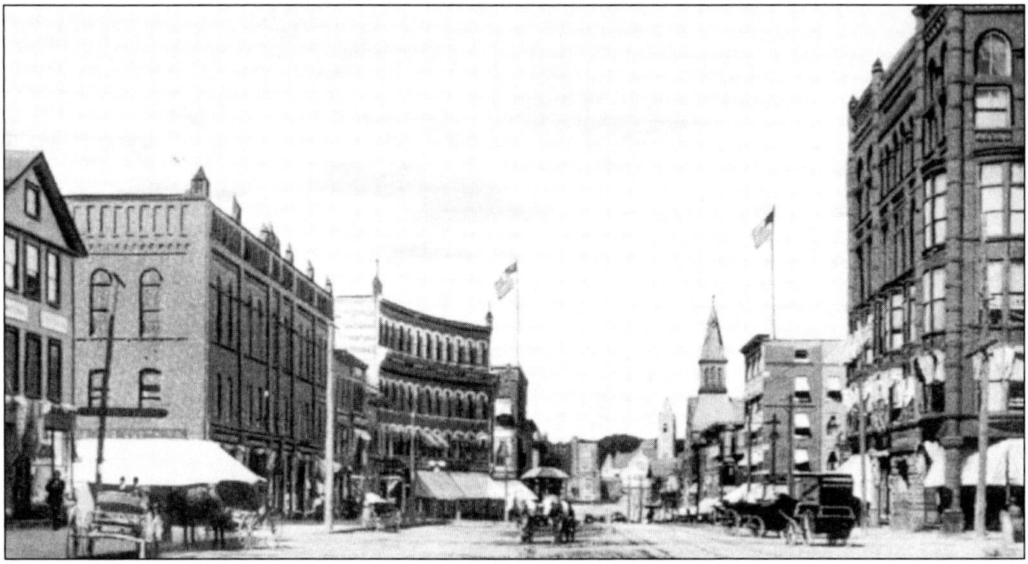

This view of Main Street in Nashua looks north in 1912. The compact part of the city lies within a radius of a mile from the intersection of Pearl and Main Streets, just south of the city hall. The width and straightness of the streets result from the plan of architect Asher Benjamin, who was engaged by the Nashua Manufacturing Company in 1825. This plan called not only for the laying out of streets, but also for the planting of shade trees. Nashua's Main Street presented a fair cross section of the city's population, which was of French-Canadian, Irish, Greek, Polish, and Lithuanian descent, with a comparatively small proportion of old New England stock.

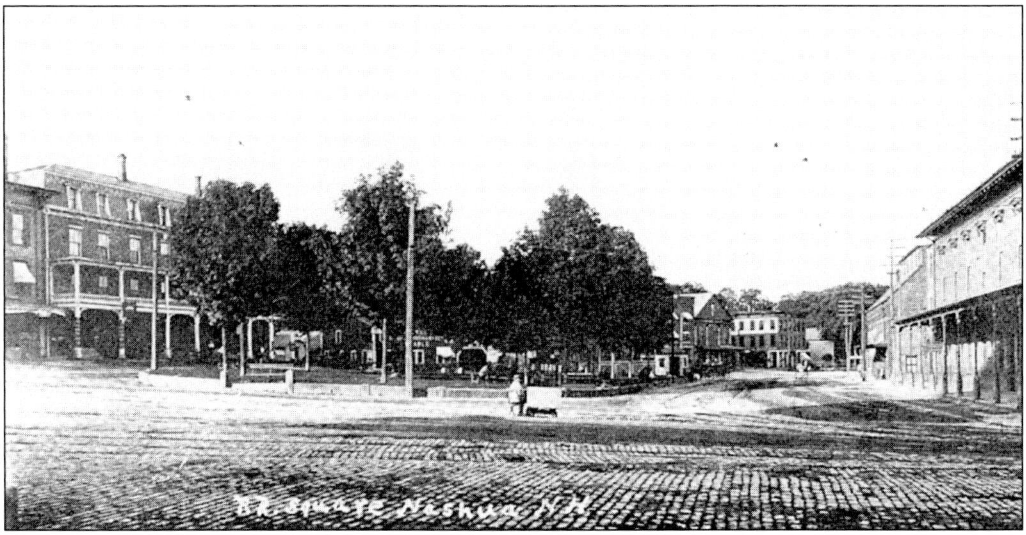

Nashua was originally a fur trading post, known by the Native American name of Watanic. Surveyed as early as 1652, its first settler, a man named Cromwell, came in 1656, and he was followed in 1660 by a group of settlers. In 1773, its grantees petitioned the General Court of Massachusetts for a town charter, which, when issued officially, named the town Dunstable, for Dunstable, England. Nashua was incorporated under its present name in 1853. By the end of the 18th century, settlement had increased, and the town had completely emerged as a farming community. Seen is Railroad Square, a major intersection of Nashua, *c.* 1900.

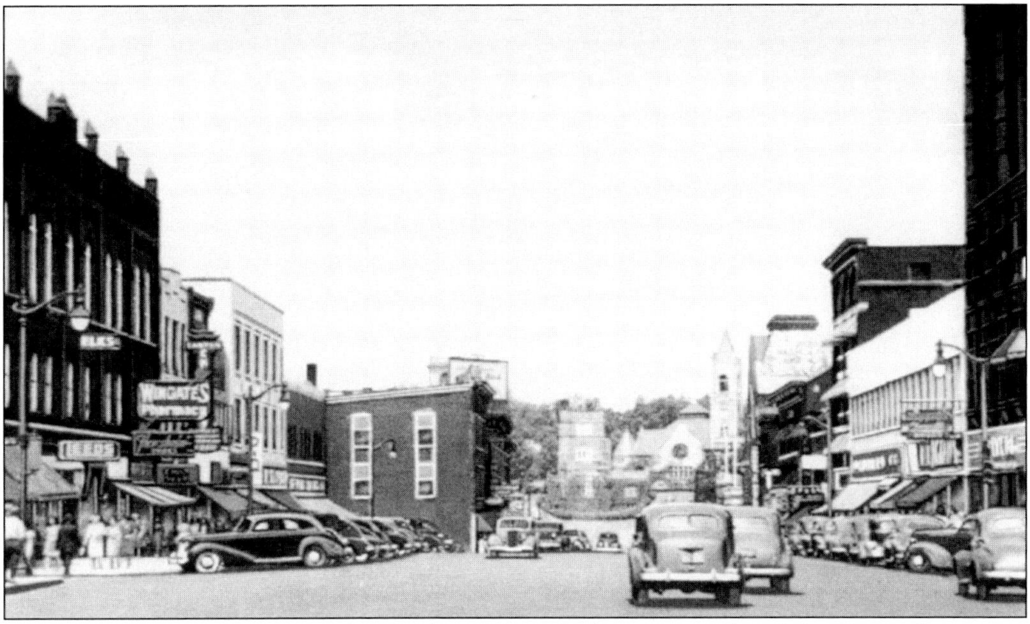

This view of Main Street in Nashua looks north in the late 1940s. Church buildings along Main Street are placed some distance back, but the commercial buildings are close to the sidewalks. Other streets spread out at right angles throughout the city's 32 square miles.

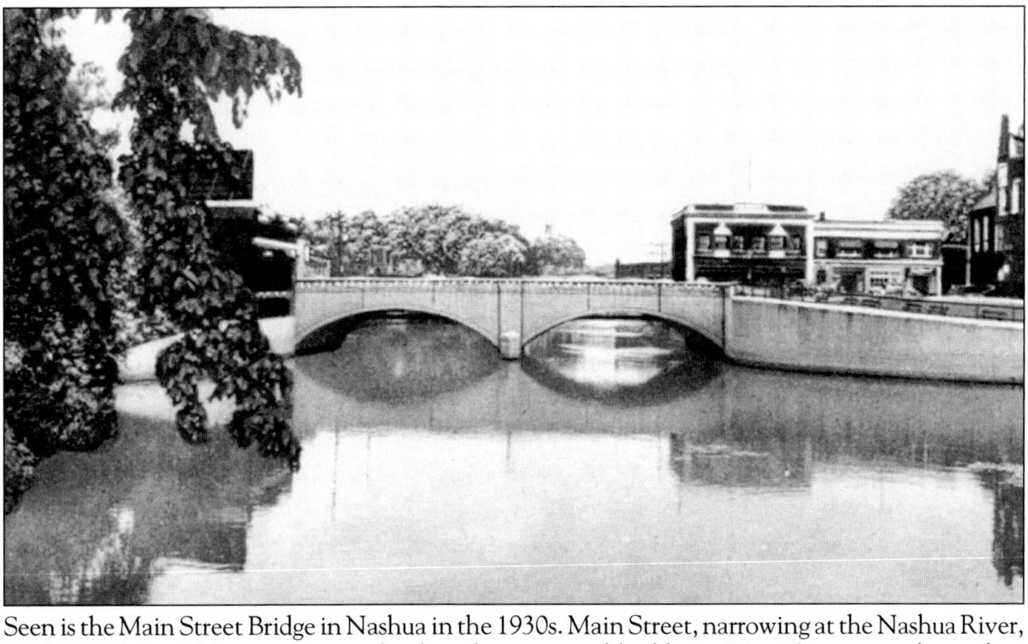

Seen is the Main Street Bridge in Nashua in the 1930s. Main Street, narrowing at the Nashua River, is a broad thoroughfare with many bank and commercial buildings. Main Street was the trading center for a large area. From the 1930s through the 1950s, the street was usually filled with cars and people; Wednesday and Saturday evenings were very popular for Main Street gatherings.

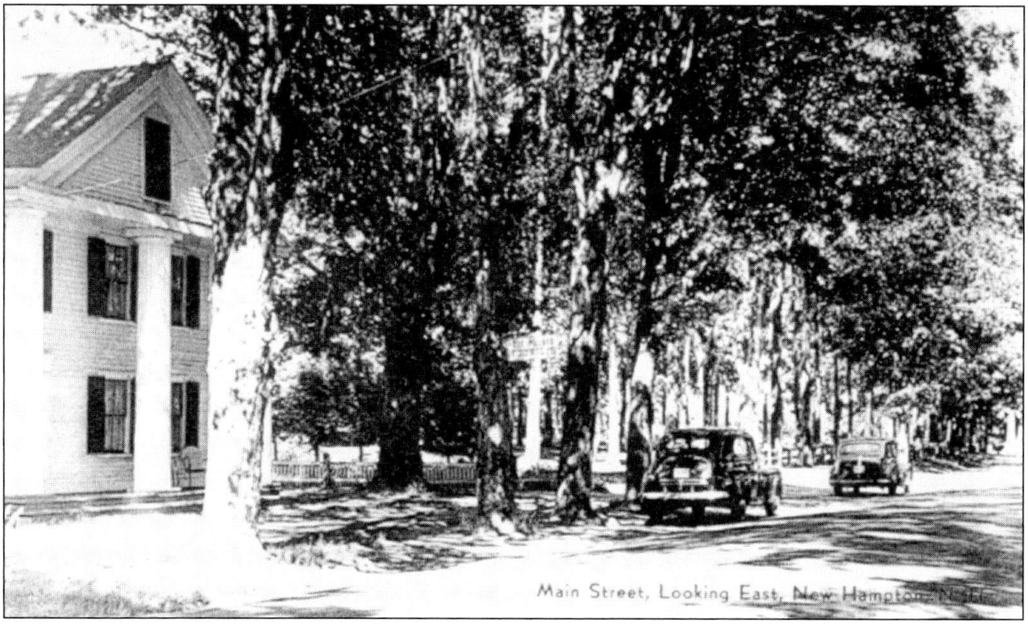

This view of New Hampton's Main Street looks east and dates from the 1940s. This picturesque village is tastefully centered around the attractive grounds of New Hampton School. As a part of the Moultonborough Addition, Gen. Jonathan Moulton, proprietor, requested the town be named for Hampton, his native town, at its incorporation in 1777. This grant was so large that a part of it was set off as the town of Center Harbor in 1797. The settlers came principally from the earlier settlements of Portsmouth, Dover, Exeter, and Hampton.

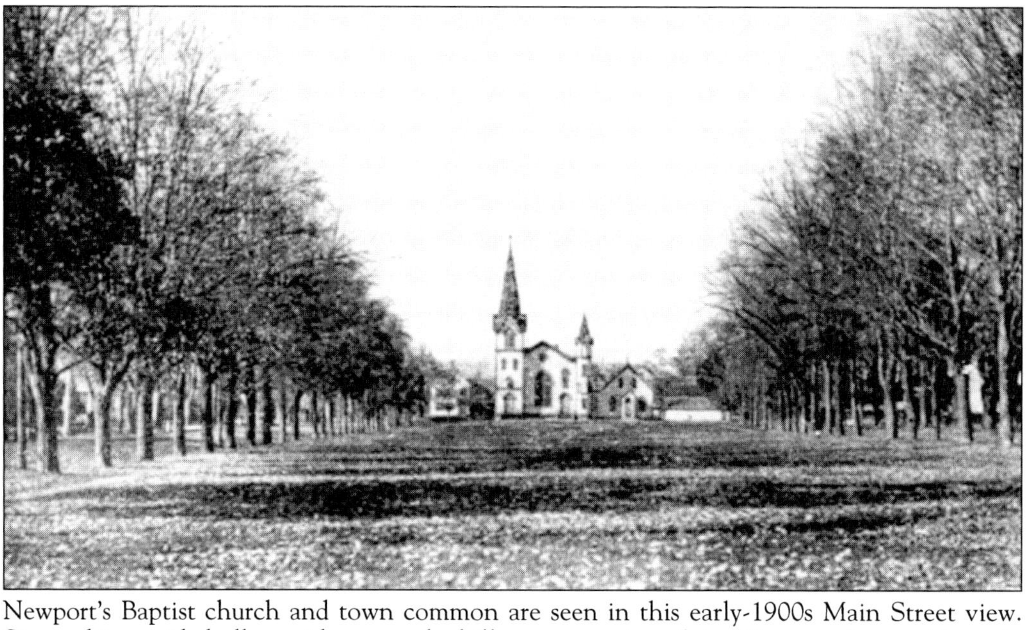

Newport's Baptist church and town common are seen in this early-1900s Main Street view. Situated in a wide hollow with no nearby hills or mountains of size, Newport has a wide main street bordered by well-spaced, attractive homes. Newport was incorporated in 1761 and supposedly named in honor of Henry Newport, a distinguished English soldier and statesman.

Four

New Castle to Woodsville

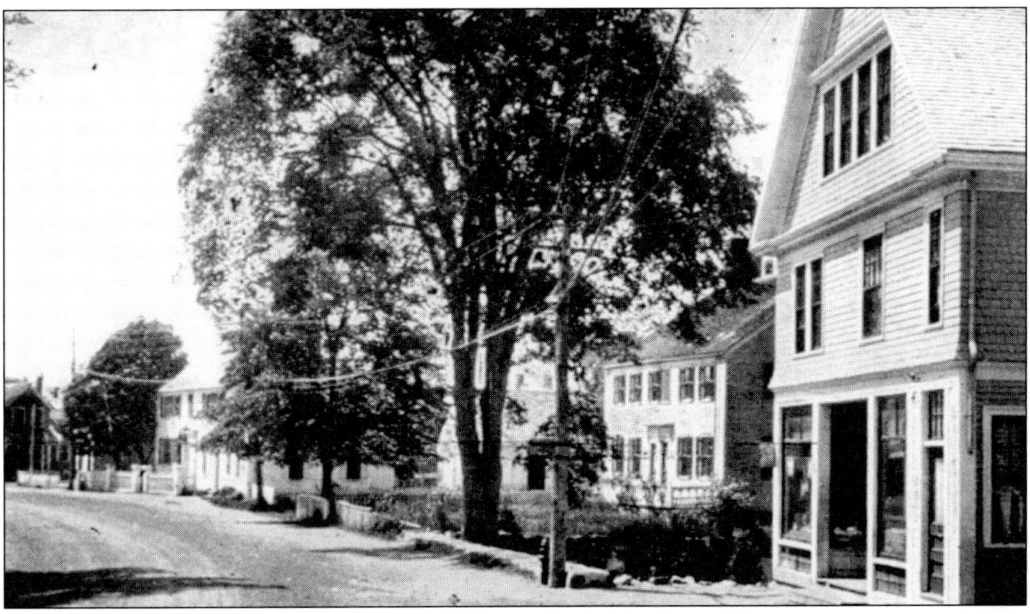

New Castle is an island town, formerly known as Great Island, and for many years was without bridges to the mainland. Horses and carriages were unknown, and the streets were outgrowths of convenient footpaths from one house to another. In 1873, the historic records of the town from 1693 to 1726, including the charter, were discovered in Hertfordshire, England, and were returned to New Castle. Today, it is considered a charming old place, but in the years preceding the Revolution, it was alive with intrigue and excitement. Its local taverns were a gathering place for philandering soldiers of fortune, and its prisons were full of traitors and ministers in danger of being sent to the Tower of London or the gallows. This view shows Main Street in New Castle in the early 1900s.

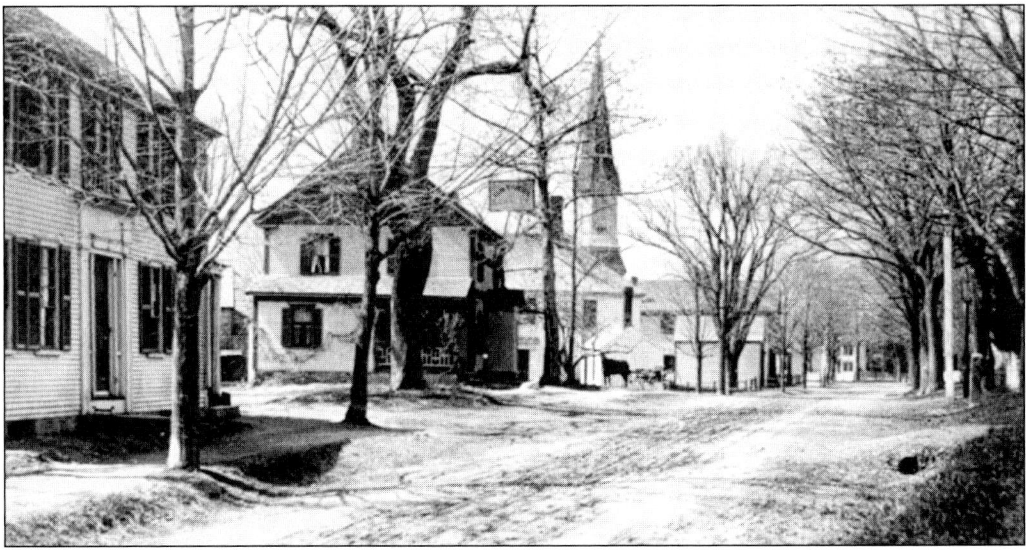

This is a view of Main Street in Newfields looking south *c.* 1908. The center of Newfields is neatly organized with the church to the left and the elegant homes at the end of the road. Originally a part of Exeter and later of Newmarket, the territory was first given the name Newfields in 1681, taking the name from a farm owned by Edward Hilton of Dover called "Mr. Hilton's New Field." In 1849, Newfields was joined to Piscassic, another local division of Newmarket, and incorporated as South Newmarket. The name was changed to Newfields in 1895.

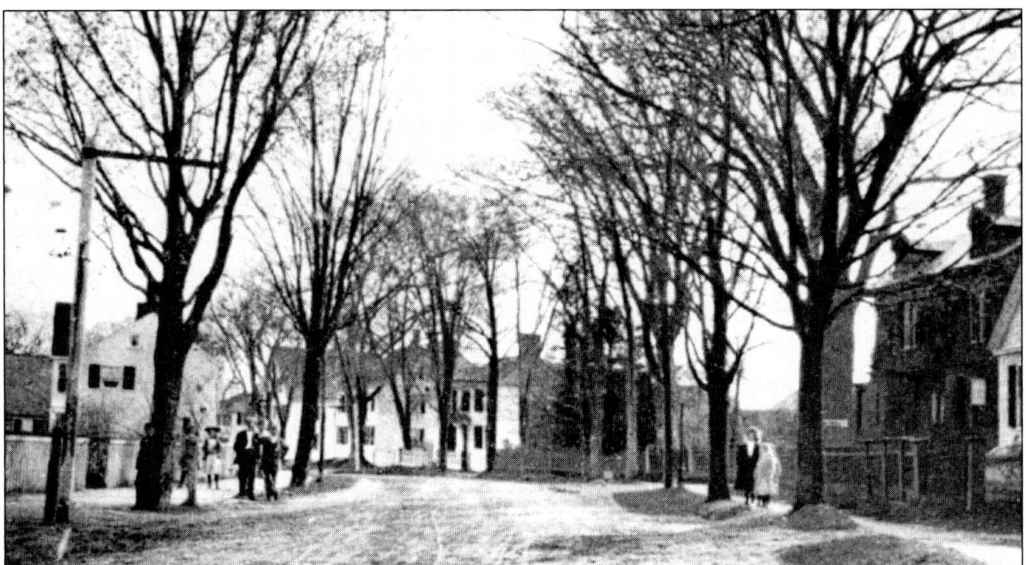

Newfields is known for its cluster of old white houses pleasantly shaded by elms and maples. This view of Main Street South dates from 1922.

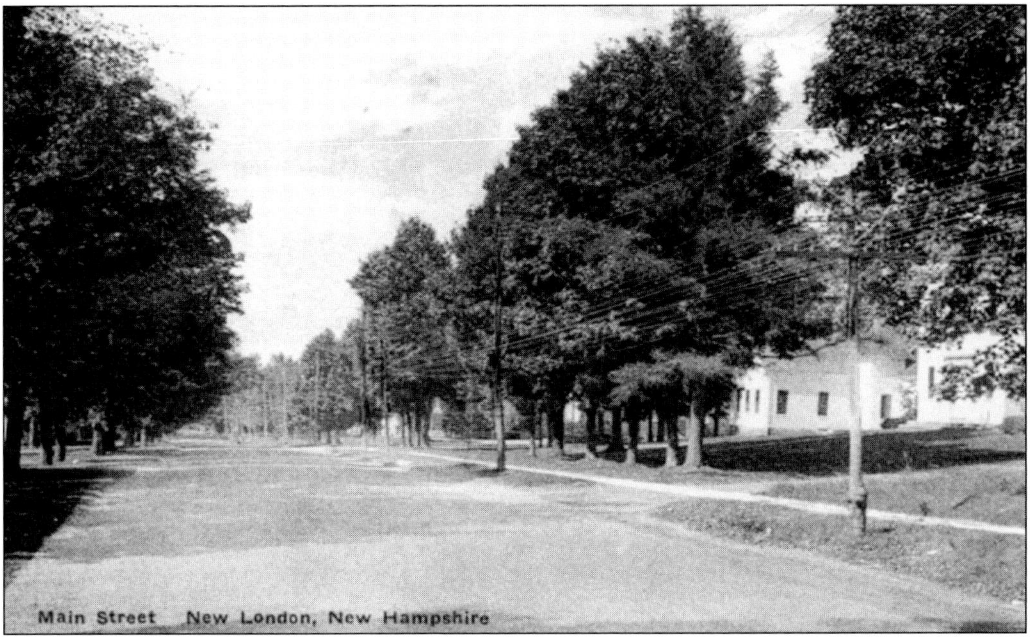

New London is ideally located on an elevation with nearby mountains. Large well-kept Colonial houses line its Main Street, interrupted by a small white church and the brick academy buildings. New London has the distinctive air of an academic town. New London was a part of an original grant by the Masonian proprietors in 1753 under the name of Heidelberg. Twenty years later, it was regranted as Alexandria Addition, and in 1779, it was incorporated and named after the English capital. This is a view of Main Street in New London in 1936.

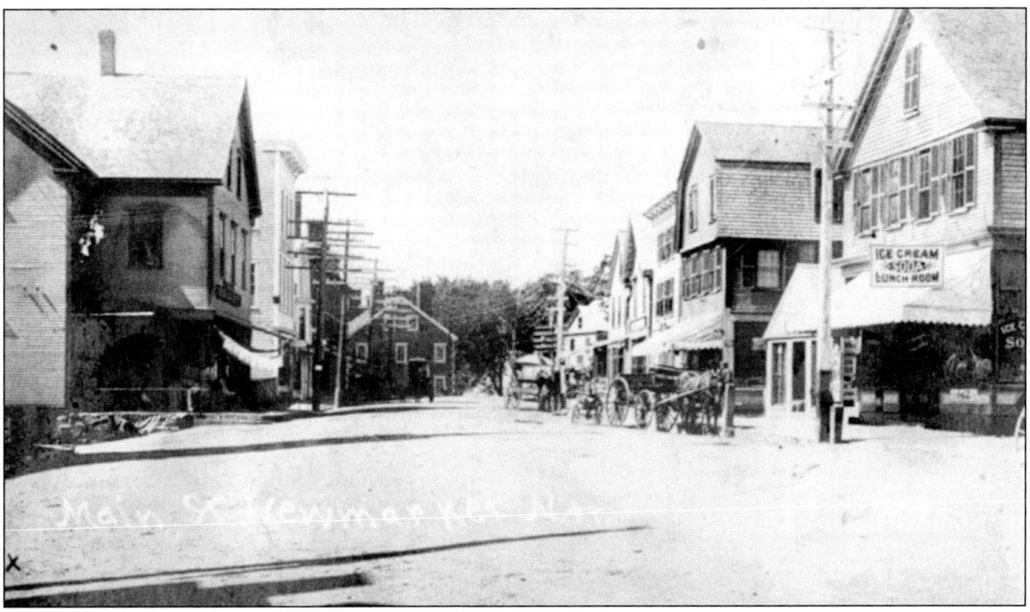

Newmarket was considered a little industrial community at the falls of the Lamprey River. This view of Main Street in Newmarket looks west *c.* 1910.

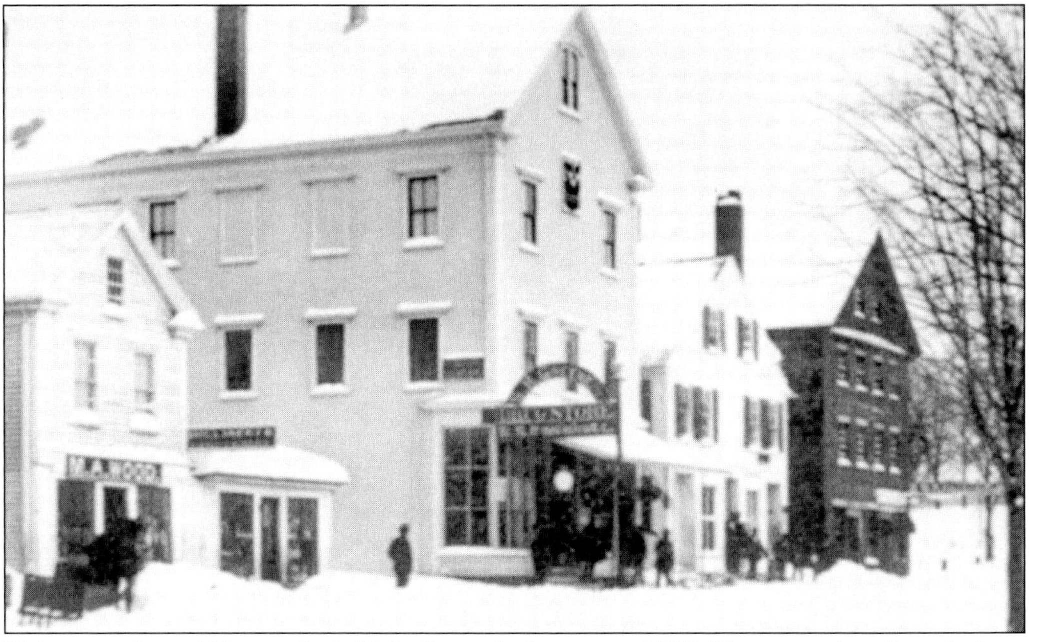

This stereoview of Newmarket's Main Street looks west *c.* 1885. The town rises abruptly from the river, with its cluster of factory buildings, to a residential section with short narrow streets and old white houses. Note the three-story building that houses the drugstore in the center of the picture. This store would hold the popular soda fountain, where many young loves began.

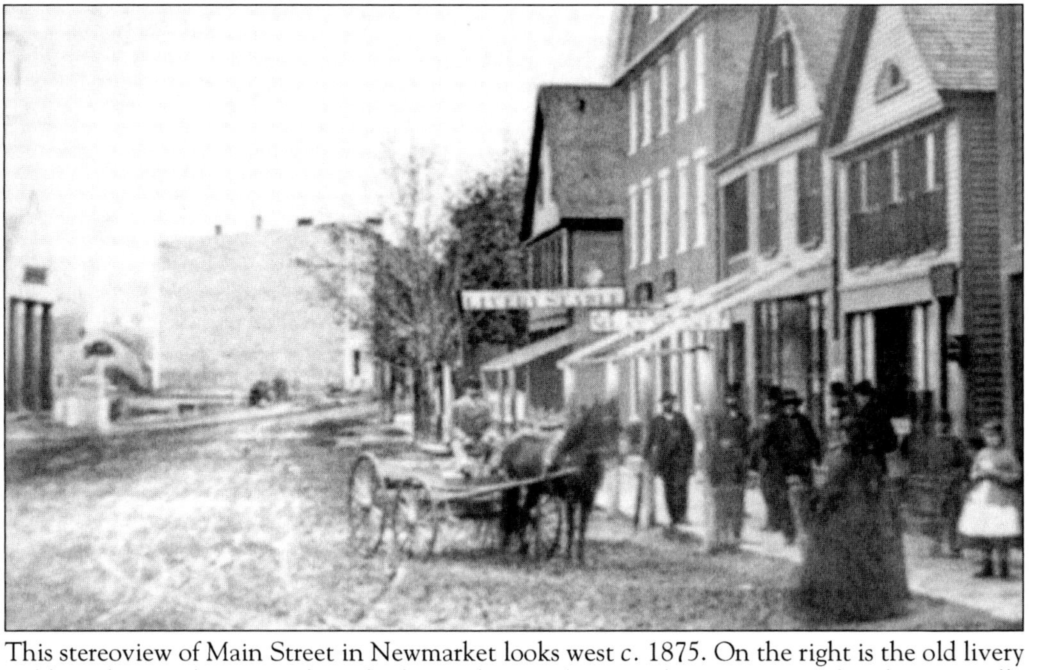

This stereoview of Main Street in Newmarket looks west *c.* 1875. On the right is the old livery stable and general store, and on the left is the Greek Revival Community Church. Originally a part of Exeter, Newmarket was set off as a parish in 1727 and incorporated as a separate town 10 years later.

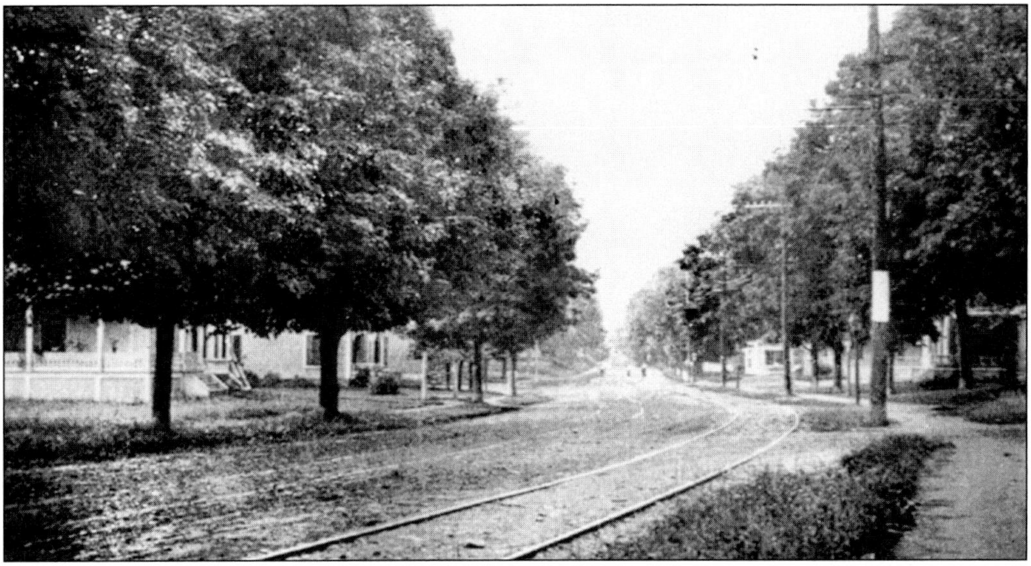

Seen is Main Street South from Highland Street in Newton in the early 1900s. Note the shade trees and the trolley tracks. Newton was the sixth settlement to be granted in the Masonian land purchase of 1746 and was one of a group of new towns in the Rockingham district set up at that time.

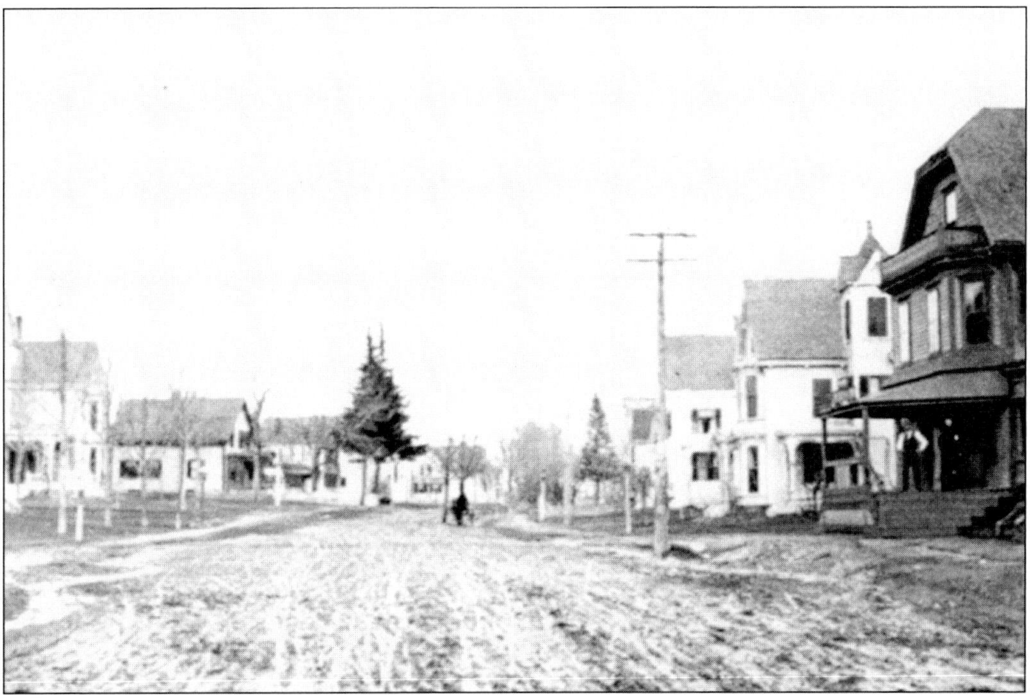

This early-20th-century view shows the prosperity of Newton; note the magnificent homes lined on Main Street. The town was first incorporated as Newtown in 1749. When the town was still a part of South Hampton, the tract of land devoted to tree cutting was known as "Loggin Plain." Newtown bore that name for nearly 100 years. In 1846, the New Hampshire legislature voted to contract it to Newton. This view of Main Street in Newton looks west *c.* 1907.

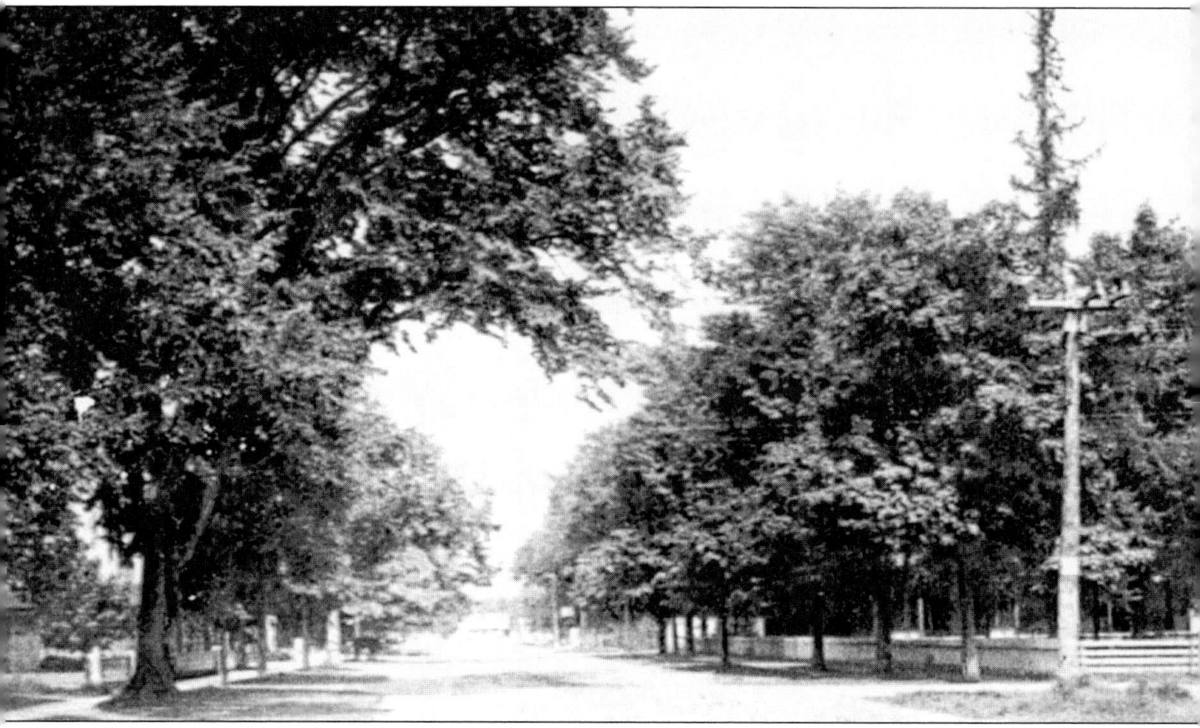

North Conway was granted in 1765. It is a year-round resort community with one long street and a number of short side streets, especially to the east, containing small houses, tourist homes, and hotels. The village is 30 feet above the meadows of the Saco River. This area was originally known to the Native Americans as Pigwacket or Pequawket, meaning "an open sandy country of plains." During the early days, the Conways were a notable stagecoach center. From here, coaches left for Concord, Dover, Littleton, and Portland. The coming of the Portland and Ogdensburg Railroad in 1872 changed all of this and was instrumental in a marked development of the community. No village in New Hampshire can surpass North Conway in its natural setting. To many, it presents the most inspiring and beautiful approach to the Presidential Range. Seen above is Main Street in North Conway in 1908.

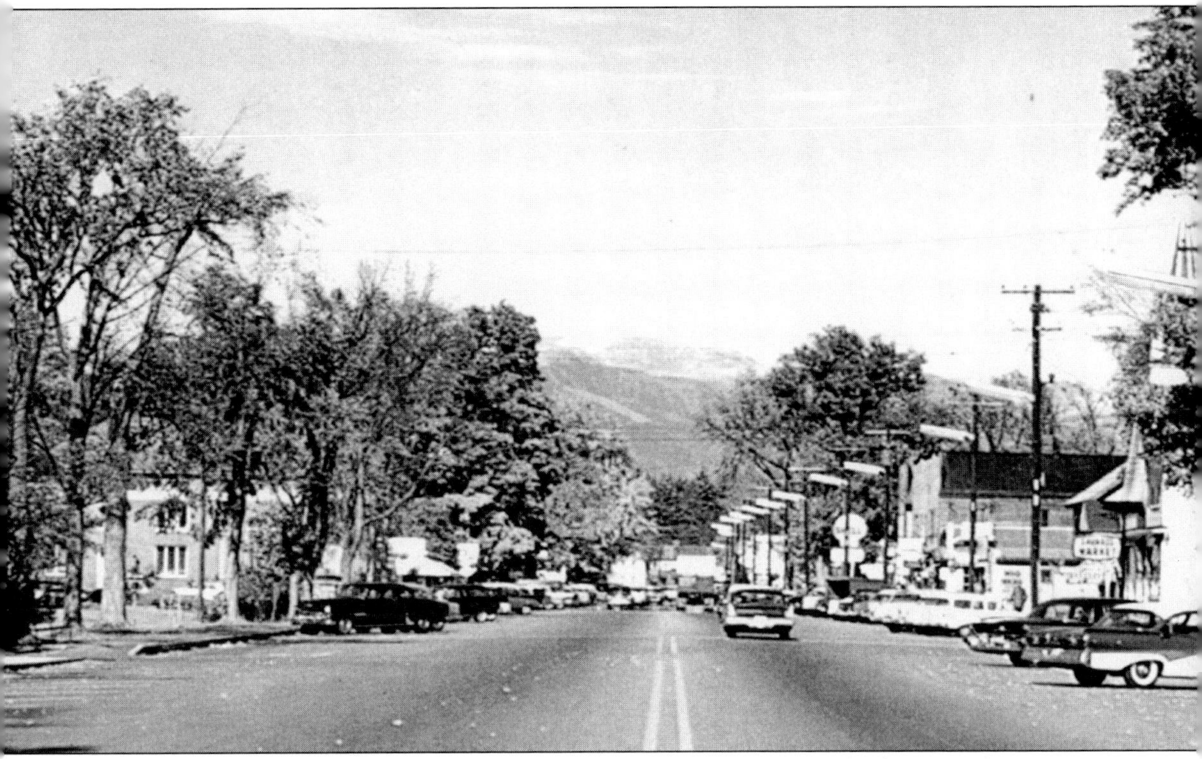

This view of North Conway's Main Street looks north in the 1950s. The business district on Main Street, with snow-capped Mount Washington rising majestically in the background, presents a natural setting for the perfect winter vacation resort. A major commercial center of the North Country, North Conway's Main Street is usually filled with automobiles, particularly during the summer and autumn months. It would not have been possible today, as it was in the 1850s, for Champney, the artist, to plant his easel in the middle of the street and leisurely paint a picture of Mount Washington.

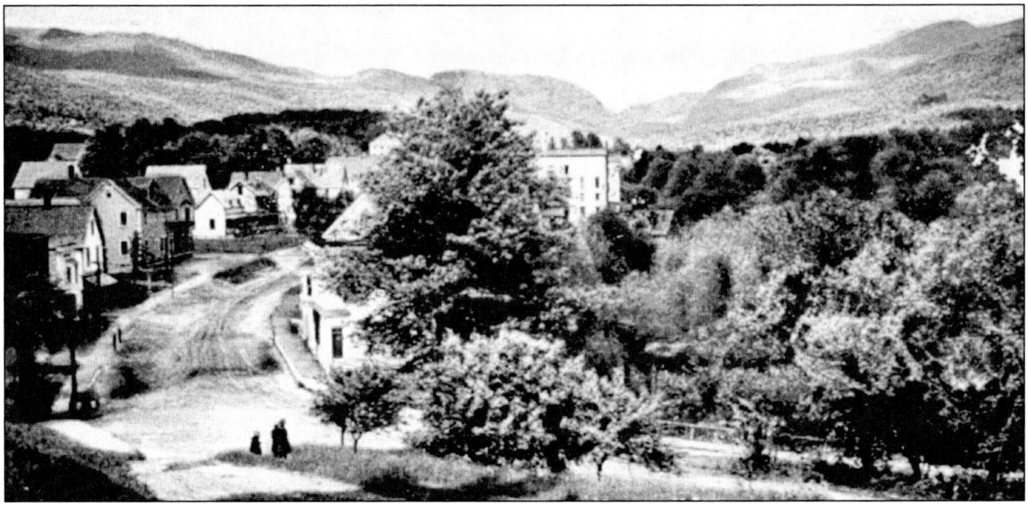

Regarded as a year-round resort community in the White Mountains, North Woodstock attracts tourists from all over the world. In 1840, the present name was given to the town. This view of Main Street in North Woodstock looks north in the 1940s.

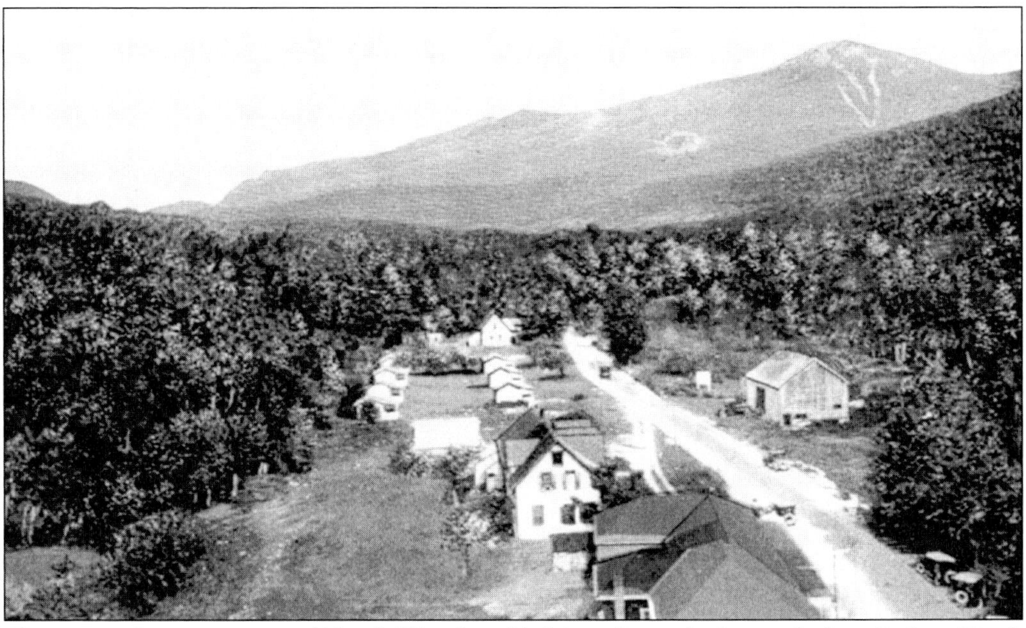

This view of an extension of North Woodstock's Main Street looks north from Indian Head. Mount Lafayette is seen in the distance on the right, and Franconia Notch is on the left.

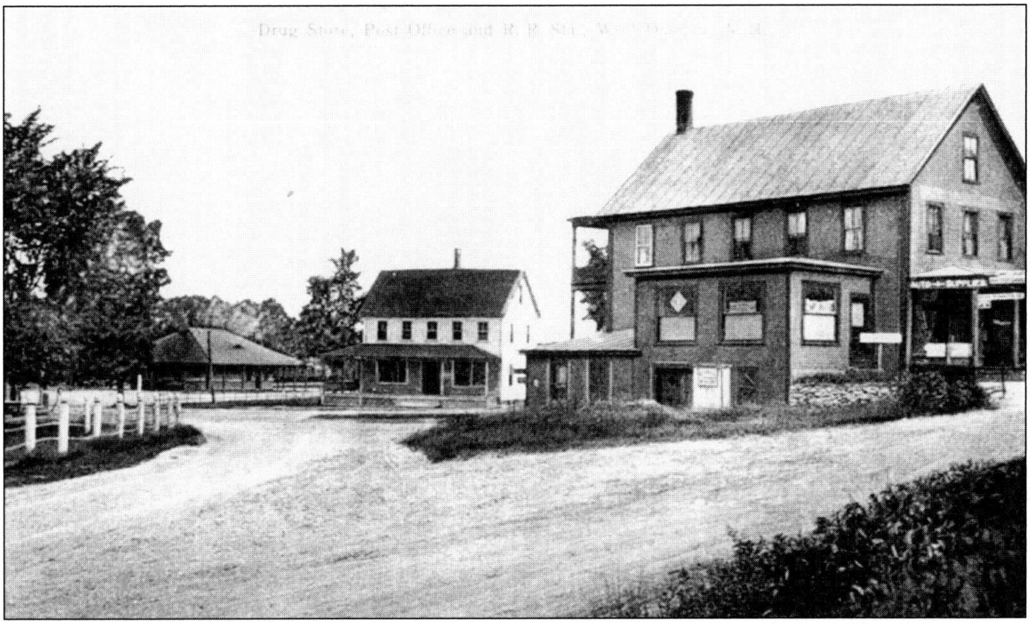

Seen is Main Street, the drugstore, the post office, and the railroad station in West Ossipee in 1928. The Ossipee region included the famous Bear Camp Valley, where poet John Greenleaf Whittier vacationed during the late 1800s. Ossipee is a little residential hamlet of modern houses in the midst of farmland. Taking its name from Koos-sipe River, or from the Native American tribe formerly occupying this section of the state, the town was once called both Ossipee Gore and New Garden. It was incorporated in 1785.

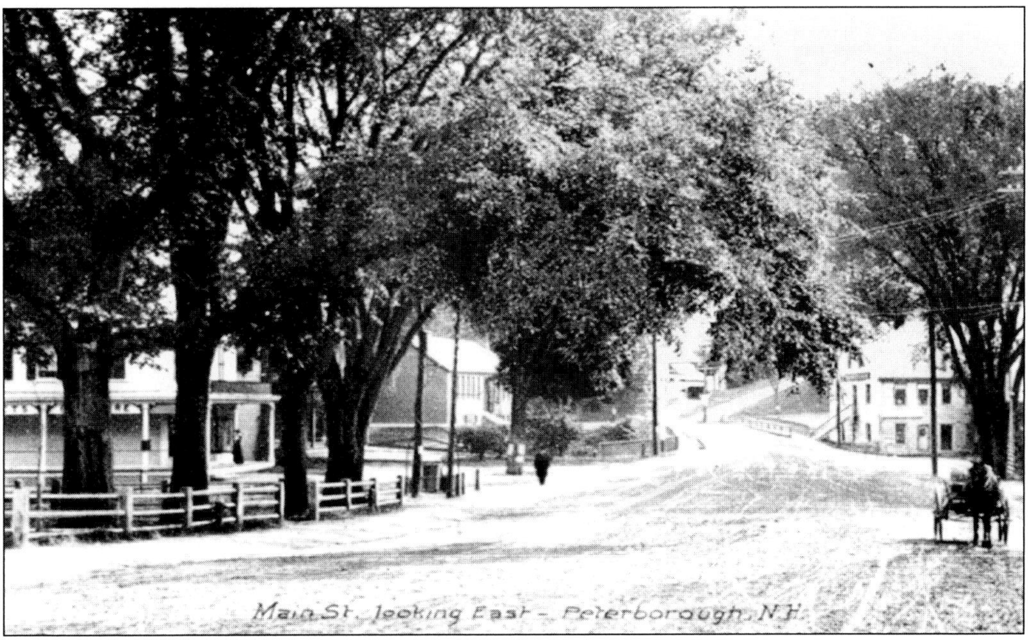

This view of Main Street in Peterborough looks east and dates from the late 1800s. Peterborough, a village of national fame through the MacDowell Colony and Sargent Camp, lies in a valley of natural beauty formed by the union of the Nubanusit and Contoocook Rivers.

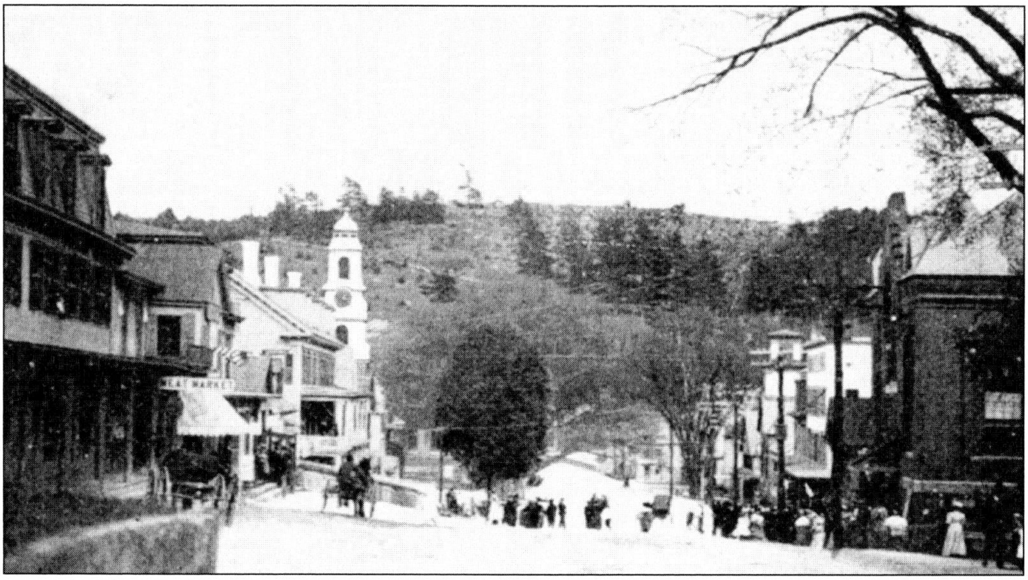

Dignified houses line Main Street in Peterborough, as seen in this 1880s view looking east. The town is set against a background of fir trees and hills, and Grand Monadnock looms behind it in the west. Taking its name from the Earl of Peterborough, the town was originally granted in 1737. Although a few pioneers found their way here in 1739, it was not until 1749 that the first permanent settlement was made in the southern part of town.

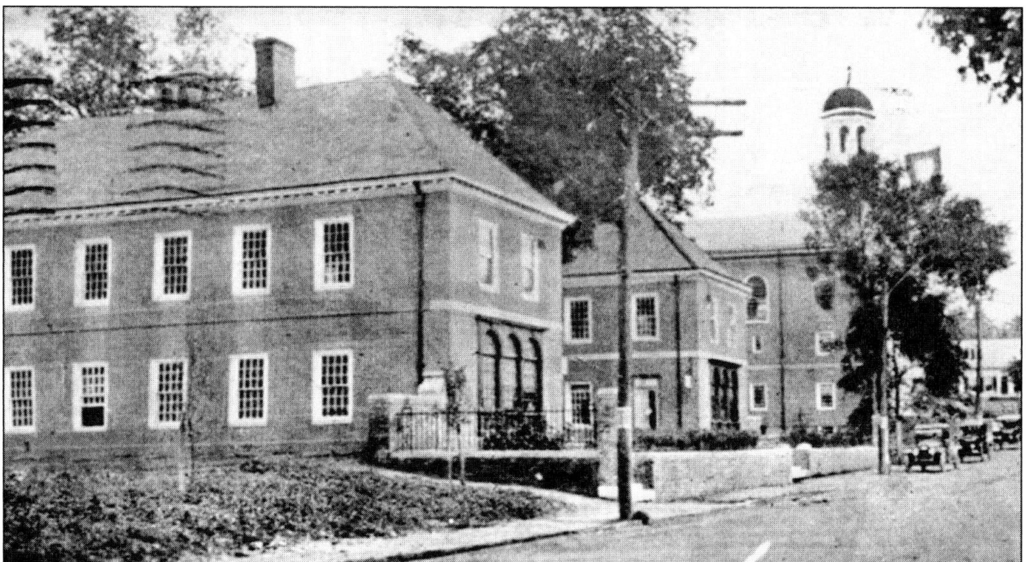

This 1932 photograph shows the historic building and townhouse of Peterborough. The townhouse, located on the corner of Grove and Main Streets, is patterned after Faneuil Hall in Boston. Constructed in 1918, the townhouse is made up of red brick with white wood trimmings and carries a low but graceful steeple. The front facade, approached by a short flight of granite steps, has three doors, surmounted in the second story by arched windows set between white Corinthian pilasters. Rounded arches that top the windows of the main auditorium add to the charm of the building.

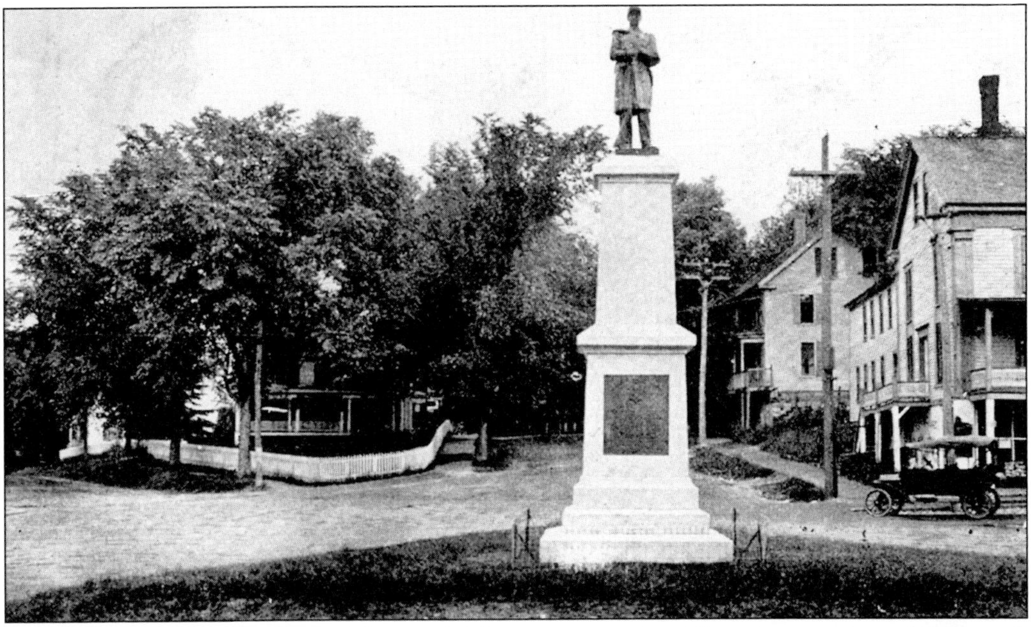

This is a view of the Soldiers Memorial Monument at the village intersection of Penacook c. the 1920s. Penacook is located at the confluence of the Contoocook and Merrimack Rivers. The small square with a nucleus of a tiny park is surrounded by brick and frame houses. In the early days of settlement, Penacook was strongly garrisoned against the Native Americans and was the scene of the skirmishes between them and the European settlers. For many years, a part of the village of Penacook was known as "the fort." The settlement itself dates from 1659, when it was granted by the Massachusetts Bay Colony.

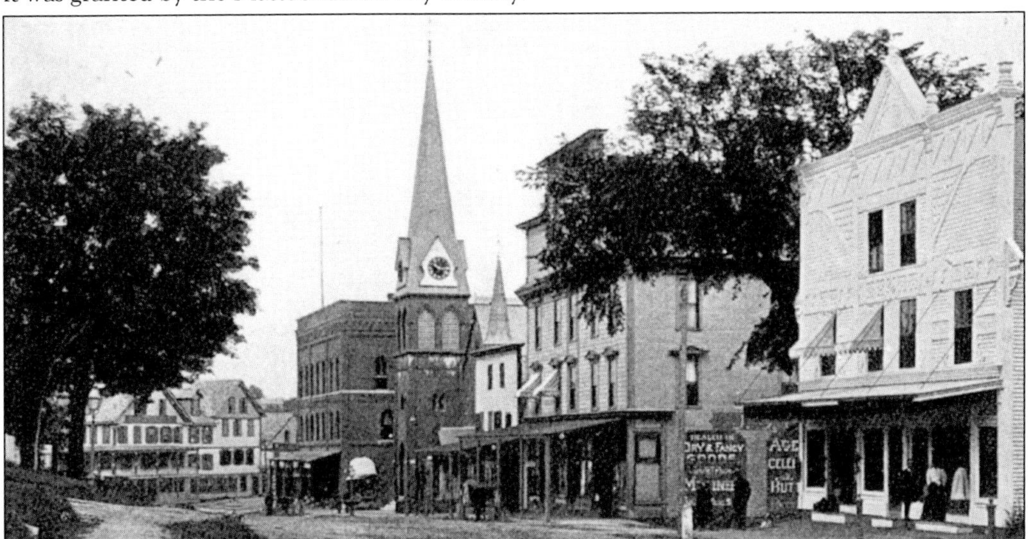

Pittsfield, an industrial village, was built on two elevations above the Suncook River. Settlement was first made in 1768, and the town was incorporated in 1782. Ten years later, sawmills and gristmills were in operation, and from that time on, Pittsfield gradually expanded into a community manufacturing shoes, textiles, and sporting clothes. This view shows Pittsfield's Main Street c. 1900.

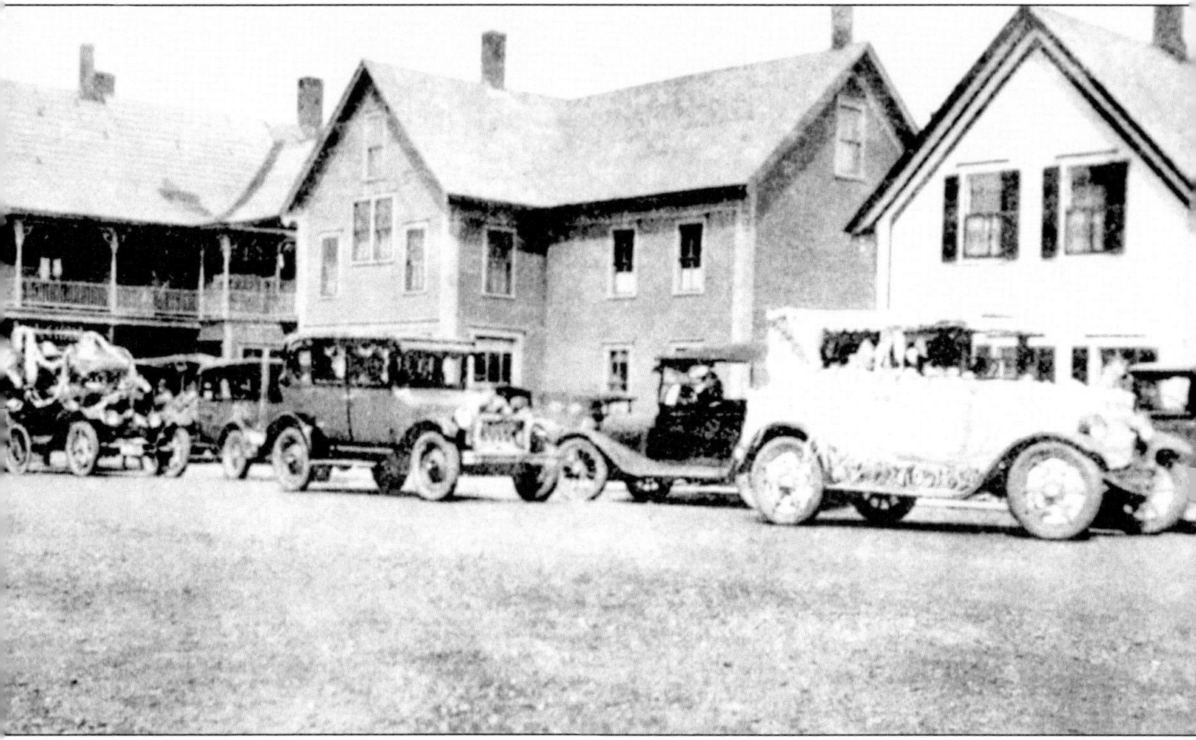

An Old Home Day parade on Main Street in Pittsburg takes place in the early 1930s. The residents proudly show-off their finest automobiles in the parade. Pittsburg is the northernmost and largest township in area in New Hampshire and includes the tracts of Carlisle, Hubbard, and Webster. Early settlers formed their own local government, and *c.* 1829, the section became known as Indian Stream Territory. On July 9, 1832, the inhabitants organized the Republic of Indian Stream, with a written constitution, council, assembly, and court. The tiny state existed for three years, but its career ended as the Indian Stream (1835–1836), when, after a dispute with the Canadian authorities, the territory was occupied by the New Hampshire militia. Incorporated as Pittsburg in 1840, the north and west lines were established in 1841, and the region was awarded to New Hampshire in the Ashburton Treaty (1842).

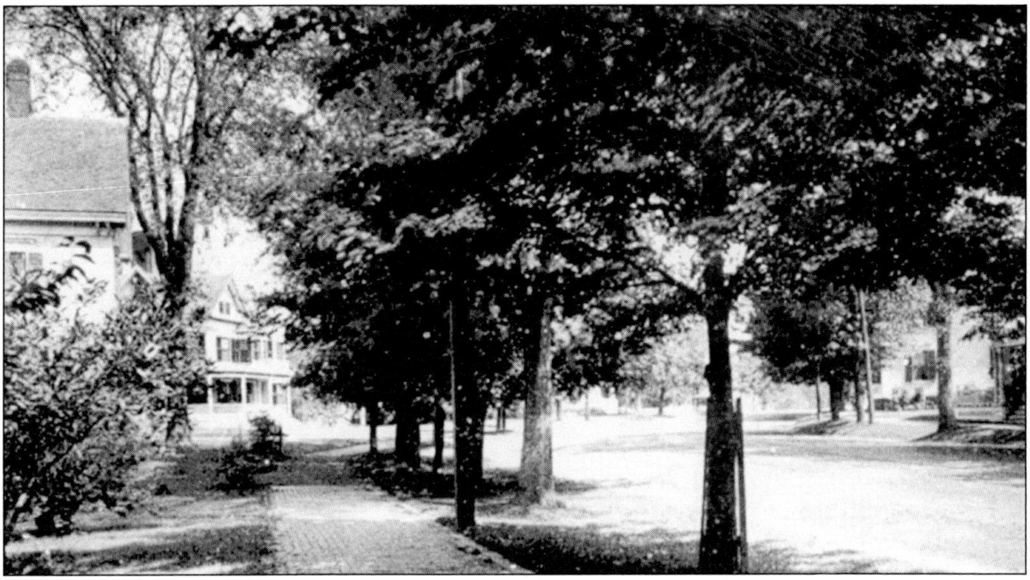

Middle Street is a major residential section of Portsmouth. Settled in 1623 and incorporated in 1849, Portsmouth is a seaport town. The glory of Portsmouth's sea trade, long since faded into the past, still lingers in the reviving waterfront and state mansions of Middle Street and Market Square.

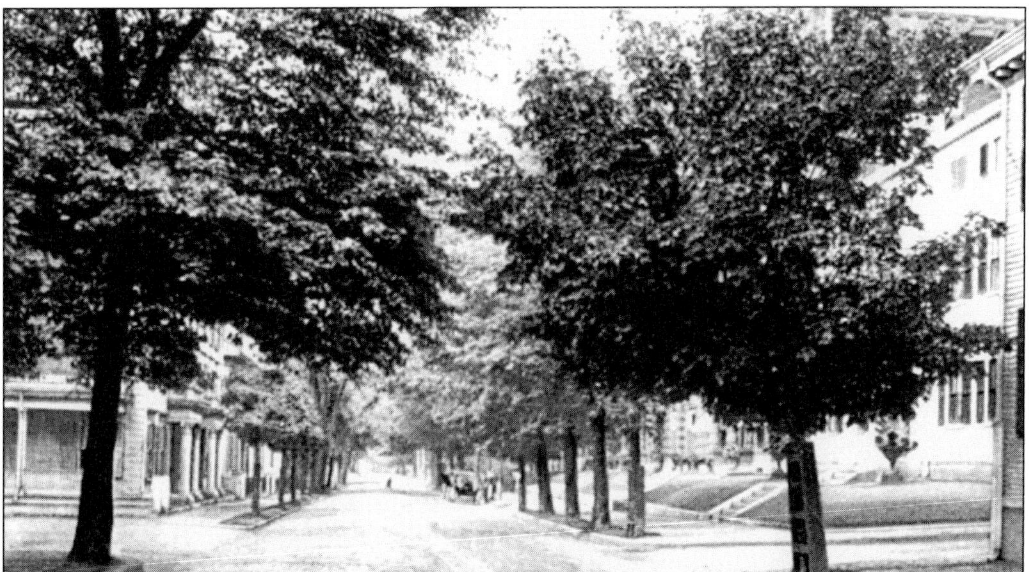

This is a view of State Street, a major thoroughfare in Portsmouth, in the early 1900s. This residential section was near the old Rockingham Hotel, a famous landmark of its day.

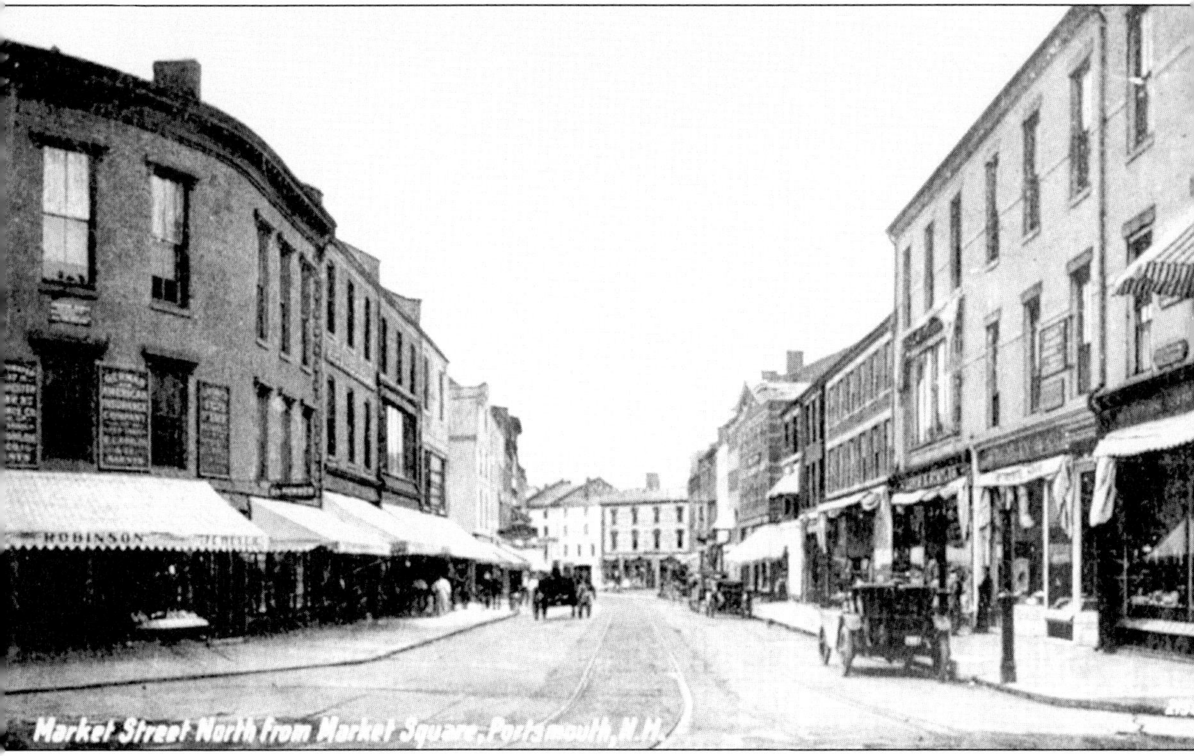

This early-1900s view looks west to the business district of Portsmouth known as Market Square. There are antique shops, specialty gift shops, and elegant eating establishments along the narrow side streets from Market Square. The city doubles in population each summer. Many of the old houses open their doors to visitors, and the narrow streets near the waterfront become busy with tourists. The influx of summer visitors adds to the prosperity of the city, particularly on Saturday evenings, when Market Square comes alive with shoppers and street entertainment.

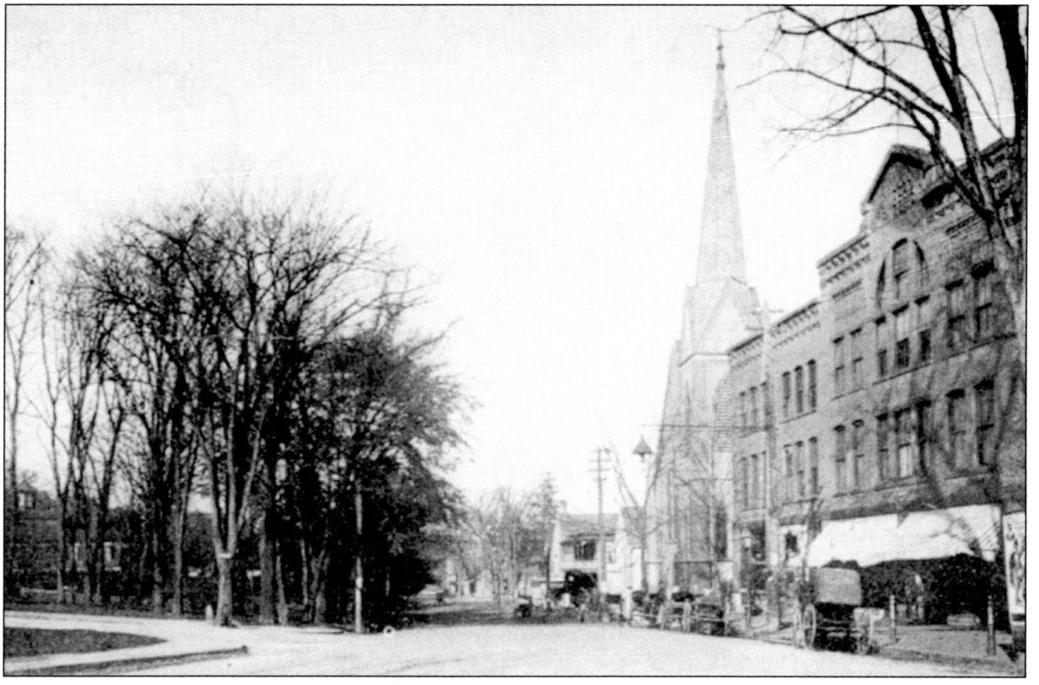

Main Street in Plymouth is seen in this 1914 view, which looks north. Retail businesses can be seen to the right, and the peaceful common, where summer concerts and political rallies were held, is on the left.

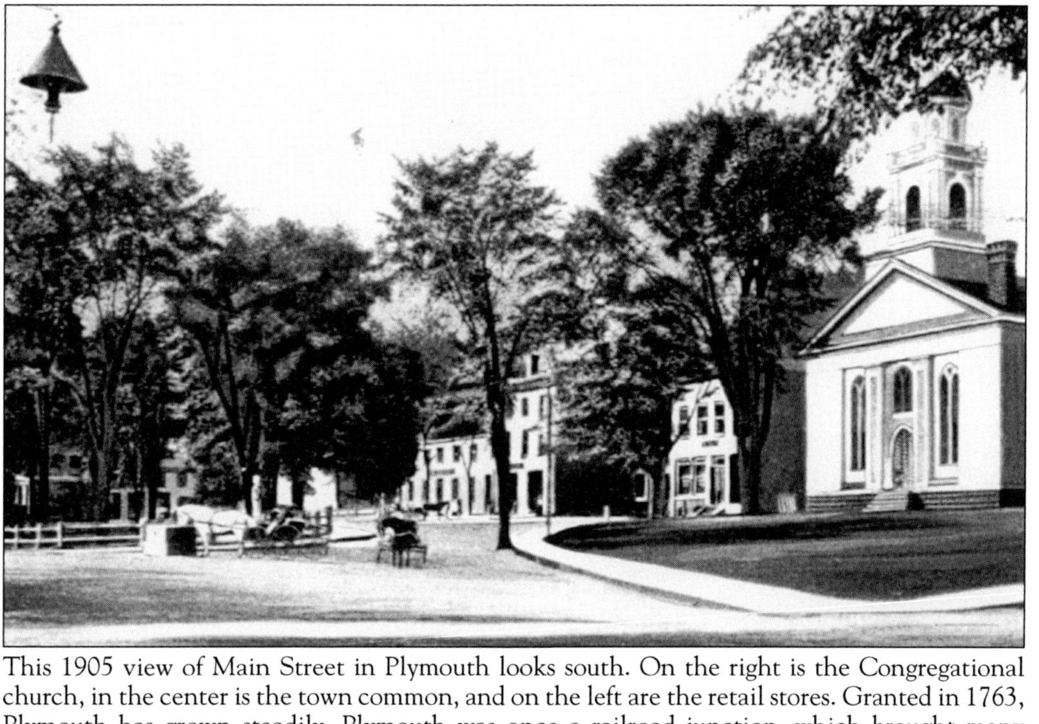

This 1905 view of Main Street in Plymouth looks south. On the right is the Congregational church, in the center is the town common, and on the left are the retail stores. Granted in 1763, Plymouth has grown steadily. Plymouth was once a railroad junction, which brought many people here to trade, and it is still considered a major business district.

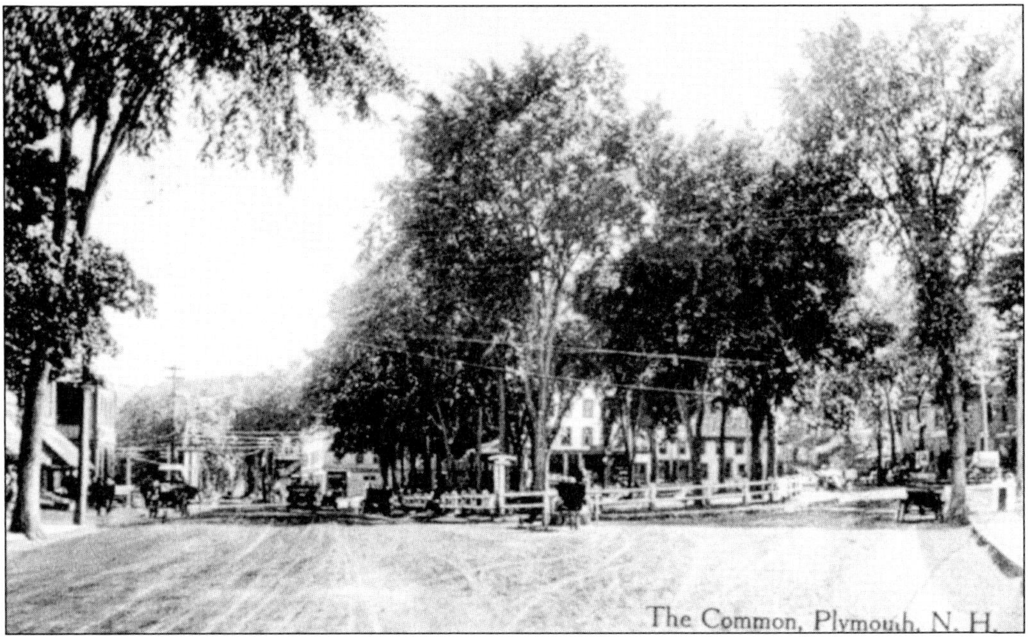

The busy college town is properly known as the gateway to Franconia Notch and the western slopes of the White Mountains. Plymouth State University is located in the center of the community, on the hill to the right, and is affiliated with the University System of New Hampshire. Plymouth is a member of the New Hampshire Main Street community. Seen is the square and Main Street in a view looking south in 1916.

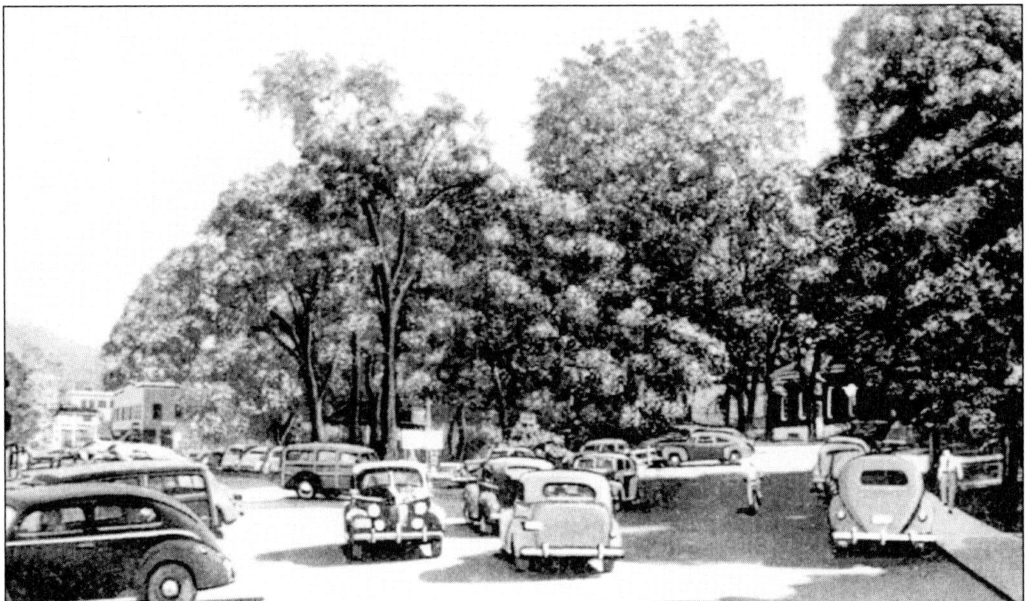

This view, looking south, shows the square, or the town common, and Main Street in 1952. Plymouth is famous as both a summer and a winter resort. The well-shaded town common, with its bandstand and benches for relaxation and Sunday afternoon concerts, is centered in the business district.

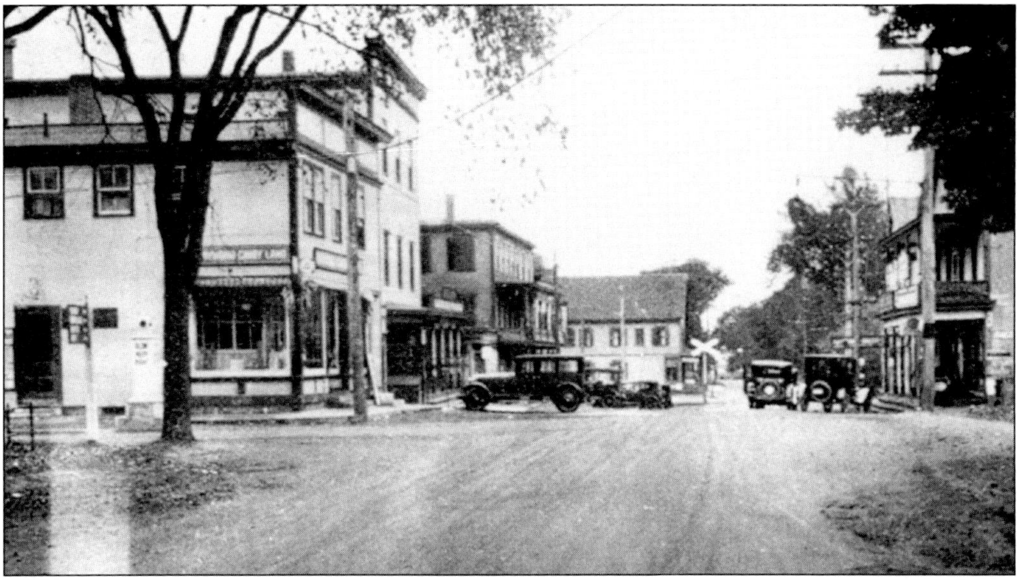

Main Street in Raymond is seen in this *c.* 1925 view looking east. The Boston and Maine Railroad crossing can be seen at the center of the business district in the distance. Col. Stephen Dudley purchased the territory, originally called Freetown, from a Native American in 1717. It was settled as a part of Chester in 1726, and in 1764, it was incorporated under the name of Raymond.

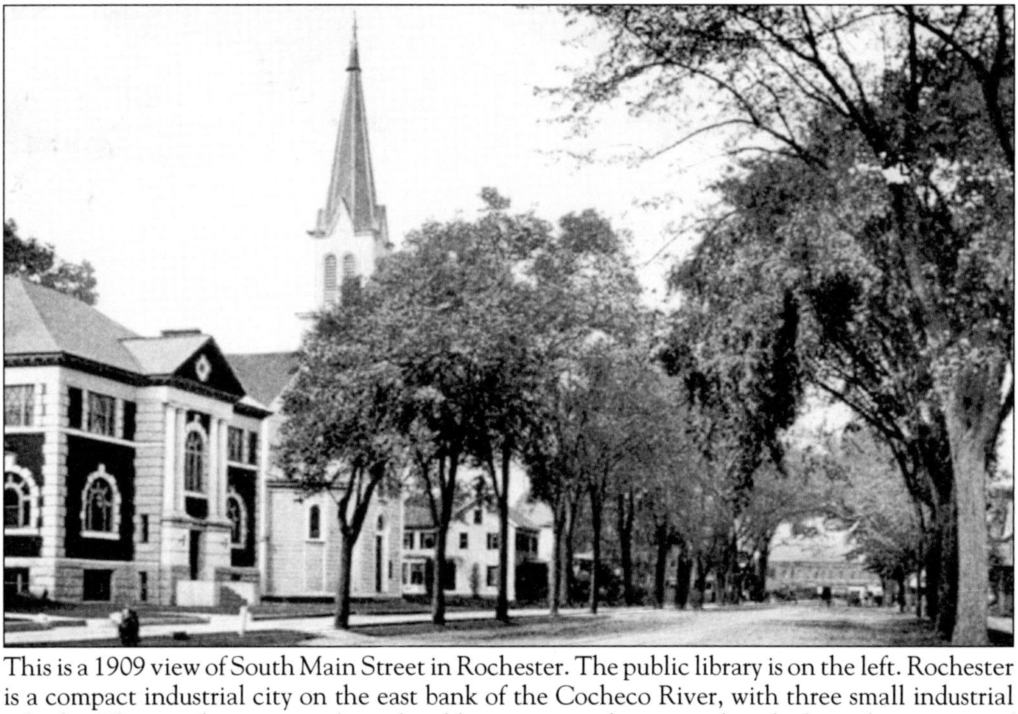

This is a 1909 view of South Main Street in Rochester. The public library is on the left. Rochester is a compact industrial city on the east bank of the Cocheco River, with three small industrial suburbs. The city has an air of comfortable prosperity that arises largely from the activity of its varied industries.

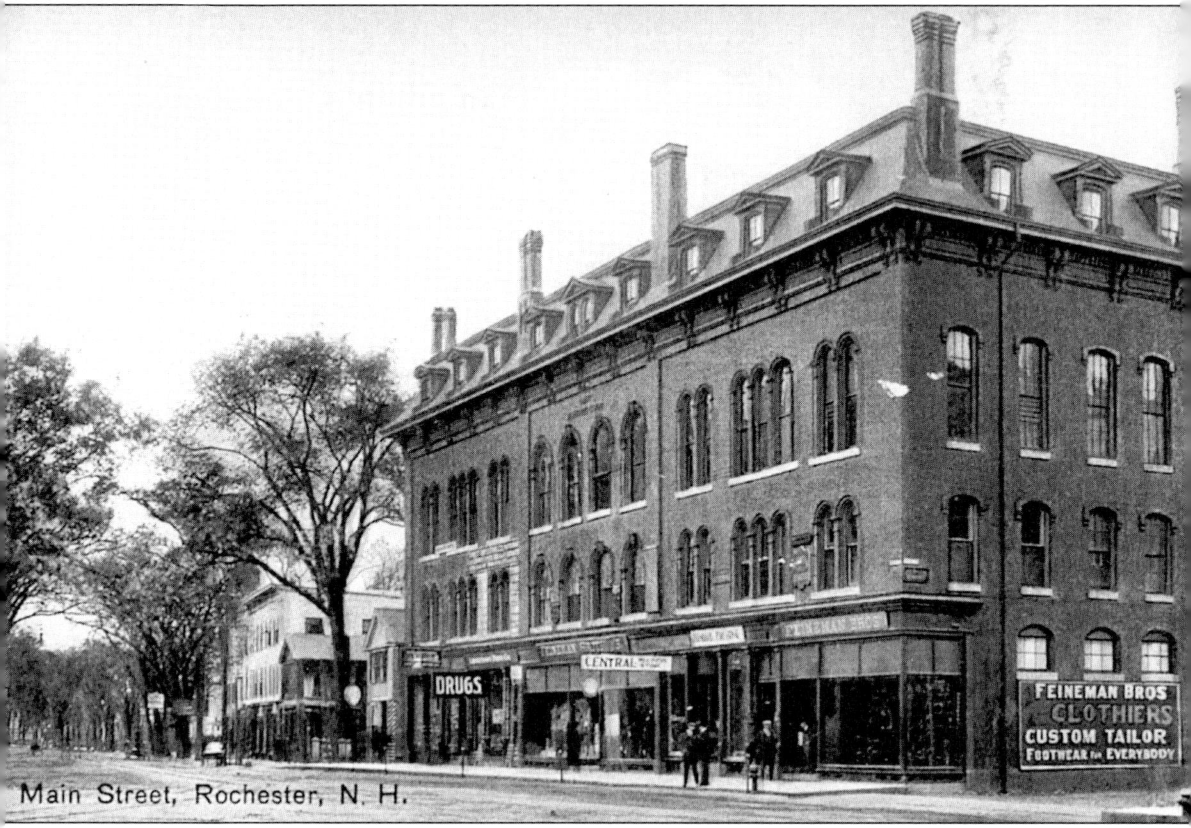

At the turn of the 20th century, Rochester's Main Street flourished with the addition of many retail stores to the business district, including the drugstore, clothing store, and hotel in the center of the district. In 1891, Rochester was incorporated as a city with full municipal rights. At this time it was a railroad center. Twenty years earlier, four separate railroads passed through the town, but these were later amalgamated into two branches of the Boston and Maine Railroad, which met in the city. This photograph shows Main Street in the early 1900s.

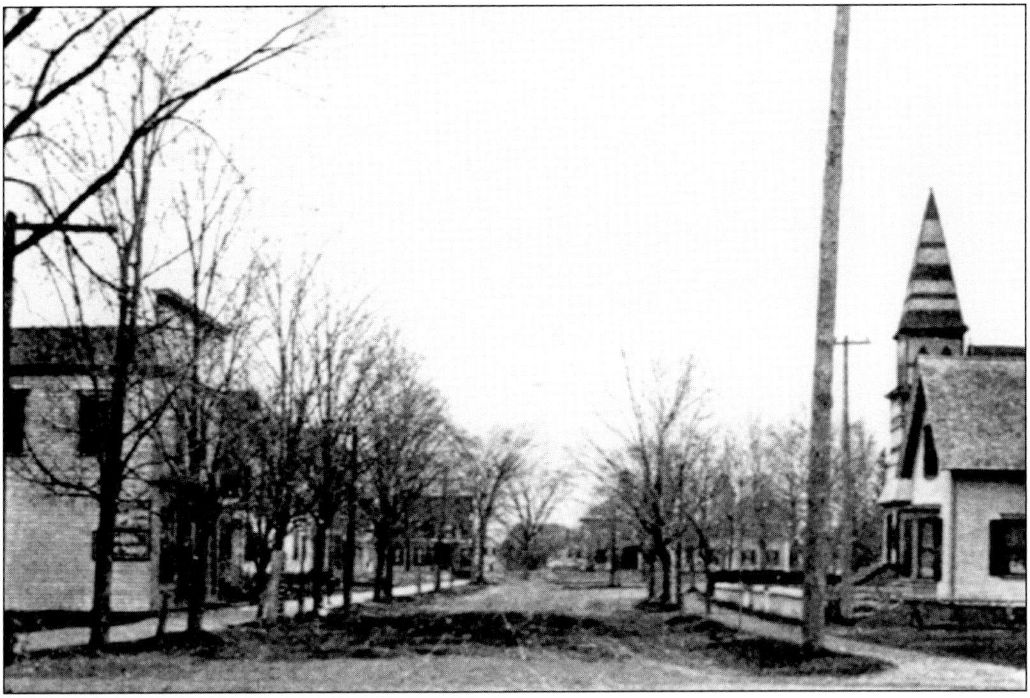

Seen is South Main Street in East Rochester in 1906. Rochester was originally part of Dover, and although it was granted in 1623, the presence of Native Americans greatly slowed settlement in the region. The first settler is believed to have been Capt. Timothy Roberts, who brought his family to the area in 1728.

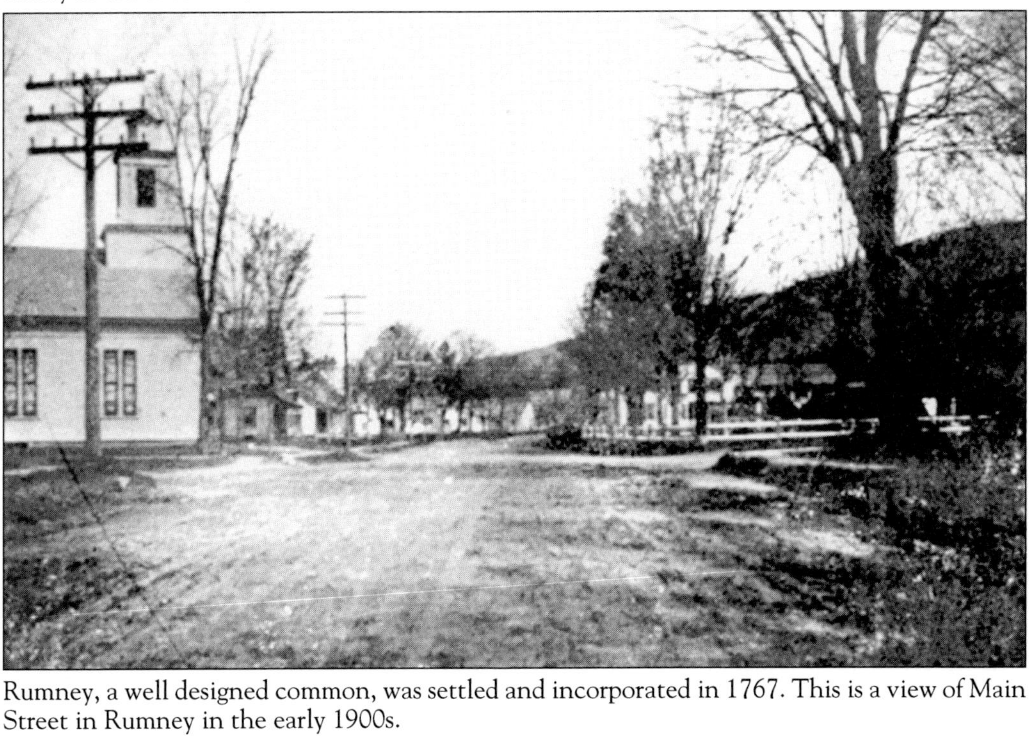

Rumney, a well designed common, was settled and incorporated in 1767. This is a view of Main Street in Rumney in the early 1900s.

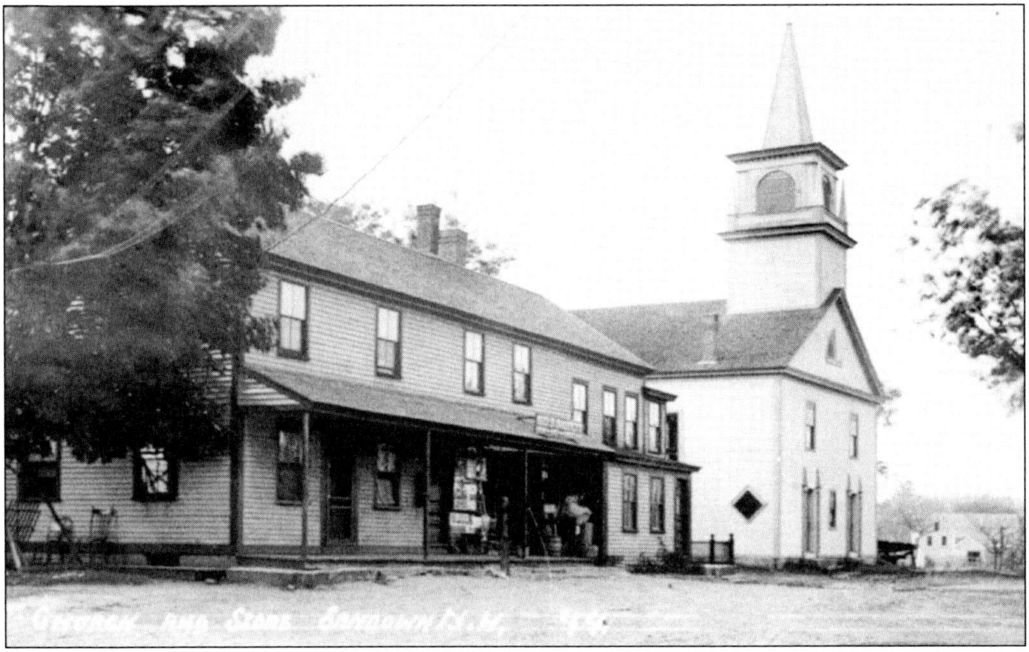

Sanborn's store and the Methodist church are seen on Main Street in Sandown in this view looking north. This photograph was taken between 1906 and 1910.

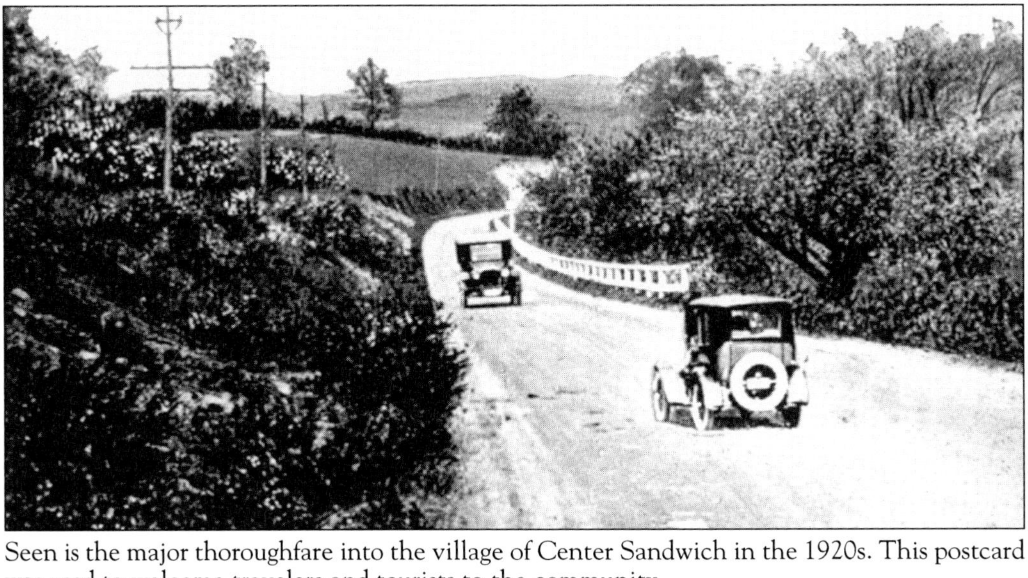

Seen is the major thoroughfare into the village of Center Sandwich in the 1920s. This postcard was used to welcome travelers and tourists to the community.

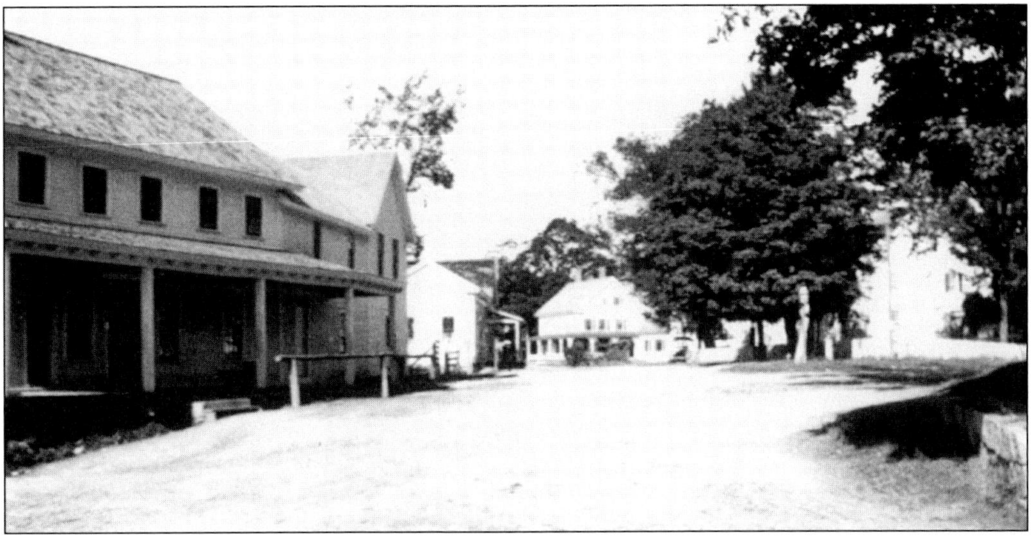

The Upper Square and Main Street in Center Sandwich are seen in this *c.* 1910 view. Sandwich was a little four-corner settlement on the hilltop. Today, it is a delightful settlement around a fine old maple-encircled church. Sandwich is a popular summer resort.

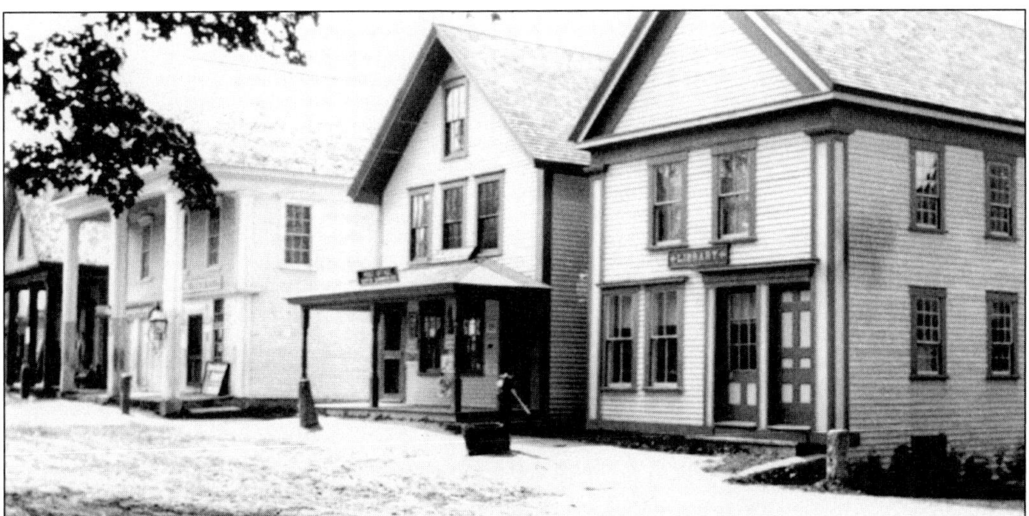

Seen is the Lower Square and Main Street in Center Sandwich *c.* 1910. Some of these fine old buildings have long since disappeared; however, the elegance of the community remains.

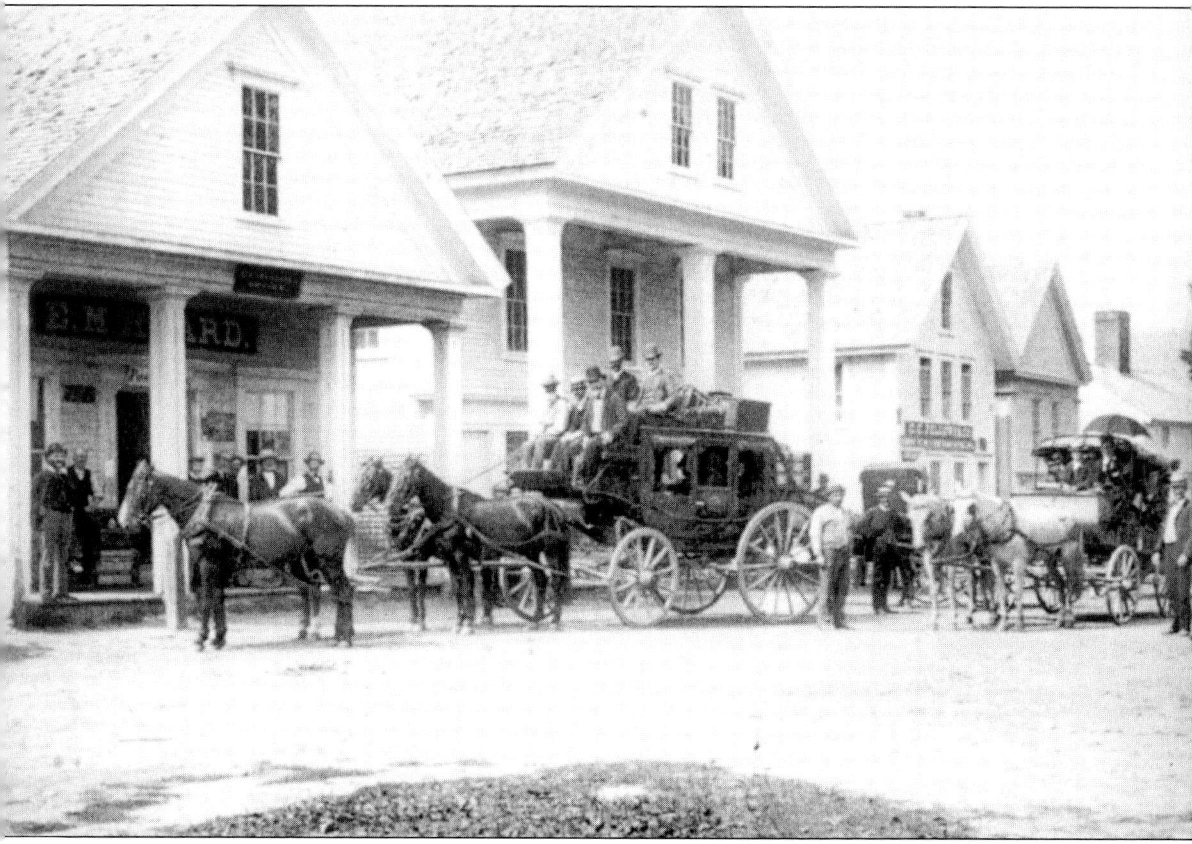

A stagecoach leaves Center Sandwich *c.* 1905. Center Sandwich is a delightful settlement located in a basin surrounded by mountains. The Ossipee, Red Hill, Squam Range, and Sandwich Range form the rim. The settlement was chartered in 1763 by Gov. Benning Wentworth and incorporated in 1770. The grantees for the new settlement were prominent families from Exeter.

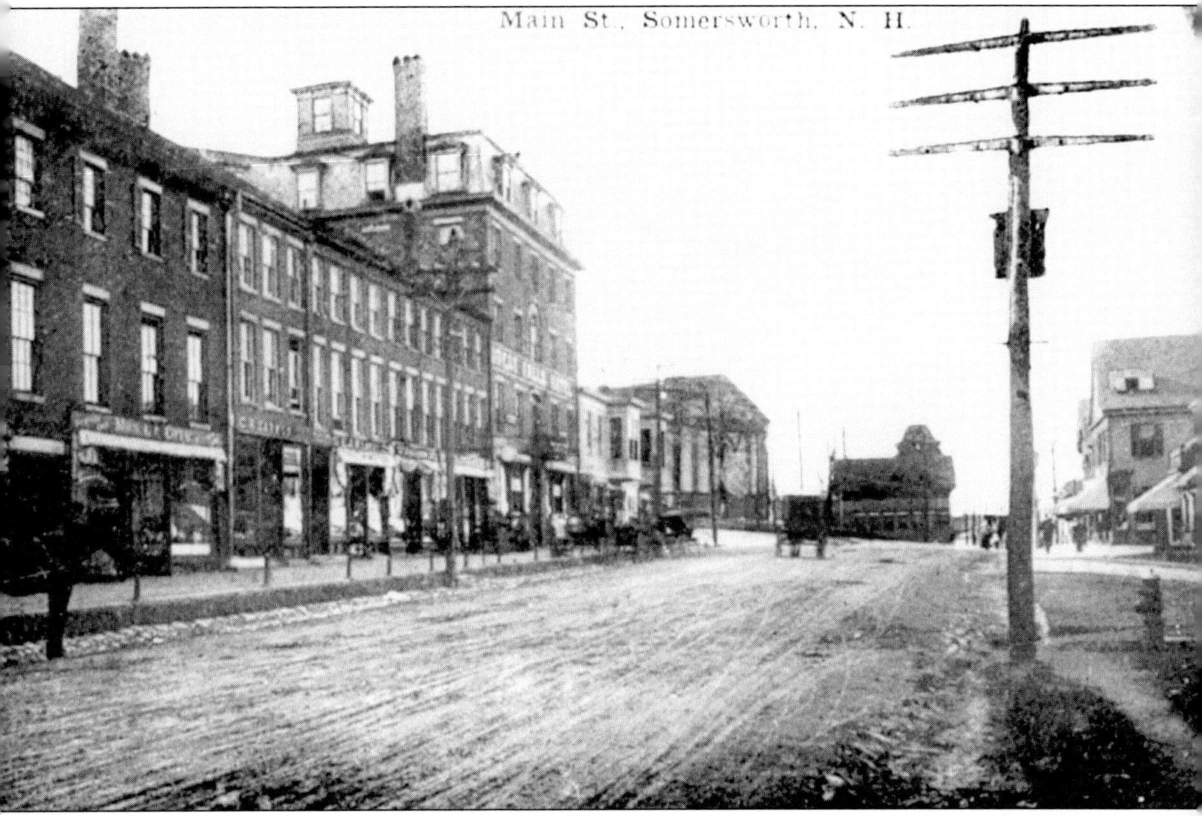

Main Street in Somersworth is seen in this 1911 view. The business section is located on the lower level of the terraced streets and is considered a trading center for many of the Maine towns along the east bank of the river. Originally a part of Dover, Somersworth was set off as a parish in 1729 and became a separate town in 1754. Its name was first spelled Summersworth and was probably derived from "Dummer-town," the name given to the town by the Rev. John Pike when he spent his summers preaching here. Originally, it was known as Great Falls, a name it retained until it was incorporated as a city in 1893.

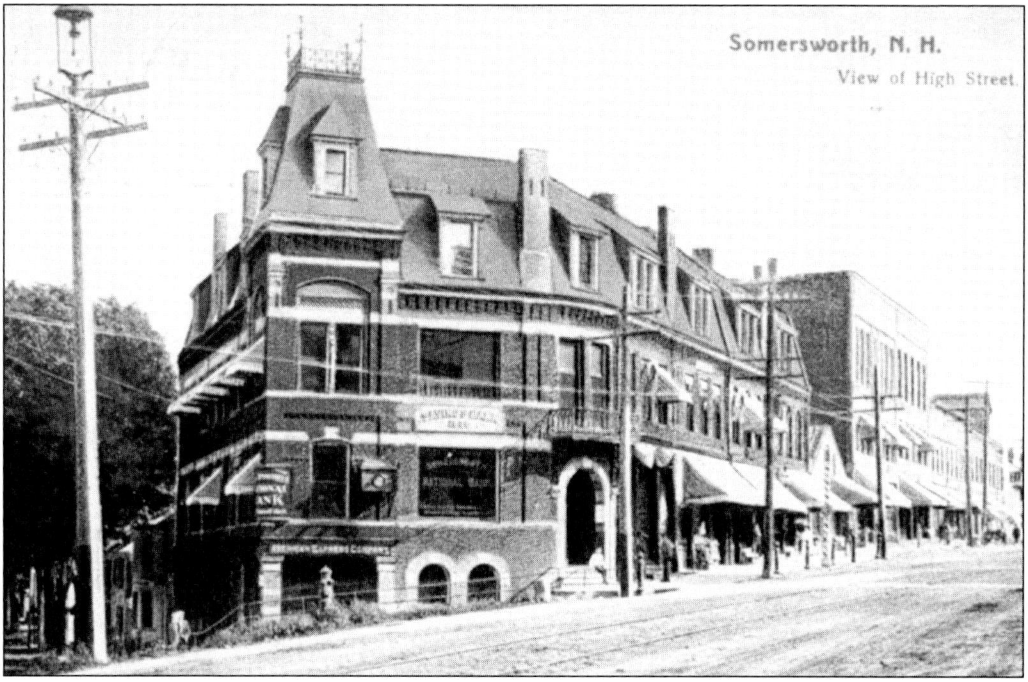

This is a view of Main Street and High Street in Somersworth in 1909. Somersworth, located on the high bank that rises abruptly from the Salmon Falls River, contains rows of white houses, mostly of the 19th century architecture. Somersworth is a member of the New Hampshire Main Street community.

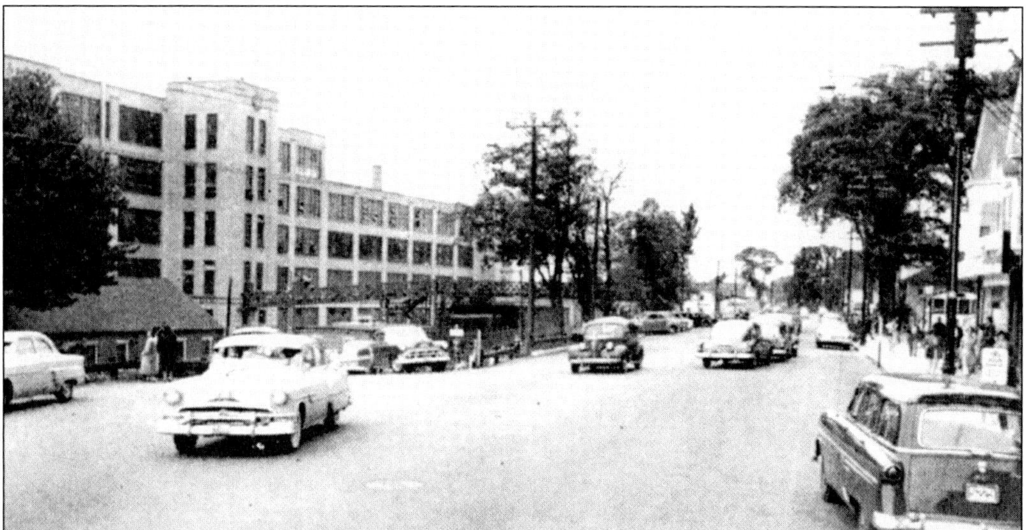

This is a view of the General Electric Plant on Main Street in Somersworth in the 1950s. Ever since the Great Falls Manufacturing Company began building here in 1823, Somersworth has been an industrial community, and its major industries played a great part in the city's well-balanced economy. In 1945, the General Electric Company's meter and instrument department in Lynn, Massachusetts, faced the need for expansion, and the company moved to Somersworth in 1947. Somersworth has steadily continued to grow and expand.

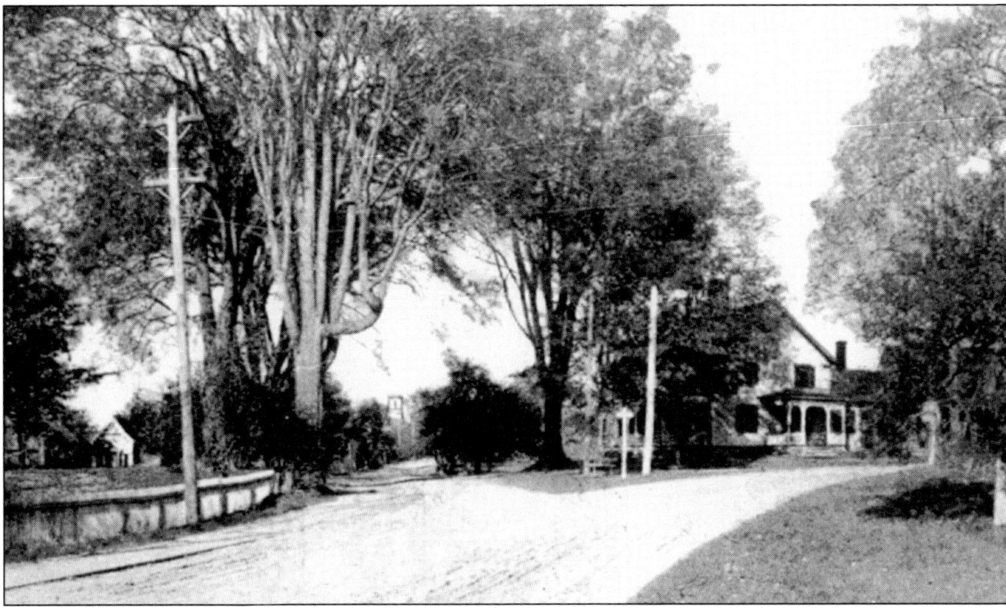

Seen is Stratham's Portsmouth Avenue, or the King's Highway, in a view looking east *c.* 1910. Note the magnificent elm trees framing the intersection. Stratham is a scattered little community whose farms, devoted mainly to market gardening, are among the most fertile in the state. In 1629, it was granted to Edward Hilton as Winnicot. The date of the first settlement is unknown, but 30 families were residing here by 1697. In 1716, it was incorporated, taking the name of Lady Stratham of England, who paid for the compliment by giving the town a church bell.

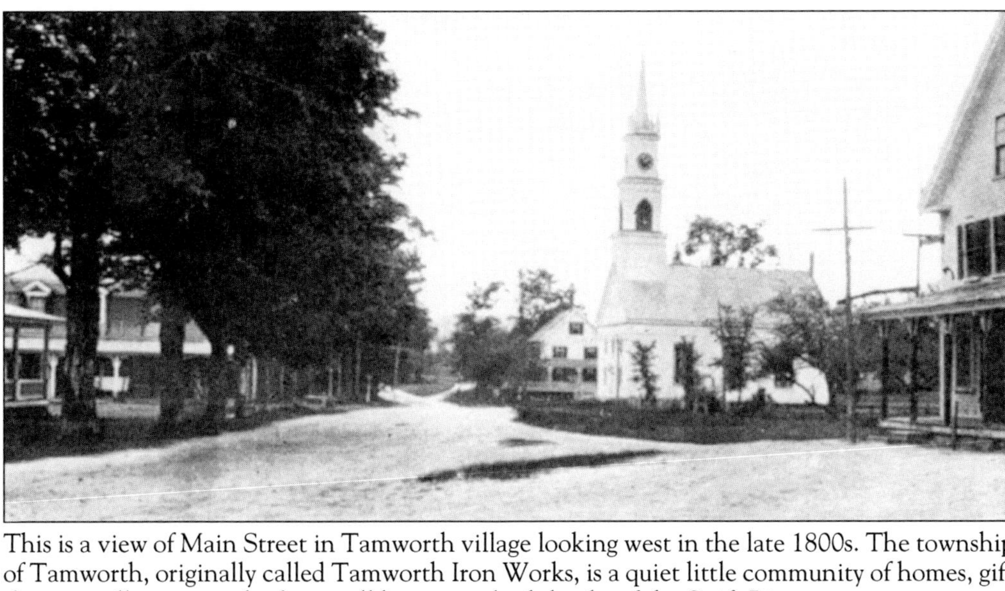

This is a view of Main Street in Tamworth village looking west in the late 1800s. The township of Tamworth, originally called Tamworth Iron Works, is a quiet little community of homes, gift shops, small stores, and a few small houses on both banks of the Swift River.

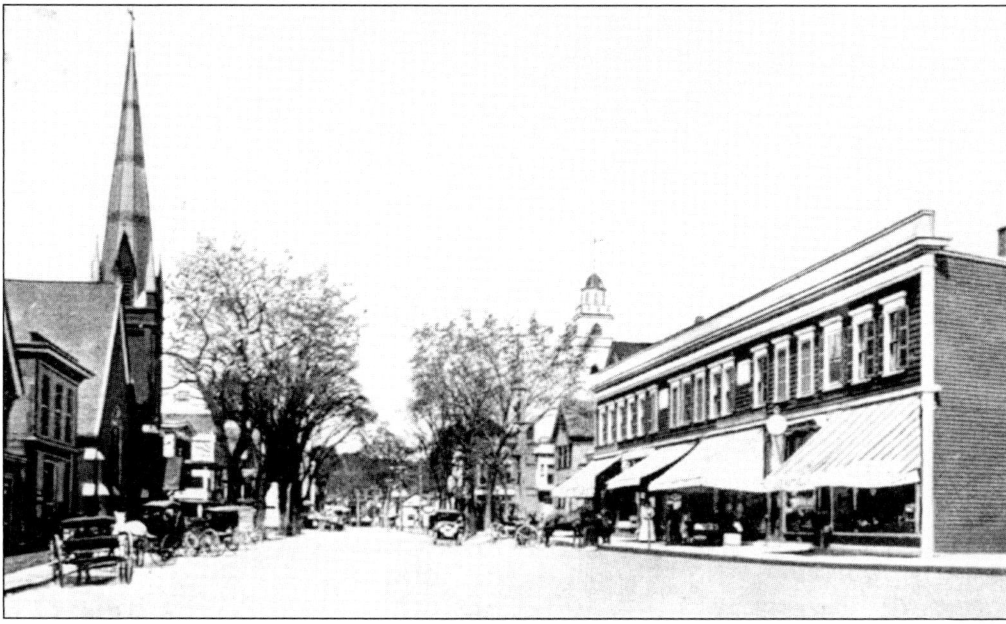

Here, Tilton's business district is shown with its retail stores, churches, and shade trees. Originally settled as a part of Sanbornton, Tilton township was not incorporated until 1869, when it took its name in honor of Nathaniel Tilton, the first settler (1768). This is a view of Main Street from Post Office Square in 1921.

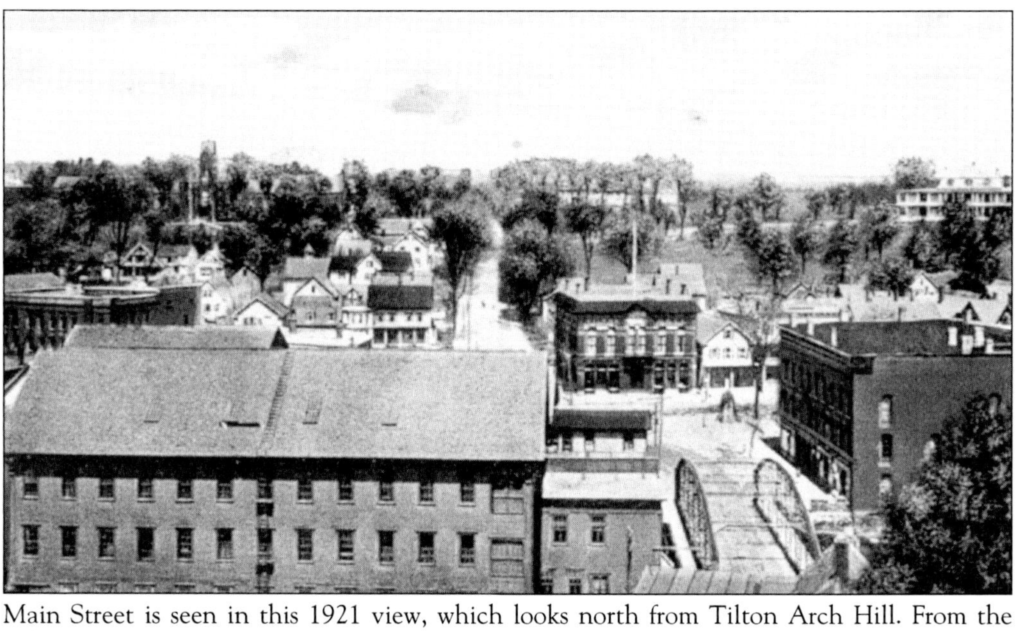

Main Street is seen in this 1921 view, which looks north from Tilton Arch Hill. From the Tilton Arch, there is an excellent view of the town. This memorial arch is on an eminence 150 feet above the Winnipesaukee River and commands a varied and extensive view of the surrounding country.

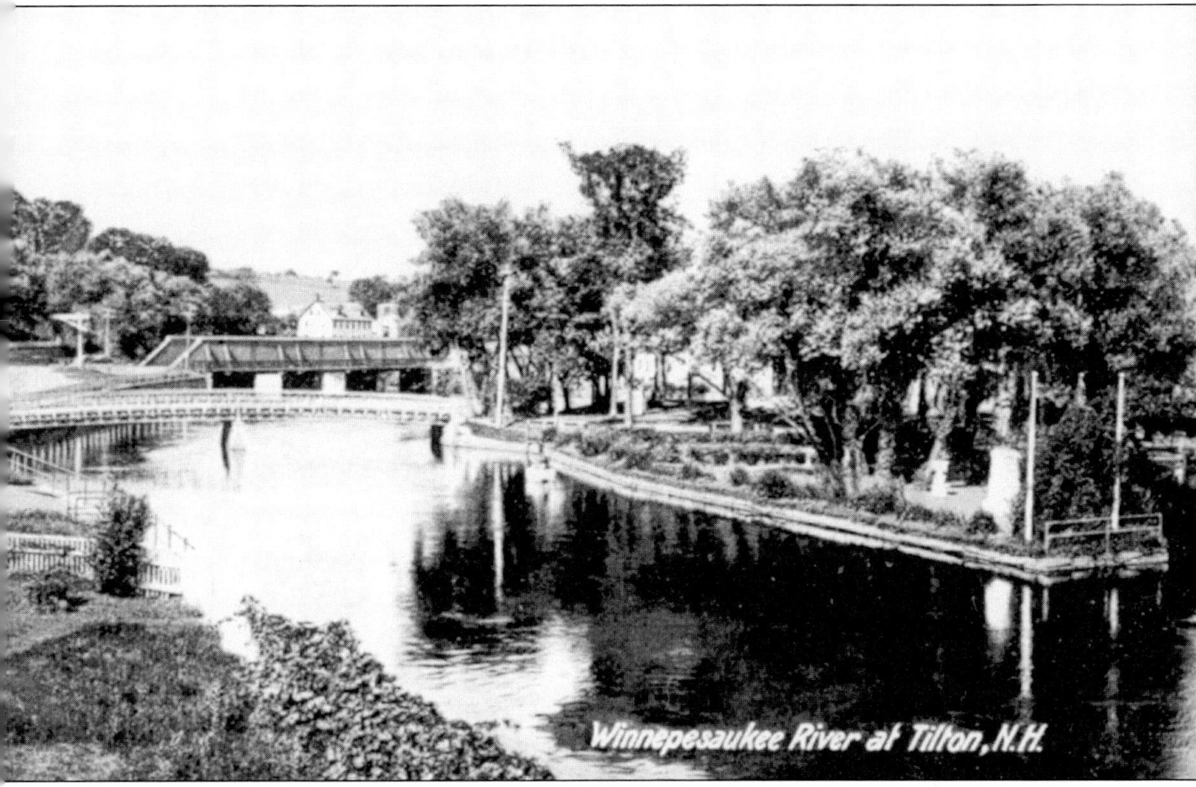

This view of Tilton's Main Street (far left) and the railroad bridge over the Winnipesaukee River dates from the early 1900s. To the left and up one block from Main Street is the Tilton School, which was established in 1845 under the aegis of the Methodist Episcopal Church. The school was incorporated in 1852 as the New Hampshire Conference Seminary. In 1923, the present Tilton School, a privately endowed educational institution, was adopted. Tilton is a member of the New Hampshire Main Street community.

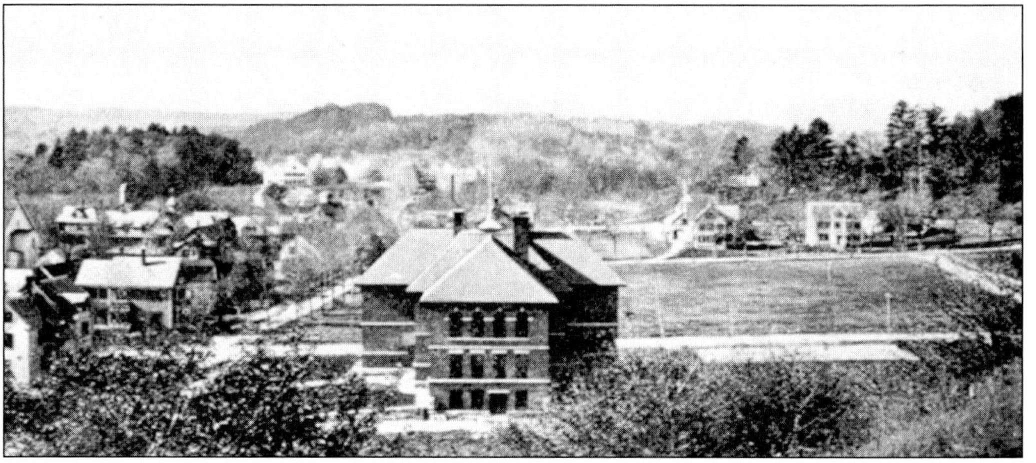

Seen is "the Square" and business district of Wilton in the early 1900s. The focal point is the grade school in the center of the picture. Wilton lies in a narrow basin of the Souhegan River, along which once stretched textile and lumber mills. This settlement looks from its hilltop to the broad range of the Temple Mountains. Many of the houses clustered around the crossroad are summer homes. Wilton received its first grant in 1749 and a regrant as Wilton in 1762. During the early days, an unbroken forest of pine stretched from the Souhegan Valley to Canada. Lumbering was a chief industry for more than a century. Wilton is a member of the New Hampshire Main Street Association.

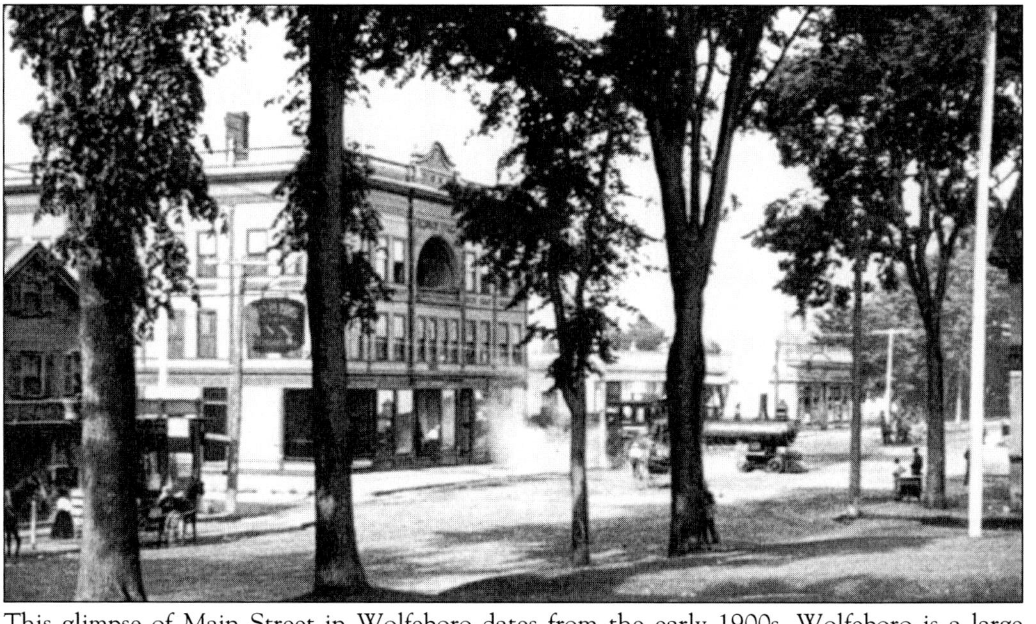

This glimpse of Main Street in Wolfeboro dates from the early 1900s. Wolfeboro is a large village of well-kept houses along a main street running down from the hills to the waterfront on Lake Winnipesaukee. This town is an important port on the lake and the most populous settlement on the east side of the lake.

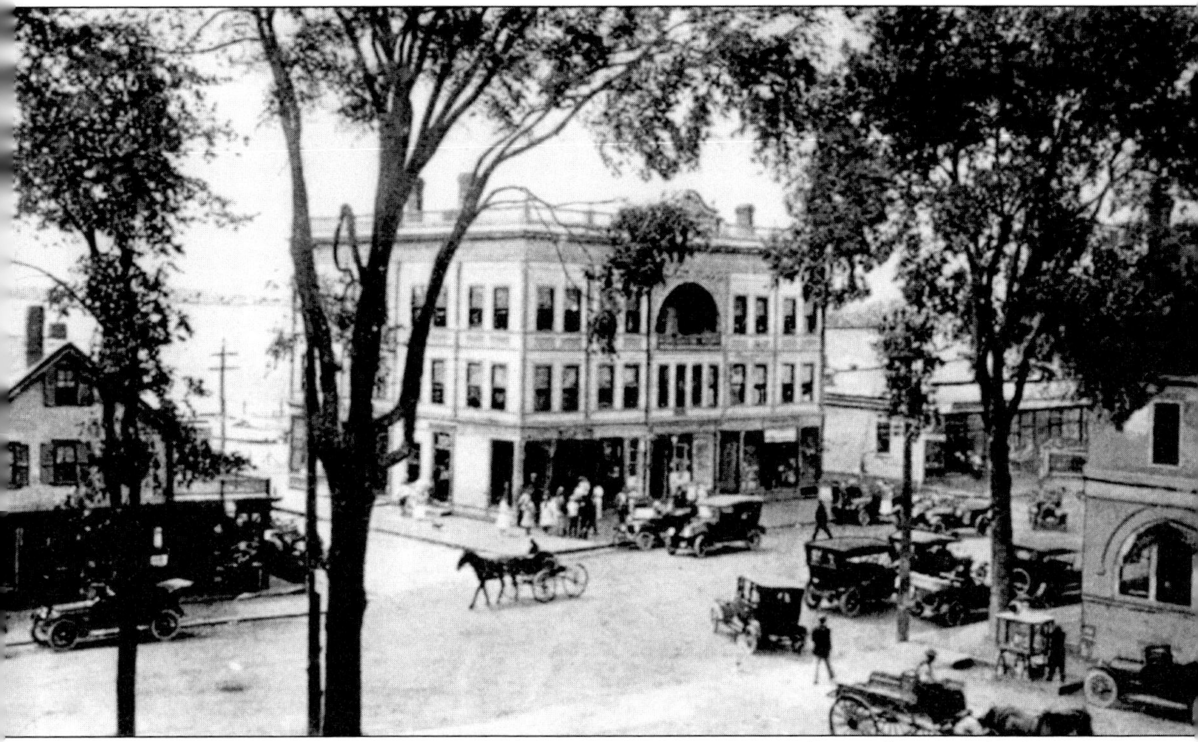

Post Office Square and Main Street in Wolfeboro are seen in this early-1900s bird's-eye view, which looks west, with Lake Winnipesaukee in the background. In 1764, Colonial Gov. John Wentworth established a summer home in Wolfeboro, giving Wolfeboro the distinction of being the "oldest summer resort in America."

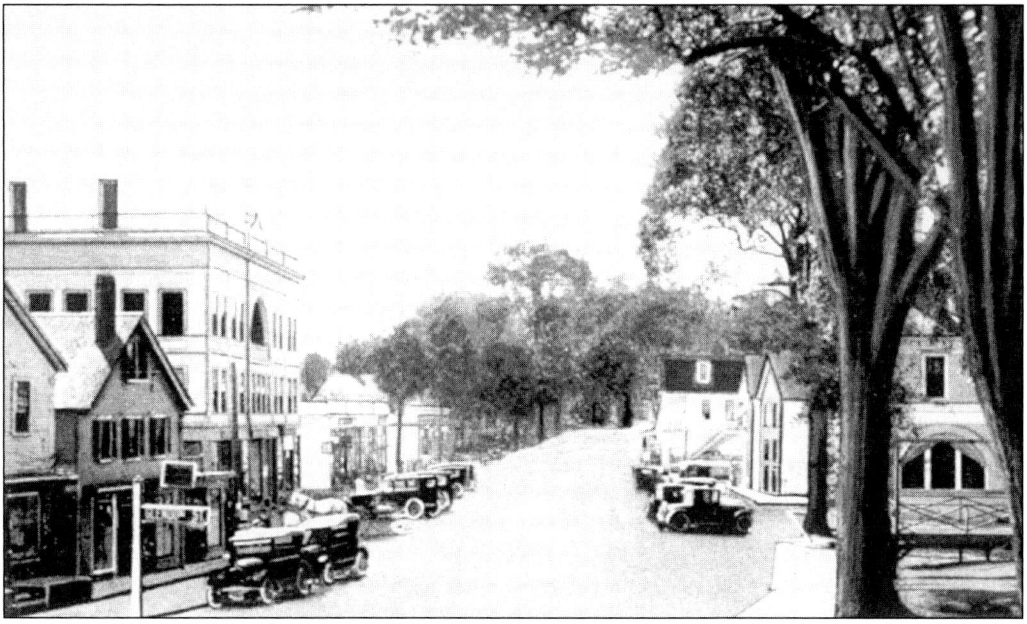

This view of Wolfeboro's Main Street looks north in the 1930s. The busy center of the business district is appropriately framed with shade trees. Lake Winnipesaukee is behind the building on the left. The side-wheelers *Lady of the Lake* and the *Mount Washington* made daily stops in Wolfeboro, which was a major port of call. The main part of Wolfeboro was granted on October 5, 1759. Five weeks later, the grantees gave it the name of Wolfe-borough, honoring Gen. James Wolfe, who had fallen at the Plains of Abraham in Quebec.

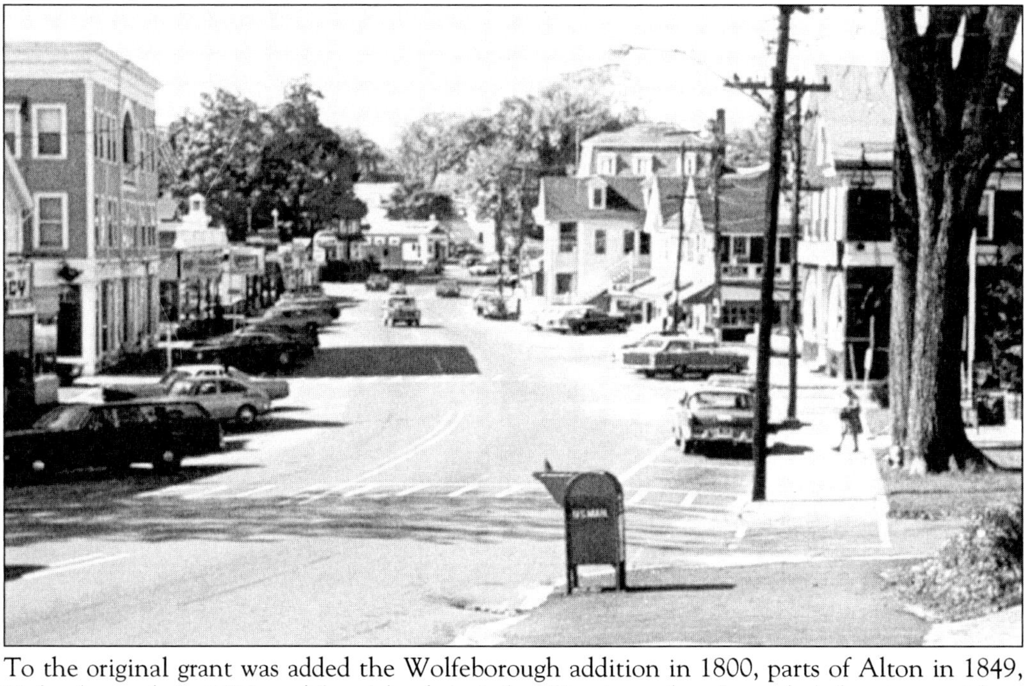

To the original grant was added the Wolfeborough addition in 1800, parts of Alton in 1849, Tuftonborough in 1858, and four islands in Lake Winnipesaukee formerly belonging to Alton in 1895. This view, looking north, shows Wolfeboro's Main Street in 1973.

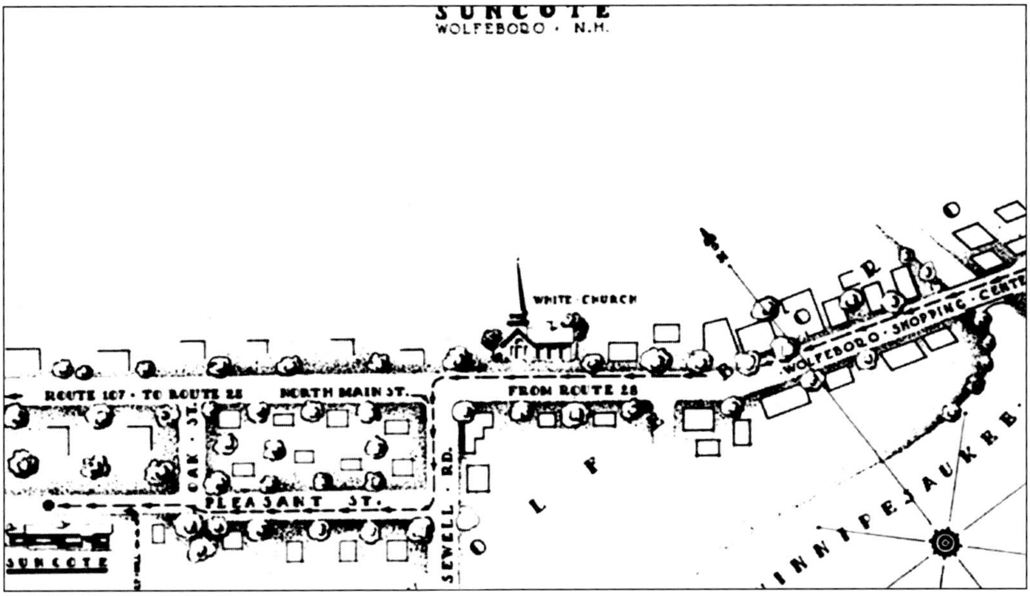

This road map of Wolfeboro's Main Street shows the town's layout, indicating the shopping center and lake to the right and the residential section on North Main Street.

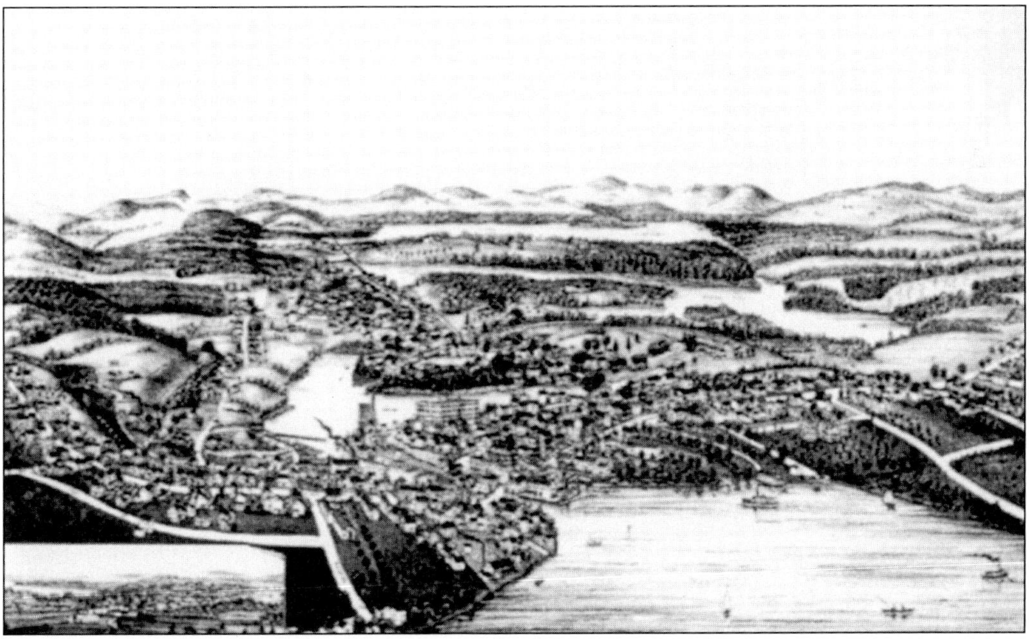

This map of Wolfeboro provides an overall view of the community that rests on two major lakes, Lake Winnipesaukee in the foreground and Lake Wentworth in the center background. This bird's-eye view, looking north, shows Wolfeboro in 1914.

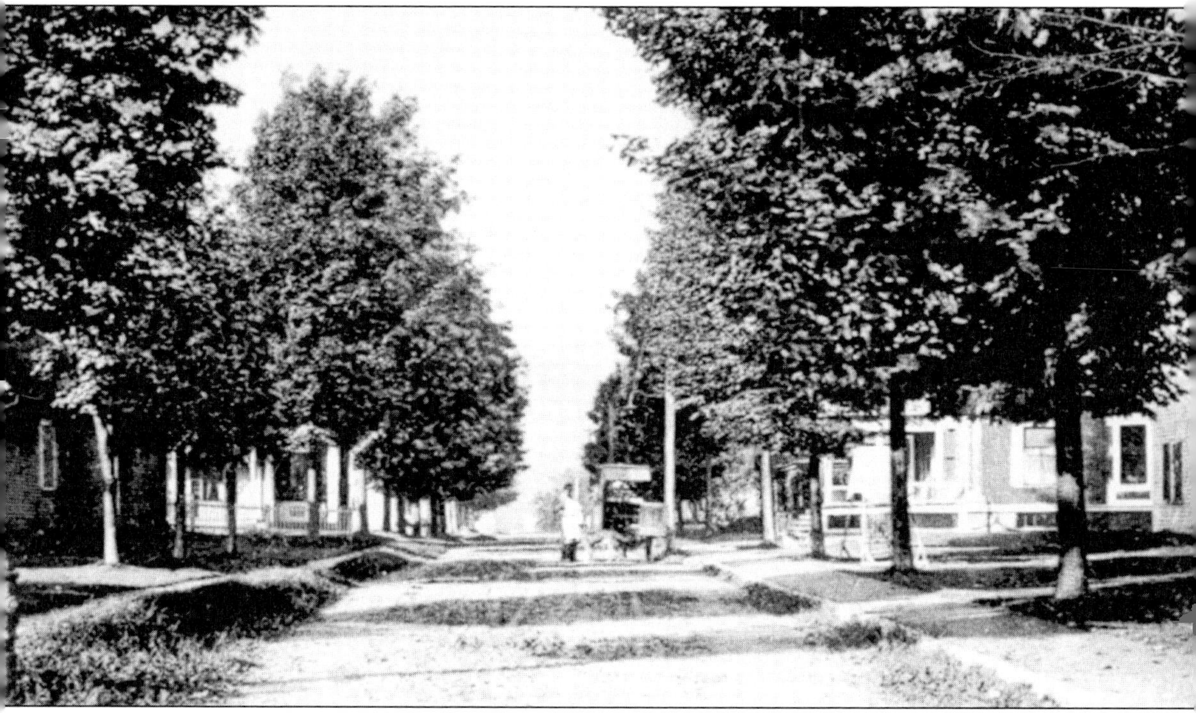

Seen is Maple Street in Woodsville in the late 1800s. This section of Haverhill was a mere group of little houses and relatively unimportant until 1854, when the Boston, Concord, and Montreal Railroad reached this point. Up to that time, the little settlement's only industry was a sawmill on the Ammonoosuc River.